D0078207

EVEN ODDER PERCEPTIONS

EVEN ODDER PERCEPTIONS

Richard L. Gregory

London and New York

First published in 1994
by Routledge
11 New Fetter Lane, London EC4P 4EE

Simultaneously published in the USA and Canada
by Routledge
29 West 35th Street, New York, NY 10001

© 1994 Richard L. Gregory

Typeset in Palatino by
Mews Photosetting, Beckenham, Kent
Printed and bound in Great Britain by
Biddles Ltd, Guildford and King's Lynn

All rights reserved. No part of this book may be reprinted or reproduced or
utilized in any form or by any electronic, mechanical, or other means, now
known or hereafter invented, including photocopying and recording, or in
any information storage or retrieval system, without permission in writing
from the publishers.

British Library Cataloguing in Publication Data
A catalogue record for this book is available from the British Library.

Library of Congress Cataloging in Publication Data
Gregory, R.L. (Richard Langton)
Even odder perceptions/Richard L. Gregory.
p. cm.
Includes bibliographical references and index.
1. Science. I.Title.
Q158.5.G74 1993
153.7–dc20   93-17929
CIP

ISBN 0–415–06106–7

To Adam and Helen Gelbtuch

CONTENTS

CONTENTS

FIGURES

PRETEXT

It is a pleasure to produce a second volume of essays, following *Odd Perceptions*, which appeared in 1986. As in *Odd Perceptions*, many of these essays started as Editorials for the journal *Perception*, which has by now been running for 21 years. Published by Pion, under the well-focused, accommodating eye of Adam Gelbtuch, it has been a pleasure editing *Perception* with my colleagues over these years.

Writing an Editorial, every couple of months, directs the mind away from its usual concerns, no doubt at some cost to other work, but if some of the Editorials in *Perception* and these expanded and re-considered essays are worth reading, this is justification enough.

Ideas come in all sorts of ways, especially through shared experience, discussions and jokes with friends. So I acknowledge a debt to all my friends and colleagues. Most particularly, I would like to thank Anne Neville for patient and careful work on the manuscript. The Leverhulme Trust has generously awarded me a Leverhulme Emeritus Fellowship for continuing research. The Gatsby Foundation most kindly supports my secretary. Janet John has not only helped on this project, but through her efficiency and tolerant understanding she makes working a pleasure and, one hopes, productive.

Richard
L
Gregory

1

TRAFFIC LIGHTS

One of my earliest memories is of an elderly policeman in tears. He was standing by a lone traffic light at a simple crossing in a quiet English village. My father, who was driving, stopped and asked the policeman what was the matter. It turned out that he had worked all his life at this crossing, directing the occasional car or van: now he was replaced by a traffic light. All that he had achieved through forty years in wet and cold and heat was now done by mindless red and green lights.

This was my introduction to poignancy.

When my children were small, sometimes we would play the game of blowing out the red to make it change to green. Of course, the glass of the car's window-screen was in the way, but this was magic. It always worked. Quite soon the red would give way to green – and we were off. By this magic the children experienced with the traffic lights the kind of power to make things start or stop that the policeman had lost with the coming of the lights. Looking back on his life on the crossing, the new lights told him he had been an automaton all those years, for now a rotating switch in a box had replaced his brain. Thirty years later the children experienced the power the policeman had lost, as the automatic traffic lights seemed to respond to their will. Perhaps both were illusions.

However this may be, we respond to traffic lights as absolute authorities. This is so whether they are time-sequenced or switched from sensory pads in the road, responding almost intelligently to traffic. We are sometimes annoyed by having to wait, and just occasionally we start to doubt. Has it gone wrong? Is it stuck? This is an odd decision that we make – with possible death the outcome – for how do we know when the light is *supposed* to change? We edge out very slowly with extreme caution, hoping no-one sees us, palpitating with guilt and nameless dread, as we violate the Law of the Light. Then, safe, we race away from the confrontation with fate – looking back to see the red change to green as it pursues us with guilt.

1

Waiting for red to change to green on a clear open road is an even odder experience. It is perfectly obvious that nothing is coming so it is perfectly safe to drive on, yet we are inhibited by the extremely strong rule that red means Stop. This is the most strongly held law in modern life, for we all accept that its universal acceptance is life-saving. The red light is the last Kantian Categorical Imperative.

Would it be imperative if traffic lights were human? Imagine a policeman on traffic duty, holding one up for several minutes with absolutely nothing in sight. One would soon assume that his body is not obeying his mind; or that his mind is elsewhere. It would be quite frightening, for one would not know quite what to think. Is he a dummy? Dead? Trying an experiment? There are no such doubts or thoughts for automatic lights, and on balance they are completely fair. Even when in a great hurry one accepts the situation; one accepts the imperative as inevitable. Preference for machine-made over human-made decisions, like most things, goes back to the Greeks. The Athenians of the fourth century BC used an automatic device of randomised tickets in slots, the *kleroterion* (Brumbaugh 1918, p. 66), for selecting juries. Jury service was an onerous duty, involving days of boredom sitting under the sun. The machine was preferred to human officials and even to the gods, who might be biased. Similarly, we accept the delay at automatic traffic lights because we know they are scrupulously fair and, being totally unintelligent though meaningful, they would not understand that we, or other contending drivers, are late for train or plane.

As for most human laws, laws of the lights are somewhat different in different countries. The universal international pedestrian–traffic war has various rules for the amber temporary truce between red and green. There are even differences between states of America as the amber has different meanings in Boston, New York and California. And within Britain there are different ambers: most crossings have a fixed amber period, cunningly phased with red and green delays; in others amber flashes, allowing a temporary contract between driver and pedestrians with human sign language and the making of faces. It is in the uncertain duration and various kinds of amber period that the driver's decision to stop or continue must be made. (There was a steamy novel called *Forever Amber*. This is totally irrelevant.)

All those lights switching on and off must be expensive. Is the amber really necessary? There is a story that they tried to get rid of amber lights in Chicago, which would mean quite a saving in bulbs. They went further: why have separate light bulbs for the red and green lights? This was a clever idea. It depends on the fact that a single bulb in a square box with four glasses – two reds opposite each other, two greens opposite each other – will give, let's say north–south red

2

and east–west green from just one bulb. A second identical box, immediately below but rotated through ninety degrees, will give the reverse: north–south green lights and east–west red lights. So, by switching on the bulbs, with only one on at a time, the lights will change from red to green and green to red for all directions. Brilliant! But there was a snag. Normally, red is always on top but with this system, though red is on top for one direction, red is below the green for the other direction. This may not matter for people with normal colour vision; but colour-blind people (who confuse red and green) can no longer use position to see which is red and which is green. How much position is used by colour-blind people with red-always-on-top is an open question, but apparently it was claimed that colour-blind people in the Chicago experiment had so many accidents, as red was not always on top, that this clever scheme was abandoned.

Years ago traffic lights were simple and unambiguous. Red meant *Stop* – green meant *Go*. But now this is different. In Britain it is common to see a red with a green arrow immediately below it. So we have red and green at the same time! The imperative red is counter-manded by the permissive green arrow. Now the sign is a mumbled *StopGoStopGo*. Ouch! As the green arrow counters what used to be the universally imperative red for straight ahead, it implies that we have to interpret what the red forbids and what it allows. It allows straight-on – which is normally forbidden by the red – and it forbids turning right or left – which are not explicitly signalled.

Presumably this system is based on research, but it certainly seems counter-intuitive and to flout several quite basic principles. The situation is made even worse by the placing of the lights to the side of the crossings, rather than suspended above as in many European countries and America (though this also has its problems).

Is there some better way? We have green, but not red arrows on traffic lights. Why don't we have red arrows for *Don't go*? It might be objected that an arrow should always mean *Go*. But, as things are, there is not this consistency in British road signs, as there are arrows with cancelling cross-lines meaning *Don't* turn left, or *Don't* turn right. So why not red arrow traffic lights, meaning *Don't go* – straight, or left, or right, as the red arrow tells you? Then red is always *Stop* and green is always *Go*.

If colour-blind people confused the red and green arrows they could be given special shapes; or, as the existing road sign cancelled-arrows have now, cross-lines. Europe has special arrows made of dots.

Quite apart from countermanding green, how sacrosanct is red? Is it ever justified to 'beat the lights'? A perpetual bother of driving is that although one can see what is happening very well in front and one can take avoiding action to what is in front, it is very different

3

behind. Even with the best mirrors, one entirely depends on the judgment of another driver to avoid collision from the rear. If he or she is coming up fast behind as the lights are about to change, what should one do at this critical moment? It may be safer to accelerate as the red appears. In Bristol (where this is written) TV cameras have been set up at some crossings to look for drivers beating the lights. A sharp increase in minor collisions from the rear has been observed at these lights. As the cameras are visible, drivers know they are being watched and can be traced from their number plates, so presumably normal on-the-turn-to-red behaviour is upset – drivers are being *too* punctilious.

Some of the British road signs are mandatory, others obligatory. The distinction is clearly important. It is represented not by the sign but by its *background*. An arrow-sign is mandatory on a circular background, and advisory on a square background. Not realizing this when it was introduced some years ago – the shape of a background is not a usual sign – I violated a mandatory *Don't turn left* arrow in London and was stopped by a policeman. When I asked why this was a violation, he explained that the sign was mandatory but he did not seem to know why, except that he had been told to stop drivers turning left at this point. He didn't seem to appreciate the distinction between a round or square background any better than I did. A week later, a summons arrived for illegally turning left against a mandatory arrow. Over the next few days I asked six policemen the difference between round and square backgrounds. None knew the difference, or that there was a difference. Armed with this, I phoned the local chief of police and told him the result of my little survey. He cancelled the summons. In my experience the police are fair and reasonable. Who would expect the shape of the background to change the meaning of a sign?

Whether the system of traffic lights is based on research is a moot question, but certainly there is extensive research on driver behaviour and accidents at lights. Allsop, Brown, Groeger and Robertson (1990) report that 20,000 people are injured at signalled-controlled road junctions each year in Britain. Considering that lights are placed at crossings to make them safer this seems a high figure, though it is small compared with the umpteen millions of crossings made by cars and pedestrians every year. It is reported (Allsop *et al* 1990, citing Olson and Sivak 1986) that in a 'surprise' situation, movement time from accelerator to brake is in the range 280–780 ms (median 400 ms) for younger drivers (18–40) years) and, surprisingly less, is 220–480 ms (median 350 ms) for older (50–84) drivers. When people were alerted with a warning, these times become 200 ms and 220 ms respectively. Perception times to a sudden red light are: 420–1020 ms (median

750 ms) for younger, and 630–1030 ms (median 750 ms) for older drivers. When alerted, both age groups have a median of 500 ms. Just how, and with what reliability, decisions are made in the 'uncertainty period' before the red changes has both theoretical and practical significance. It is not 'merely academic'.

Driving requires fine judgment. As for all symbols, traffic lights and road signs need to be interpreted with intelligent appreciation of context and other drivers' intentions, with prediction and evaluations of possible outcomes. Much of this highly complex, ever-changing decision making – remarkably – is below the level of conscious awareness. Indeed, becoming analytically aware can make us dither, creating uncertainty and confusion. It is amazing that almost anyone can drive reasonably safely – possibly because the cortex is not much involved! – though the task is difficult and inherently dangerous.

Perhaps necessarily, the lights and the law require – yet also penalise – intelligence.

REFERENCES

Allsop, R.E., Brown, I.D., Groeger, F.A. and Robertson, S.A. (1990) *Approaches to modelling driver behaviour at actual and simulated traffic signals*, Final report by the Transport Studies Group and MRC Applied Psychology Unit Cambridge to the Transport and Road Research Laboratory on contract 9834/35. (UCL Reference ECW3.)

Brumbaugh, Robert S. (1918) *Ancient Greek Gadgets and Machines* (Westport, Connecticut: Greenwood Press).

Olson, P.L. and Sivak, M. (1986) 'Perception-response time to unexpected roadway hazards', *Human Factors* 28(1), 91–6.

2

THE CASE OF THE SUGARED ALMONDS

Some tiny events stay in one's memory as gems to be treasured, every now and again to be re-examined. This is a very special private gem, not really to be revealed. Please treat it as such.

Just after we married we dined in a very grand restaurant in Scotland. It was one of those places with too much of everything: over-large dazzling white tablecloths; so many waiters they were faceless smiles; massive silver so polished it was invisible, reflecting a world of secure assumptions we hardly understood. There were even odder reflections from the too-many gilt mirrors, Escher-worlds away.

My wife was in a dreamy mood. What were her thoughts?

With the coffee, an absolutely enormous bowl full of sugared almonds was placed on our table. There must have been at least a hundred almonds, lying there to be selected, each identical to its sugary companions. To my astonishment – lasting to this day, years later – my young wife picked up the huge bowl and poured practically all the sugared almonds into her handbag.

'Is that *right*?' I asked.

'Of *course*,' she answered.

The rights and wrongs of this remained a topic of debate for years. Here is the issue:

She: If the sugared almonds are provided – and they were put on our table to be taken by us and no-one else – why shouldn't we have *any* number of them?

Me: Too many are deliberately provided, so that we have the luxury and freedom of choice.

She: But I made my choice – I took lots of almonds.

Me: But you aren't supposed to take so many.

She: Then where is the freedom of choice? What's the point of being offered lots of them, if one can't actually take lots of them?

Me: Um – well, you see – because in a place like this one has the feeling of opulence and that one has the best of everything – which makes one feel special.

She: But what is so special, if we can't have more than two or three almonds?

Me: Well – you could – only you shouldn't have put them in your handbag!

She: Why not – I couldn't eat any more now.

Me: Well – you see – *that's the point*.

Unfortunately she didn't see this point. I never was able to explain it effectively, to her or to myself.

Just what *is* the point?

3

PERCEPTIONS OF *HAMLET*

This essay was inspired (breathed in) by a splendid weekend organized by Lord and Lady Hylton at Ammerdown House where some twenty Shakespeare scholars, led by Professor Desai, and a few interested though relatively ignorant people such as myself, discussed the characters and meanings of the most celebrated play ever written – Hamlet.

This one play, *Hamlet, Prince of Denmark*, written by William Shakespeare in about 1606, has excited questions about its meanings over centuries, and in many languages by generations of theatre audiences and scholars. It has grown a literature of tens of thousands of learned papers and books of comment, and at least one journal, edited by Professor Desai in Delhi, is entirely devoted to studies of *Hamlet*. Hamlet appears in *Chambers Biographical Dictionary* as though he had really lived, and we learn there that he first appeared in the legend of Hamlet, in the twelfth-century Latin history of Denmark by Saxo Grammaticus.

   In the action of the play there are eight violent deaths, adultery, a mad woman, a fight in a grave – and a ghost, whom only Hamlet hears. This is the ghost of his father, who after almost interminable delay (Hamlet's famous procrastination, as it is often called) sets him to revenge his father's murder and the violation of his wife Gertrude, Hamlet's mother, by demanding that Hamlet must kill his uncle, the murderer King Claudius. What makes this violent, improbable plot so interesting to so many people?

   There are many questions that have been asked by scholars and lovers of the theatre over three centuries; but they focus on a single aspect of the play: why did Hamlet procrastinate? According to the first editor of Shakespeare's works, Sir Thomas Hanmer (1773, quoted by Bradley 1904), 'There appears to be no reason at all in nature why this young prince did not put the usurper to death as soon as poss-ible'. Hanmer explains this most famous, most discussed procrastina-tion of all time as necessary for the author to avoid the play coming to end before it had fairly started. Most commentators, however, explain it in terms of the character of Hamlet. Either his character simply lacks decision, or his concern with philosophy unfits him for action. This last view has no doubt been accepted as a general criticism of the academic world and its ways of looking at and dealing with (or not dealing with) the 'real' world. Yet to those with an intellectual cast of mind it is absurd to make rapid decisions when delay may allow better judgement to prevail.

Looking at this more generally, there are certain questions that have been asked for thousands of years of philosophy, science, art, and the morality of right and wrong conduct. They have been considered without so far finding any resolution after these millenia of consideration and debate. But, living as we do in real-time, hasty and often arbitrary actions must be determined upon to catch situations while they can be mastered; and new events may overtake the wisest delayed decisions, to make them 'merely academic'. So, procrastinating scholars (it is is often thought) are best locked up in colleges – which is the supreme advantage for all concerned – of Oxford and Cambridge. Students are often impatient with experiments and explanations that do not yield immediate results of practical consequence. The answer to this is that deep explanations allow us to surface with better practical decisions and more powerful techniques for solving 'real' problems. If this is so for science, why should it not also be so for individuals? Why should it not be right for Hamlet to experiment in his mind, for as long as possible, to find the best, perhaps far-from-obvious decision? What's the rush, when eternity is at stake?

Hamlet's soliloquies might be seen as the medium for the bard to express his own thoughts; or they might be Hamlet's protracted thought experiments, necessary for his considered action. Here we meet a curious question. We speak of Hamlet as thinking; Hamlet as procrastinating; even, Hamlet as being conscious. But Hamlet never lived. He is but a product of the bard's wonderful imagination. Even Shakespeare's identity has been questioned, and certainly we have no independent record of his thoughts, or consciousness, or intentions. *Hamlet* commentators concern themselves with the prince's psychology, rather than the bard's. Most, until recently, discuss fictional Hamlet as though he were a living, intelligent man. This is, surely, his interest for us – making him relevant now, long after the death of his creator, the bard, and the demise of the society in which Hamlet's actions (had he ever lived) would have had any direct effect.

Is it important that this play was written by Shakespeare? Suppose *Hamlet* had been written by a committee. Would Hamlet have the same interest for us, if the play had been written by a computer? The feat of producing these wonderful words by machine would certainly enthral us technically. We would ask how a machine could do it, how much human help it needed. If it turned out that the computer was self-guided, following internal rules it had built up for itself, perhaps jolted from time to time by chance as in a poker game or roulette, then our technical interest would be maximal – but correspondingly our psychological interest would surely wane to vanishing point. The famous procrastination would have no more significance than following the rules of a game, from time to time jolted by the run of the dice. As we find the play *Hamlet* so psychologically enthralling, though we do not and we cannot explain Hamlet's behaviour from Shakespeare's psychology, evidently we do see Hamlet the man as an alive, independent being, and the bard as a human with normal though incredibly enhanced psychology.

If we knew more about Shakespeare, would we understand Hamlet better? *Hamlet* is a great work of art. What of a great work of science? We know far more about Newton than we do about Shakespeare, though Newton's psychology is quite mysterious (Cohen 1980, Westfall 1980). On any account, this lack of knowledge of the psychology of the author is less important for our appreciating the achievements of Newton than those of Shakespeare. If we discovered, now, that Newton was a secret computer, much of his work would appear to us unchanged. What would look different would, for example, be the Queries in the *Opticks* which speculate beyond available evidence or structured theory. Reading these we assume, and somehow we need to assume, that they were written by a highly intelligent human author. For the far more mathematical *Principia* (or, say, the *Nautical Almanac*) it would not much matter if it was (and most of the *Nautical Almanac* is) written by a computer. The only passages where it would matter are where decisions are made outside the rules of a calculus or theory. Thus, Newton's assumptions and leaps of imagination remain essentially Newton's. We find Newton interesting for having created them, very much as we find Shakespeare interesting for having created Hamlet. But this interest in the authors follows from our interest in the character of Hamlet and, so to say, the character Newton gives the universe.

Most truly interesting works of creation are products of procrastination, and action without context is as boring as zapping arcade games which, though fun for the moment, are too restricted and do not open doors to new possibilities. Surely *Hamlet* is so interesting because it is rich with hinted possibilities. We see the prince (though he never lived) as a man, and we are privileged to share the dramatic tensions of his doubts and conflicts preceding the decisions which lead to events with terrible outcomes. The event-action is robust blood and thunder, stemming from earlier traditions of dramatic tragic drama. As a work of art *Hamlet* does not stand alone and could not be understood without reference to earlier plays – any more than Newton's *Principia* stands alone or could at all be understood without reference to the discoveries and ideas of many earlier scientists.

Newton was criticised in his time for mysterious action-at-a-distance, and lack of initiating principles. Shakespeare initiates *Hamlet* with a ghost. This is the ghost of Hamlet's father. The reality of the ghost is questioned and tested in the very first scene of Act I, by the officers Marcellus and Bernardo and by Hamlet's friend Horatio:

Marcellus. Horatio says 'tis but our fantasy,
And will not let belief take hold of him
Touching this dreaded sight twice seen of us.
Therefore I have entreated him along
With us to watch the minutes of this night;
That if again this apparition come,
He may approve our eyes and speak to it.
Horatio. Tush, tush! 'twill not appear.

But the ghost does appear, though he does not yet speak:

Marcellus. Thou art a scholar; speak to it, Horatio.
. . . . . It is offended.
Bernado. See! it stalks away.
Horatio. Stay! speak: speak, I charge thee. Speak!

Following a wonderful passage, where nothing happens:

Horatio. A mote it is to trouble the mind's eye.
. . . The graves stood tenantless and the sheeted dead
Did squeak and gibber in the Roman streets
As stars with trains of fire and dews of blood
. . . Was sick almost to doomsday with eclipse
. . . But, soft! behold! lo! where it comes again.

The ghost returns, and Horatio continues:

Horatio: I'll cross it, though it blast me. Stay, illusion!
If thou hast any sound, or use of voice, speak to me.
Marcellus: Shall I strike at it with my partisan?
Horatio: Do, if it will not stand.
Bernardo: 'tis here!
Horatio: 'tis here!   [*Exit* Ghost.]
Marcellus: 'Tis gone!

Then they give explanations, half-appropriate to a living man, a king, for its departure:

11

Marcellus. We do it wrong, being so majestical
To offer it the show of violence
For it is, as the air, invulnerable
And our vain blows malicious mockery ...
Horatio. And then it started like a guilty thing
Upon a fearful summons.

Later, the ghost speaks to Hamlet:

Ghost.　　　　　　My hour is almost come,
When I to sulphurous and tormenting flames
Must render up myself.
Hamlet.　　　　　　Alas! poor ghost!
Ghost. Pity me not, but lend thy serious hearing
To what I shall unfold.

This is that he was murdered through poison by:

that incestuous, that adulterate beast
... So to seduce – won with his shameful lust
The will of my most seeming virtuous queen.

Thus was Hamlet commanded to revenge his father's murder. His musings, doubtings, testing and discovery of his own mind (Act III) are so well known they sound like echoes:

Hamlet. To be, or not to be: that is the question!
Whether 'tis nobler in the mind to suffer
The slings and arrows of outrageous fortune,
Or to take arms against a sea of troubles,
And by opposing end them? To die: to sleep;
. . . . . .
To sleep: perchance to dream: aye, there's the
　　rub;
For in that sleep of death what dreams may come
When we have shuffled off this mortal coil,
Must give us pause. There's the respect
That makes calamity of so long life;
For who would bear the whips and scorns of time,
The oppressor's wrong, the proud man's contumely,
The pangs of despis'd love, the law's delay,
. . . . . .
Thus conscience does make cowards of us all;
And thus the native hue of resolution
Is sicklied o'er with the pale cast of thought,
And enterprise of great pitch and moment
With this regard their currents turn awry,
And lose the name of action.

12

Yet he cannot remain inactive (Act IV):

> How stand I then,
> That have a father kill'd, a mother stain'd,
> Excitements of my reason and my blood,
> And let all sleep, while, to my shame, I see
> The imminent death of twenty thousand men.

Now let's ask again: What sense of interest would any of this have, if we did not think of Hamlet as a living man? What sense the ghost, if we did not think of him as a man recently dead, though able to speak? Yet, as I understand it, recent literary criticism denies independent life to the characters of plays and novels.

How should we perceive fictional characters? This is an interesting question. They can live in our minds more vividly than do some of our friends and colleagues. Recently, an English television actor, William Roache, successfully sued a reviewer who found Ken Barlow – the *character* he plays – boring. Actors have a hard time knowing who they are: they become the stage or the TV characters they play. Surely we all create ourselves – write our own parts, stage our own performances – throughout life. We become very different at home or at work; with intimate friends or formal colleagues; playing with children; playing host or guest with adults. The line between reality and fiction of personal identity is very hard to draw. As an author with his creations, no doubt we let parts of ourselves live, and allow other bit-players within us to die.

Hamlet dies, waiting for news from England:

> O! I die, Horatio;
> The potent poison quite o'er-crows my spirit;
> I cannot live to hear the news from England,
> But I do prophesy the election lights
> On Fortinbras: he has my dying voice;
> So tell him, with the occurrents, more and less,
> Which have solicited. – The rest is silence.

If we return to the best-known Shakespeare commentator, Andrew Cecil Bradley (brother of the Oxford philosopher, Francis Herbert Bradley), we find that Hamlet was by him and his generation regarded as a once-living man, with both conscious and unconscious motives. Of the passage just quoted, he writes (Bradley 1904, p. 101):

> Is it not clear that he [Hamlet] is speculating just as vainly now, and that this question of conscience is but one of his many unconscious excuses for delay? And, lastly, is it not so that Horatio takes it? He [Horatio] declines to discuss that unreal question, and answers simply,

13

> It must be shortly known to him from England
> What is the issue of the business there.

In other words, 'Enough of this endless procrastination. What is wanted is not reasons for the deed, but the deed itself.'

Bradley considers a rather different version of this conscience account (p. 102):

> Hamlet, so far as his explicit consciousness went, was sure that he ought to obey the ghost; but in the depths of his nature, and unknown to himself, there was a moral repulsion to the deed.

This Bradley rejects on three grounds: that on this account Hamlet would not have concealed that meaning until the last act (though surely this should apply to Shakespeare rather than to Hamlet); that if this were so, Hamlet wouldn't have hesitated to kill his uncle while at prayer, to save his enemy's soul from going to Heaven; that (though here again I would have thought this should refer to the bard rather than to Hamlet):

> The theory requires us to suppose that, when the ghost enjoins Hamlet to avenge his father, it is laying on him a duty which *we* are to understand to be no duty but the very reverse. And is not that supposition wholly contrary to the natural impression which we all receive in reading the play? Surely it is clear that, whatever we in the twentieth century may think about Hamlet's duty, we are meant in the play to assume that he *ought* to have obeyed the Ghost.

This is subtle stuff. It refers both to Hamlet as a conscious person, also to his unconscious motives, and to the bard's intentions with respect to us his audience, and our reactions to the plot and the characters of the play. These are all intertwined – in what we would now call incomprehensible, unpredictable *chaos*! But this is also so, surely, for life itself. In real life there is just this interplay of events, having uncertain causes and effects, guessed-at motives and conflicting claims making decisions difficult, with a corresponding need for procrastination in real time. If we accept Bradley's view that Hamlet is real, he is no more difficult to understand than anyone else of our acquaintance. If we deny him existence (as recent Structuralism seems to do) we are denied our own experience for understanding the play; then it becomes arbitrary and dull. A literary theory that can make *Hamlet* dull certainly has remarkable power, but this is not sufficient to make it a useful theory, or true.

What is Structuralism? For years I have procrastinated over finding out. Following admittedly cursory and hurried reading, I find that

14

Structuralism attempts to make literary criticism scientific. Like science, it has developed its own (impenetrable) jargon. It derives from continental *semiotic* notions of symbols and meaning. Well-known names in the field include Roland Barthes, Pierre Corneille, Jacques Derrida, Michel Foucault, Roman Jakobson, Claude Lévi-Strauss and Ferdinand de Saussure. The novelist David Lodge (1986) describes what Structuralism is more clearly than in any other account I have so far found. He distinguishes two main branches (p. ix):

> One is the extension of what I would call classical Structuralism. It is concerned with the analysis and understanding of culture as a system of systems, of which language is usually taken as the ideal model for explanatory purposes. This Structuralism seems to do for literature – or myth, or food or fashion – what grammar does for language: to understand and explain how these systems work, what are the rules and constraints within which, and by virtue of which, meaning is generated and communicated. It is essentially formalist, and aspires to the status of science.

The second branch is

> ideological in orientation. It combines the anti-empirical methodology of classical Structuralism with ideas derived from Marxism, psycho-analysis and philosophy ... this Structuralism is polemical and *engagé*.

At least the first branch seems to the uninitiated understandable and interesting. But does it kill off characters of fiction, in favour of scientific-looking analyses of texts? Does it destroy what it classifies? Explanations in science reveal wonders of the world, described by symbols: is this so, also, for these explanations of symbols in literature? Or do they destroy the meanings and kill the characters they hope to capture?

Men are captured in chess, but they have no characters, apart from the roles they play. Kings, bishops, knights, pawns have powers and vulnerabilities entirely from the rules and their place in the game. Any one, or all at once, could be substituted for different men, of wood, marble, china or humans costumed in chess clothes – it does not matter who or what they are provided that they follow the rules and play their parts appropriately. This is the same for the planets in the Newtonian universe: if planets were substituted for bodies of the same masses, there would be no differences in the dynamics of the solar system, and with crude sight all would seem the same as before. This is quite unlike the classical planets seen as characters, gods and goddesses, acting out their courtly ritual as individual intelligences in the sky. Is Structuralism attempting this Newtonian revolution of the

15

heavens, from individuals to rule-bound cyphers, for characters of literature? The laws of the physical world are essential keys to the understanding of physics, and some psychological laws are revealed by observations and experiments on people; but only on the crudest accounts are individual objects or people submerged in the generalities of laws. With greater astronomical knowledge, each planet – while obeying the general laws of physics – is seen to have its own individual characteristics, with the interest individuality confers. If in the quest of scientific respectability Structuralism reduces Hamlet's character to an anonymous piece as in a game of chess, or to a substitutable object of physics, surely science will look askance at such a misuse of its methods, and literature will suffer as its characters drown and are lost in a meaningless sea of rules.

In the year *Hamlet* was written the telescope was invented, allowing a close look at the heavens. Turning this cardboard tube with lentil-shaped glasses to the sky, Galileo observed the planets as individually different. He saw the Queen Moon not as a perfect golden sphere, but pock-marked wth mountains and shadows. Saturn he saw not with its ring, which was too fanciful for acceptance, but as a face with ears, or two handles of a jug – which through the months mysteriously disappeared. That it was an encircling ring that vanished when it became edge-on was realized by Christian Huygens nearly half a century later. Galileo saw Jupiter with four changing and sometimes disappearing encircling moons, the very model of the solar system with central sun that the Inquisition had imprisoned him for believing, tantalizingly only just out of reach of unaided eyes. The sun blinded him. Before the instrument of discovery lost him his eyes, Galileo saw ever-changing disfiguring dark spots upon the Sun King's face. So the heavens were more ugly and more beautiful, less constant but more challenging, than had been thought before this closer look with these wonderful glass lentils. When the light the stars emit was analysed it was found possible to discern the individual substances of the stars and learn why they burn. By these clever, careful observations, the lawful moving points of light and the bland bodies of sun and moon became fascinating individuals, to be studied not only for the parts they play in the structure of the universe, but each for its own individual interest. As we increase our understanding of how we think and feel and live, doesn't this extension of understanding through closer seeing apply also to the characters of literature?

REFERENCES

Bradley, A.C. (1904) *Shakespearean Tragedy: Lectures on Hamlet, Othello, King Lear and Macbeth*. (London: Macmillan). Reprinted 1991, with foreword by John Baley (London: Penguin).

Cohen, I.B. (1980) *The Newtonian Revolution*. (Cambridge: Cambridge University Press).

Lodge, D. (1986) *Working with Structuralism*. (London: Routledge & Kegan Paul).

Smith, N.D. (1903) (ed.) *Eighteenth-Century Essays on Shakespeare*. (Glasgow: James MacLehode).

Westfall, R.S. (1980) *Never at Rest: A Biography of Newton*. (Cambridge: Cambridge University Press).

4

WHAT USE IS A JELLY BABY?

A man about 46 years of age giving the name of Joshua Copper-smith, has been arrested in New York for attempting to extort funds from ignorant and superstitious people by exhibiting a device which he says will convey the human voice any distance over metallic wires so that it will be heard by the listener at the other end. He calls the instrument a 'telephone' which is obvious-ly intended to imitate the word 'telegraph' and win the con-fidence of those who know the success of the latter instrument without understanding the principles on which it is based. Well-informed people know that it is impossible to transmit the human voice over wires as may be done with dots and dashes of Morse code, and that, were it possible to do so, the thing would be of no practical value.

The authorities who apprehended this criminal are to be con-gratulated and it is to be hoped that his punishment will be prompt and fitting, that it may serve as an example to other *con-scienceless schemers* who enrich themselves at the expense of their fellow creatures.

Quoted by Edison's assistant, Francis Jehl
(Jehl 1937, pp. 1937) from a Boston Newspaper of 1865.
This was written 11 years before Bell's telephone
(1876): the most valuable of any patent.

When Michael Faraday was asked 'What use is electricity?' he replied 'What use is a baby?' Like babies, how discoveries and inventions grow is unpredictable. Most are forgotten. A few change the world. Babies are wonderful toys for adults!

Children growing to adult powers are nurtured and tended and influenced by many people in a co-operative enterprise where we can all question and learn. Certainly we learn from children.

New discoveries and young inventions are like this: a scientist can-not resist playing with them, teasing them into new tricks, while

18

looking for what they may do and what they might become. Like bringing up children, science depends on hoped-for futures, with shared intentions; yet, when the roll of the dice lands upon success, there are some unintentional inventions and discoveries. There is this element of chance for children and for ideas. Most fade away, but for a few the elements come together and jell with a life of their own. These are *Jelly Babies*.

GOO JELL

The universally useful 'goo jell' Vaseline (whose history is described in Panati (1987)) was invented in 1859 by a Brooklyn chemist, Robert Chesebrough. He was looking at oil wells in Pennsylvania to try to get rid of an annoying sticky substance which gummed up the drilling rods and blocked the pumps. This slimy goo was believed, by the oil men, to heal cuts. Chesebrough took a sample back to Brooklyn. Purifying the dark, oily mess in his laboratory, he obtained a clear jell. Then he most certainly demonstrated intention, for he tested its supposed but most probably mythical curative powers on self-inflicted wounds. It seemed to work. So perhaps he was on to something interesting. His jell soon took off as a remarkable product, finding more and more totally unexpected uses.

At first it was called 'petroleum jelly' then it became famous as Vaseline. Within a short time it was used for: bait for catching trout; simulated tears for actresses to catch sympathy; preventing machines from rusting at the North Pole, by Robert Peary; preventing frostbite; softening leather; a coating for long-distance swimmers; preventing the green corrosion of the terminals of car batteries; by Amazonian natives who cooked with it as it did not go rancid, and they also used jars of Vaseline as money. There were many other applications. Having found so many uses for his omnipotent jell, Robert Chesebrough became extremely rich. Taking a mouthful daily, he lived happily to extreme old age.

Vaseline started out as unwanted goo which jelled into innumerable unpredictable successes. This, however, had nothing of the interest of our second jell – though this turned out not to exist.

MATHEMATICAL JELL

The Aether was supposed to fill all space – carry light and everything else in the universe that seemed to act-at-a-distance. This all-pervading universal jell had its ancient origins as the quintessential matter of the planets and stars of the Greeks. Two thousand years later, after many changes and adventures (Whittaker 1910), the universal 'aether jell' linking everything was the strongest, most certain and most useful belief of physics in the nineteenth century. Yet now, the Aether is abandoned – another myth.

We might say that the universal jell, the aether, was invented to carry light by analogy with sound carried by air. At least by the seventeenth century, sound was known to be waves travelling in air. There was no problem about the existence of air for though not itself visible, it could be felt, and its effects could be seen in winds propelling ships and, with super-human strength, turning windmill sails to grind grain. By the time of the flowering of science in the middle of the seventeenth century it was clear that air affected barometers, allowing non-mystical predictions of capricious air-borne weather. Through the experiments of Robert Boyle who removed air with vacuum pumps – though the supposed aether could not be removed, which made its presence impossible to establish experimentally – it became clear that air carries sound; that it had chemical properties; that it is necessary for fire; necessary for life.

Only a little earlier air had 'looked' very different. It seemed that flames rose because they possessed 'levity'. It was thought that 'Nature abhorred a vacuum'. Then Galileo's pupil Torricelli showed, with Viviani in 1643, that – absurdly – Nature only abhors a vacuum up to 33 feet. They found that the height 'supported by a vacuum' is much less for the much heavier mercury. Then it became clear that the old notion of 'abhorrence of a vacuum' is a joke. It looks funny when it is realized that the water, or the mercury column, is balanced by the weight of the atmosphere reaching right up to space. From this simple experiment a whole new way of seeing was born. How often does scientific insight, especially with an invention as useful as the barometer, generate a joke?

Pascal showed (in 1646) that the 'abhorrence to a vacuum' was less up a mountain. Then the atmosphere was no longer seen in the psychological terms of the Greeks (air giving us 'inspirations') but in terms of mechanical and chemical principles – though the weather be beyond a joke.

Light was supposed to be waves much like sounds in air, travelling in a medium though a very peculiar medium – the aether. The great nineteenth-century physicist James Thomson, Lord Kelvin, deduced properties of the aether from observing smoke rings, concluding that atoms are aether vortices. Unlike air, aether was curiously hard to detect for it seemed to have no extra properties and, unlike air, aether couldn't be pumped away or in any way removed. It seemed too good to be true. Just as the existence of this elusive universal jell began to be questioned it was defined mathematically by the Scottish physicist James Clerk-Maxwell – with equations which still have immense importance today even though the aether they depended upon has now disappeared as a fiction. Clerk-Maxwell predicted (1831–79):

> The vast interplanetary and interstellar regions will no longer be regarded as waste places in the universe. . . . We shall find them to be already full of this wonderful medium; so full that no human power can remove it from the smallest portion of space, or produce the slightest flaw in its continuity.

It was just this that made its existence hard to test; though there were some doubts.

Michael Faraday became fascinated by what was called 'electric light' as early as the eighteenth century – the luminous discharges in glass vacuum tubes. In the 1850s he became particularly interested in the striations in the glow, including 'Faraday's Dark Space'. It is fascinating that though the *glow* is affected by a magnet the *striations* are not. Faraday wrote (in a letter to J. Plucker on 27 January 1857):

> Then again the question of transmission of the discharge across a perfect vacuum or whether a vacuum exists or not? is to me a continual thought and seems connected with the hypothesis of the ether. What a pity one can't get hold of these points by some *experiments* more close and searching than any we have yet decided.

Faraday had come to reject the notion that electricity is a fluid and had begun to doubt the aether when he devised his notion of Lines of Force in space.

John Meurig Thomas has recently written (1991):

> Faraday demonstrated the existence of his conceived *lines of force*. . . . Events were to show that this was probably Faraday's greatest contribution to physics and certainly his most important theoretical one. His lines of force ushered a new era of physics and cosmology; an era built on the concept of field, which pervaded the space around a magnet and around an electric current, and, in the words of Maxwell (much later) 'weaves a web through the sky'.

The aether was evaporated from physics by the concepts of Einstein's Theory of Relativity (1905), and by the experiments of Michelson and Morley in America which showed that light has the same speed whatever the direction their measuring apparatus was carried by the earth's motion through space.

This most famous null-result experiment was conceived in 1881 and carried out in its definitive form in 1897. Its unexpected result was not, at first, interpreted by Michelson as showing there is no aether.

Like any other experiment, this needed assumptions to interpret it and what these assumptions should be was not at all clear. Michelson preferred to think of the earth dragging the aether with it (like the atmosphere) and so avoiding a change in the velocity of light. Only later did a theory emerge that made the meaning of his extremely surprising result, of no change of light's velocity with or across the earth's motion, 'obvious'.

It was obvious through Einstein's eyes. It is a much wondered-at marvel that Maxwell's equations for the aether inspired, and were essential for Einstein's theory – yet it was Einstein's theory that banished the aether! Newton had thought of light as particles travelling through space – but waves? Before Einstein, generations of physicists depended on the aether for their conceptual sanity. How could waves travel in *nothing*?

As late as 1925, the distinguished physicist Sir Oliver Lodge (1851–1940) still accepted, without doubts, the aether. He saw it as explaining just about everything; action-at-a-distance, gravity, light, magnetism, electricity, matter, mind – even God. In his *Ether and Reality* (1925) Oliver Lodge invoked the aether not only for the sense of sight but also for touch. The book ends:

> Touch seems to be a purely material sensation, the result of direct contact with matter: it is indeed what we call 'contact'. But when we come to analyse touch, we learn that atoms are never in contact. They approach each other within an infinitesimal distance; but there is always a cushion, what may be called a repulsive force, between them – a cushion of Ether. Hence, even our apparently most omnipresent medium, on which alone we can directly act, and through which all our information comes. It is the primary instrument of Mind, the vehicle of Soul, the habitation of Spirit. Truly it may be called the living garment of God.

The properties of the aether became ever more bizarre. Following Lord Kelvin, who calculated it should have a rigidity greater than steel, Lodge described the aether as having a density 1,000,000,000,000 times the density of water, yet with a viscosity of zero. He says (p. 99):

> Resistance to motion is due to viscosity, not to density; and the Ether certainly has no viscosity; it is not at all like treacle, it is perfectly limpid. Density is no cause of friction, but it is a cause of inertia, and inertia is just what moving bodies exhibit.

So he gives the invisible, untouchable aether just those properties that need explaining.

Oliver Lodge was interested in the philosophy of science (he stated clearly that exceptions may refute, but confirmations cannot prove a generalization) yet he fell for the notion of an all-embracing *something* supposed to explain *everything*, and so explaining *nothing*. It fails to explain because the questions are merely restated as properties of this otherwise unknown substance. Thus the aether was endowed with the properties of light, magnetism, inertia and so on that it was invoked to explain – until it became mystery incarnate. Is this the fate of any Theory of Everything?

The same objection holds for Vitalism – supposing a substance of life – which does not explain life because *it* would need explaining and nothing can explain itself. Yet, curiously, although aether and vital spirit are not explanations, somehow they focused explanations towards conceptual inventions of great power. This is so for that most romantic, largely serendipitous invention – radio. Radio was born of fundamental discoveries undreamed of before the nineteenth century, in a flurry of invention that exceeded knowledge. Radio was more than a discovery because it did not already exist in nature: it was more than an invention because its principles were not understood.

Maxwell believed in the aether. He visualised aether as a perfect jell. He said that it 'weaves a web through the sky'. To give his aether equations substance, he conceived a mechanism of imaginary gears that he could visualise (Fig. 4.1).

Radio was first seen as a possibility from the mathematical work of James Clerk-Maxwell, around 1865. His theory of light as electromagnetic waves predicted there should be similar waves with a great range of frequencies, all travelling at the same speed as light in space. But different kinds of detectors are needed for different frequency bands, for although the waves are essentially the same for all frequencies they interact with matter differently, and so have to be detected or observed by different means. With our eye's narrow (one octave) frequency response, we can't see X-rays, ultra-violet, infra-red or radio waves, as they do not resonate with the micro-structure of our retinas. It is remarkable that a simple length of copper wire responds to the comparatively long waves of radio, to which the complex subtleties of the millions of rods and cones receptors of a retina are blind.

What are now called radio waves were first generated and detected in 1887 by Heinrich Hertz. Hertz was a student of the modern founder of the study of vision, Hermann von Helmholtz. Hertz's apparatus was absurdly simple, like a child's science-pretend toy: a shocking coil and a loop of wire with a small gap. This showed that an electric spark could produce another tiny spark, a few feet away, in the gap of a loop of wire. Action-at-a-distance! Yet, no more so than for eye-light. Hertz found that the invisible waves predicted by Clerk-Maxwell

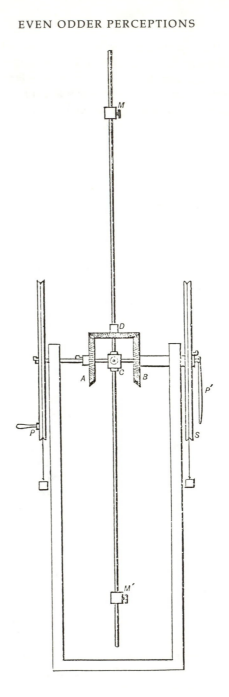

Figure 4.1 An original drawing of James Clerk-Maxwell's aether gears

could be reflected, refracted and polarized just as for familiar light, except that the mirrors and prisms and lenses must be made of different materials.

We think of radio as invented by Guglielmo Marconi (1874–1937), and indeed it was Marconi who brought wireless communication into being. This was an immense achievement especially as (or because?) Marconi had only limited formal training in science. Here science did not simply show the way. The secrets were unlocked by intentional, largely intuitive invention, as much as by scientific discovery. The inventor Guglielmo Marconi started from where the scientist Heinrich Hertz left off, though the essentials of Hertz's apparatus lived on for years in wirelesses, transmitting and receiving Morse code.

Marconi started experimenting in his parents' home near Bologna. When he needed solid support, the Italian government did not help. In 1896 he moved to England and was assured the help of the Post Office. He very soon demonstrated wireless communication across the Bristol Channel. But the next year he set up his own company, as the British government declined to pay for his patents. In 1899 he communicated over 50 kilometres across the English Channel and his work was seen as extremely significant, especially for communicating to and between ships. Indeed, the Chief Engineer of the British Post Office, William Preece, had seen the importance and the possibility of communicating over long distances without wires as early as 1884, when he had tried to extend Michael Faraday's electric induction to communicate to islands and across rivers. This attempt, however, was doomed to failure because the induction effect (the principle of transformers) falls off very rapidly with distance. Early demonstrations of radio were often dismissed as 'merely' induction. The new principle took time to be recognized. It must have looked too good to be true!

Perhaps because he was not a trained scientist, Marconi was not afraid to challenge and, indeed, flout the science of his day. One of his greatest, most idiosyncratic achievements, that no committee would have backed, was transmitting across the Atlantic, in 1901. This experiment should have failed – for like light, radio waves should not have bent round the earth anything like as much as Marconi found that they did. When he reported that he heard the letter S in Morse code at his receiver in Newfoundland, transmitted from Cornwall over 3500 kilometres of sea, he claimed something impossible. It was questioned, and there was no real proof, as the three faint dots of the Morse Code S might have been imagined. Accepted proof came in 1902, when Marconi got inked-paper records of communication between Poldhu in Cornwall and the ship *Philadelphia* which was 2500 kilometres distant. But how did the waves bend round the earth? This question led to the surprising discovery of layers of ionized gas high in the atmosphere, which reflect radio wavelengths though not light.

The invention challenged science – and won. In turn – science gained from the invention.

There were many contenders for the prize of inventing radio, including the greatest inventor of all time, Thomas Alva Edison (1847–1931) who was granted over a thousand patents for a remarkably wide range of inventions which had immense practical use and very considerable scientific interest. His Black Box demonstrated what he called 'etheric force'. This was on 22 November 1875, at his Menlo Park laboratory in New Jersey. His Black Box was very similar to Hertz's apparatus, displaying faint sparks that seemed to Edison quite different from any other sparks he had seen in all his experience of telegraphy. He found that this new kind of spark would not charge a Leyden jar, did not affect an electroscope, or a galvanometer (Jehl 1937, p. 82). This discovery was made twelve years before the experiments of Heinrich Hertz, but they lacked any theoretical basis. Although Edison sent messages without wires two years before Hertz, this work was not recognised and has been largely forgotten. Oliver Lodge said of Edison's 'etheric force' experiments, that they were: 'a small part of this very thing, only the time was not ripe; theoretical knowledge was not ready for it.'

Oliver Lodge demonstrated wireless telegraphy over a short distance in London at the Royal Institution in 1894. He wrote several early books on wireless telegraphy (including *Signalling Across Space Without Wires* in 1897). He also spent a lot of time on psychical research. Sadly, he tried for years to hear the voice of his dead son Raymond by radio through the signs and crackles of the aether. Sometimes he thought he succeeded. It may be no accident that many pioneers of radio were convinced of telepathy, clairvoyance and messages from the dead, for radio seemed hardly less miraculous.

Sir William Crookes, OM, (President of the Royal Society, inventor of the radiometer, discoverer of the metal thallium and also a pioneer in psychical research) predicted, in 1892, with remarkable prescience, what wireless communication would be like. In a lecture published in *The Fortnightly Review* of February 1892, (quoted by Constable (1980) p. 10):

> Rays of light will not pierce through a wall, nor, as we know only too well, through a London fog. But the electrical vibrations of a yard or more of wavelength, of which I have spoken, will easily pierce such mediums, and which to them will be transparent. Here, then, is revealed the bewildering possibility of telegraphy without wires, posts, cables, or any of our present

costly appliances. Granted a few reasonable postulates, the whole thing comes well within the realms of possible fulfilment.

Crookes even predicted at the same time what a domestic radio set would be like:

> I assume here that the progress of discovery would give instruments capable of adjustment by turning a screw or altering a length of a wire, so as to become receptive of wavelengths of any preconcerted length. Thus, when adjusted to fifty yards, the transmitter might emit, and the receiver respond to, rays varying between forty-five and fifty yards, and be silent to all others.

What is remarkable is his realization that tuning for wanted and rejecting unwanted transmitters would be possible. Sir William Crookes was almost there – before there were the needed discoveries and inventions that would make the goal achievable. He saw it as possible before the science existed. This goal drove him to discover and invent, helping it to be reached. And this article very likely inspired others to invent what was needed to make the dream come true. He patented the principle of electrical resonance in 1897 with his 'syntonized [tuned] telegraphy', which later allowed radio stations to be separated. Marconi, seeing the same goal even more clearly, though his knowledge of science was far less, patented his version of resonant tuned circuits (originally serving a somewhat different purpose) in 1900.

There were many other contenders. A remarkable early inventor of radio (though more successful for alternating current power distribution and for his invention of the induction motor, who also tried to transmit power through space) was the Croation-born American inventor Nikola Tesla. The Tesla coil produced very low-frequency radio waves which could travel great distances, even through water to submarines. He conceived and actually built a massive steel tower for worldwide radio communication in 1900. His backers failed him, so his dream was destroyed: the great steel tower was sold for a paltry sum as scrap metal.

David Hughes, an ingenious professor of music, claimed to have transmitted signals over several hundred yards up Great Portland Street in London several years before Hertz's demonstration. But he was discouraged by lack of appreciation from the Royal Society, as he did not conduct systematic experiments or have a proper basis of theory. Hughes thought he was extrapolating Faraday's magnetic induction so he got there through a wrong analogy, but may indeed have demonstrated the first true radio communication. A wrong analogy not infrequently leads to surprising success. The much earlier invention of the Leyden jar for storing electricity was suggested by the false notion that electricity is a fluid. Fluids can be stored in glass bottles – electricity is a fluid – so electricity could be stored in a glass bottle. It worked!

It was Marconi who put together the working package of radio communication through hints from science and several key inventions; especially the Russian physicist Alexander Popov's aerial which was used for detecting lightning, Hertz's spark gap oscillator and Edouard Branley's coherer of 1890. This was a glass tube containing powered metal that mysteriously 'cohered' by the action of radio frequencies to give a lower resistance and was originally used to detect lightning. This first radio-frequency detector was used by many experimenters before Marconi. Why it works is still mysterious. Often the needed invention comes before the understanding that makes it seemingly possible.

The drama of unexpected discoveries from fundamental scientific research leading to entirely new industries of revolutionary importance is surely more significant than any political revolutions. Out of the as we now think non-existent aether, have emerged the electrical, the electro-chemical, and the communication industries that have in one century transformed our world. This has come about through questioning and finding answers from the imaginary jell of the aether.

COMPUTER JELL

We come to 'computer jell'. Imagine a liquid that can be turned solid with a beam of light. Now imagine controlling the light beam with a computer – so that the liquid solidifies into any conceivable shape. Then with computer graphics one could draw a three-dimensional object and ask the computer to turn it into an actual object, to be touched and handled and used. Science fiction? No – fact. Technology turns some science fictions into facts.

This technique, which is called stereoLithography, was invented by an American polymer scientist, Charles Hill, in 1982. Working on UV coatings for the printing industry, in which ultra-violet light is used to set polymers, he realized that '3-D printing' might be made possible by laying down successive coatings of a special polymer, developed in Switzerland by Ciba Geigy, hardened with a UV laser. It worked. So now computer drawings can jell into real objects.

Stewart Dickson (1991) says of stereoLithography:

The language of Mathematics predates computers by thousands of years. We now have in the computer a way of representing

Mathematics in its natural form. We also now have a way of transmigrating forms which have evolved in an abstract vacuum and allow them to have substance. We can put into physical form a demonstrably accurate representation of a human thought process.

Invention is transactions between fantasies and realities. In the future, machines may rival and come to overtake our inventive abilities. Meanwhile, machines can measure and calculate and they can detect and see into places we cannot reach. Machines are extra eyes, ears, and probes of new kinds, exploring across space and into the atom.

So far it is us who set up intentions – though what actually happens is seldom predicted! The crunch comes when machines decide what we should do. As our world is built from unpredicted discoveries and serendipitous inventions, we cannot know where we are going. We might – fellow jelly babies – grow up in computer minds, and as adults live in computer-created realities.

REFERENCES

Constable, A. (1980) *Early Wireless*. (Tunbridge Wells, UK: Midas Books).

Dickson, S. (1991) 'StereoLithography of Mathematical Surfaces', *Ciba-Geigy Resin Aspects*, 26, 3. Plastic Division (KU 3. 12; 4002). (Switzerland: Basle).

Jehl, Francis (1937) *Menlo Park Reminiscences*, Vol. I. (Dearborn, Michigan: The Edison Institute). Reprinted 1990, (Mineola, NY: Dover).

Jewkes, John, Sawers, David and Stillerman, Rich, (1958, revised 1962) *The Sources of Invention*. (London: Macmillan).

Lodge, Oliver (1925) *Ether and Reality*. (London: Hodder and Stoughton).

Napier, S. (ed.) (1991) *Ciba-Geigy Resin Aspects* 26. Plastic Division (KU 3. 12; 4002). (Switzerland: Basle).

Panati, Charles (1987) *Extraordinary Origins of Everyday Things*.(New York: Harper Row), p. 247–50.

Shlesinger, Edward B. (1973) *How to Invent: A Text for Teachers*. (New York: IFI/Plenum).

Thomas, John Meurig (1991) *Michael Faraday and the Royal Institution*. (Bristol: Adam Hilger).

Whittaker, Edmund (1910, expanded 1951) *Aether and Electricity*. (London: Nelson).

5

IS SCIENCE BAD FOR THE SOUL?

Once upon a time a boy aged six, with his classmates in a small school, made a box with a glass window with leaves and twigs inside, to see the incredible transformation of a dragonfly. After weeks of waiting, we arrived one morning at school to find there were the first motions of the wings as our dragonfly started to enter the world in its new form, its second coming. My friends and I were transfixed by wonder. What happened then? The teacher made us leave the miracle before it was complete, to go to another room – to sing 'All Things Bright and Beautiful'. This damaged my soul.

Several recent books claim that science is bad for the soul. This is nothing new: science–religion conflicts of various kinds have been evident for centuries and have cost lives, though far fewer than have inter-religious conflicts. The present attacks on science seem to be triggered by cosmologists who get into theological territory on the origin of the universe with the Big Bang, promising to explain everything with an equation, (particularly with Stephen Hawking's *A Brief History of Time*, 1989). Remarkably, this remained on the best-seller list for longer than any other book. It may be a cult, coffee-table talisman, seldom actually read, but its outstanding sales indicate a new interest in theological cosmology. Also, it is a just tribute to its author who, in spite of a severe physical disability, holds with very great distinction Newton's Chair at Cambridge. *A Brief History of Time* ends with the often quoted promise:

> We shall all, philosophers, scientists, and just ordinary people, be able to take part in the discussion of why it is that we and the universe exist. If we find the answer to that, it would be the ultimate triumph of human reason – then we should know the mind of God.

Is this pi in the sky?

Some will see such extrapolations from cosmology as overstepping the limits of science, though there is a clear precedent for this in

Newton's writings, as he thought of space as God's mind, and the laws of nature as ideas in the mind of God. For Newton, his mathematics worked because he intuited God's thoughts. Newton spent at least as much time on alchemy and theology as on science. Although we can now transmute elements, we are supposed to have grown out of the mystiques of alchemy and see religion separately from science, yet several recent writers see science as painting a bleak landscape for the soul.

Such claims are made in *Understanding the Present* by Bryan Appleyard (1992). Subtitled *Science and the Soul of Modern Man*, this book suggests that science takes away the securities, the rich poetic myths, the warm comfort of religion which are seen as central to human happiness. This is also a theme of *The Corrupted Sciences* by Arnold (1992), subtitled *Challenging the Myths of Modern Science*, which attacks the 'truths' of science as being intellectually misleading modern myths. Arnold sees religion as necessary for the early stages of science (p. 130):

> true religion is a pre-scientific recognition that fundamental laws of nature rule our existence and perceptions. These laws can be codified and expressed by feelings, beliefs and ecumenical rituals to celebrate what could not be formally demonstrated in scientific or philosophical terms. All genuine religions share common archetypal roots embedded in natural law, truth and ethical behaviour.

For Arnold, science destroys its own origins in poetry and by explaining mind it destroys us (p. 130):

> For as long as subjective processes and their meanings remained inaccessible via the scientific method, they could be approached only via art, poetry, philosophy and religions. However, now that we can model and demonstrate how subjective processes work in geometric, mathematical terms (including those that apply to human behaviour) we can relegate an uncaused and eternal God to the realm of fiction.

He concludes that although science has usurped faith and destroyed religion's balm:

> True religions can none the less continue to serve a useful purpose in so far as poetic truths always precede the discovery of scientific ones, even when the former are merely elegant metaphors of what eventually turn out to be laws of nature.

For Bryan Appleyard the problem is just the opposite: the accounts of science are so unexpected we have trouble living with them, as they are not related to any previous beliefs (p. 227):

31

A new and unprecedently effective form of knowledge and way of doing things appeared suddenly in Europe about 400 years ago. This is what we now know as science.

This science inspired a version of the universe, of the world of man that was utterly opposed to all preceding versions. Most importantly, it denied man the possibility of finding an ultimate meaning and purpose for his life within the facts of the world. If there were such things as meanings and purposes, they must exist outside the universe describable by science.

Appleyard goes on to say that science has created modern liberal-democratic society, and it answers questions *as if* it were a religion, though:

It confronts none of the spiritual issues of purpose and meaning. And, meanwhile, its growing power enables it to drive the very systems that did confront those issues to the margins of our concern and, ultimately, out of existence.

He agrees with Arnold that science and religion are incompatible: 'Our science, whatever it may pretend, is incapable of co-existence.' This is explored in depth by Mary Midgley (1992) in her book *Science and Salvation*.

This brings to mind Richard Dawkins' powerful notion that some *memes* (mental and software equivalents to genes) are pathological viruses of the mind that take over reason. For Dawkins, religious ideas are damaging viral memes which dull the mind by blocking questioning with facile answers – so absurd that to hold them tests belief. What of the memes of science? For Dawkins they are not damaging viruses, because they have evolved and are tested by the selective challenges of scientific method. So religions are pathological bad memes and sciences are logical good memes. This raises the question: is the selection of ideas and beliefs by the methods of science too drastic? Does it reject some important, in some sense true (though hard to justify) beliefs? It is striking that science does not throw out the arts of music and poetry (or for that matter cooking) though they are hard to justify intellectually. Many 'hard' scientists are active musicians, painters, or cooks, though the public image of scientists is that for them the arts are relatively inferior. Yet for scientists, just as for other people, the arts are life-enhancing and can be wonderful beyond compare, though we don't begin to understand why! Need we worry about not seeing *everything* through science's window? Surely the arts, and humour and, some will say, religion are valid ways of seeing things – if not the same things.

Scientists are active players of a game against nature. As for any game, it is very different for the active players and the passive watchers. All games have players, who enjoy the activity (and may make their living from it; supporters, who are interested (and willingly provide funds); and the much larger public who neither know nor care (though they may have to contribute funds). Science must look very different to the active players, to the passive supporters and to the general public, for whom it may look too expensive – and also too expansive when it encroaches on their beliefs. This is so because the science game transforms our view of the universe, of society and of our selves. But not everyone appreciates the view from science's window. It is very hard to escape ancient dreams and ghosts, and poetic images, and fathers and mothers, and retribution and reward from powers above. This may be inertia from our childhood experiences when indeed there were powerful fathers and mothers and inexplicable punishments and rewards. Whatever the cause, science is incapable of guiding people where they most need help and fails to remove 'irrational' views of everyday experience.

A central issue is *meaning*. For scientists, the meaning of things increases with greater understanding, and there are always plenty of mysteries left to evoke fresh wonder. Thus, a buttercup does not lose its charm when we see its similarity to a radio telescope. As the enormous steel dish accepts information from across the universe, so the little flower's petals accept and focus energy from space to warm the aerial-like stamen, to enable the buttercup to reproduce more efficiently. This insight adds to the wonder of flowers but not everyone is impelled by such wonder; for many people such analogies and explanations are irritating distractions from what to them really matters. For these people science appals – though some of its products appeal.

It might be worth trying to classify some of these complicated issues. The most basic distinction is between effects of the findings of science, and the image of scientists as being a kind of priestcraft claiming special knowledge. Here the public understanding of science (or lack of it) is very important. Sometimes we speak of 'public understanding of science' when we mean public understanding of the universe. This difference is important. The first may refer to the practice and profession of science as an activity aimed at seeking truth and creating inventions. The second is appreciating what science has discovered and holds to be true. To see this requires some science education (which is generally deplorable, though it may be improving). The aim is to make science, like the arts, a central part of our culture.

It is hard to believe that science challenges or in any way diminishes the appeal of the arts. There is, however, an unfortunate asymmetry here, for scientists can enjoy the arts but knowledge of the arts does not give access to science. There are grounds for accepting that science, unlike the arts, challenges religion. Whether this is bad for the soul is not so clear. We may consider science–religion issues such as these:

• There is plenty of scientific evidence that the universe is not designed for us. The discovery, at the start of modern science, that the earth is not in the middle of things demoted us from centre-stage. (Although this was a major issue for the Inquisition, this loss of pride of place seems puerile to us now.)

• The attitudes of science and religion are essentially different, and opposed, as science questions everything rather than accepts traditional beliefs. Although questioning is intellectually exciting to almost everyone, carried to extremes it might conceivably be over-challenging and too time-consuming, for one does have to accept answers for action. So there have to be practical limits to questioning – which presumably is why philosophers are kept in colleges.

• Scientific method cannot be applied in most real-life situations. It is too slow, there is inadequate evidence and no control groups for comparisons. Although we may look at groups, for example of married and unmarried people, we cannot ourselves be both married and unmarried, so it is hard to learn how to live – which drives us to accept often dubious precepts.

• Science seems incapable of providing value judgements of good or bad, right or wrong, ugly or beautiful. Yet these are very important for everyday behaviour. So science is not adequate. The response is often simple-minded gap-filling.

• Science does not answer questions of personal interest, so it cannot replace theology for providing comfort or advice. Hence the very widespread interest in astrology, despite its obvious absurdity. And may one add a large part of psychoanalysis. (Even academic book shops have bigger sections on astrology than astronomy.)

• There are some direct conflicts between the findings and theories of science and tennets of theologies. Many are well known: the stated age of the universe has gradually increased from its start on 23 March 4004 BC (according to Archbishop James Usher, 1581–1656), to the recent estimate of 15 billion BC; Newton's notion of inertial frictionless perpetual motion of the solar system, dispensing with machine-minders to keep the universe running; evolution is seen as being incompatible with a prior design. (I hear that some theologians are now adopting Chaos Theory – suggesting that God is The Great Attractor.)

• Science is too complicated and too difficult. It is counter-intuitive, so it cannot be understood by private contemplation but requires a lot of knowledge and unusual kinds of thought. Theologies are also counter-intuitive (or at least are very hard to believe) but they are largely based on human experience and are concerned with human problems. Science can seem cold and indifferent, even though intellectually it is uniquely exciting.

• Science is seen as a priestcraft but, disturbingly, its theories quite often change, so why should they be believed? Scientists may prefer live uncertainty to dead certainty – the questioning hook '?' to the exclamatory spear '!' – but most people are hooked on using spears, to protect their beliefs and attack others.

• Sciences, especially the science of perception, make us doubt the evidence of our own senses. Thus we come to depend on instruments and statistics and all manner of checks from the tools and methods of science. So science is a procrustian bed, extending us but also cutting us down to size.

There is a widespread fear of science. This is not only fear of some of its technologies but of what science's explanations do to our minds or souls. Could it be dangerous to turn science's window upon ourselves? Is psychology bad for the soul? It would be of great interest to explain, for example, why music has such power to move us; but is it possible that knowing the cognitive processes involved would blight our appreciation? If it is true that science has exorcised mind from the heavens, could it also exorcise our minds from our brains? It might be said that this was the aim of Behaviourism. Behaviourism is dead. But artificial intelligence presents similarly challenging issues. Just possibly, building robots will change us into robots. It is far more likely, though, that by understanding intelligence we will extend our perception without losing anything much that matters, such as poetry and the strange power of music, the delights of questioning and making discoveries.

If more people understood the methods and accounts of science would there be fewer complaints, fewer fears? We may conclude that science education is very important – for science's powerful insights are available only to those with some knowledge of its methods and findings and of how they can be applied. The increasing public understanding of science enlarges the arena of the debate and it is vitally important for decision-making in technological societies, where general ignorance of science is dangerous. That so few in political power are science graduates makes the inherent dangers of applying new discoveries even more risky. Just how and what kinds of science – facts, methods, theories, hands-on experience? – should be presented to the uninvolved public, for science to be accepted as the most exciting intellectual adventure and principal window to the universe and to ourselves, is another story.

REFERENCES

Appleyard, B. (1992) *Understanding the Present: Science and the Soul of Modern Man*. (London: Picador).

Arnold, A. (1992) *The Corrupted Sciences: Challenging the Myths of Modern Science*. (London: Paladin).

Dawkins, R. (1976) *The Selfish Gene*. (Oxford: Oxford University Press).

Dawkins, R. (1986) *The Blind Watchmaker*. (London: Longman).

Hawking, S. (1988) *A Brief History of Time*. (London: Bantam).

Midgley, M. (1992) *Science as Salvation: A Modern Myth and its Meaning*. (London: Routledge).

6

IS SCIENCE GOOD FOR THE SOUL?

> The subtlety of nature is greater many times over than the subtlety of the senses and understanding; so that all those specious meditations, speculations, and glosses in which men indulge are quite from the purpose, only there is no one by to observe it.
>
> Francis Bacon (1620) *Novum Organon*, Aphorism X

Let's begin at the beginning. Science as we know it, science as an organized activity with recognised social implications, started early in the seventeenth century; its beginnings were seen with remarkable prescience by Francis Bacon (1561–1626) who was an important laywer – Lord Keeper of the Seal, Lord Chancellor – a fine and indeed the first essayist, expounder of educational doctrine, defender of learning, above all founder of modern scientific method. In *The Great Instauration* (of which *New Organon* (*Novum Organum*) was separately published and is the best-known part) he set out to change society by means of inductive sciences. In science he foresaw immense power for human good. Bacon was distressed by the limitations of the science of his time (*Novum Organum* (1620) Aphorism V):

> The study of nature with a view to works is engaged in by the mechanic, the physician, the alchemist, and the magician; but by all (as things now are) with slight endeavour and scanty success.

For Bacon science is separate from religion: 'We do not presume by the contemplation of nature to attain to the mysteries of God.' Here he differs from Newton, some seventy years later, who thought of the laws of physics as ideas in God's mind – so observational and mathematical astronomy, and alchemy, should reveal the mind of God. Newton saw science and mathematics as revealing God and the soul of man; but Bacon generally separated science and religion. For Bacon (*The Advancement of Learning* (1605) Book 1):

Neither is it any quantity of knowledge, how great soever, that can make the mind of man to swell; for nothing can fill, much less extend the soul of man, but God and the contemplation of God; and therefore Salomon, speaking the two principal senses of inquisition, the eye and the ear, affirmeth that 'the eye is never satisfied with seeing, nor the ear with hearing' ... so of knowledge itself, and the mind of man, whereto the senses are but reporters ...

Bacon argues that we should not presume to solve questions of Deity and that, in any case, science is powerless for this as the natural world is a closed system with God outside and above it. He warns of the dangers to pushing science in this direction:

For if any man shall think by view and inquiry into these sensible and material things to attain that light, whereby he may reveal unto himself the nature of or will of God, then indeed is he spoiled by vain philosophy ... As most aptly said by one of Plato's school, ''That the sense of man carrieth a resemblance with the sun, which (as we see) openeth and revealeth all the terrestrial globe; but then again it obscureth and concealeth the stars and the celestial globe: so doth the sense discover natural things, but it darkeneth and shutteth up divine.'' And hence .. great learned men have been heretical, whilst they have sought to fly up to the secrets of Deity by the waxen wings of the senses.

Bacon anticipated that practical products of science, with more use of logic, would improve not only the material wellbeing of workers and indeed everyone, but also increase powers of mind. He would have loved computers! Aphorism IX states:

The cause and root of all evils in the sciences is this – that while we falsely admire and extol the powers of the human mind we neglect to seek for its true helps.

Most important, Bacon clearly saw that science should penetrate appearances and seek explanations beneath the surface, below how things seem to be. So sometimes at least, he did see science as challenging how things appear, and thus attacking beliefs (Aphorism XVIII):

The discoveries which have hitherto been made in the sciences are such as lie close to vulgar notions, scarcely beneath the surface. In order to penetrate into the inner and further recesses of nature, it is necessary that both notions and axioms be derived from things by a more sure and guarded way, and that a method of intellectual operation be introduced altogether better and more certain.

In the Proem to the *Novum Organum*, where he looks at his own work, he is convinced that:

> the human mind makes its own difficulties, not using the true helps which are at man's disposal ... whence follows manifold ignorance of things ... because the primary notions of things which the mind readily and passively imbines, stores up and accumulates (and it is from them all the rest flow) are false, confused, and overhastily abstracted from the facts ... whence it follows that the entire fabric of human reason which we employ for the inquisition of nature is badly put together and built up, like some magnificent structure without any foundation ... There was but one course left, therefore – to try the whole thing anew upon a better plan, and to commence a total reconstruction of science, arts, and all human knowledge, raised upon proper foundations.

This was the promise of the new method for science – the engine he conceived for generating truth – and indeed to a great extent it has come to pass. The point is that it has changed how and what we think: Baconian science has changed the human mind. The question now is whether or not this is good for the soul.

The particular power of Baconian – that is, modern – science is not only that it challenges and changes belief, but also and perhaps more important, that it makes *explicit* what is assumed and believed implicitly (though indeed this goes back to Socrates and we all know what happened to him). Bacon also was punished, near the end of his life losing his wealth and suffering a hardly justified disgrace, and finally died from a cold caught while experimentally freezing a hen in the snow near Highgate, then a village north of London.

Is it good to make things explicit? This must depend on what kinds of things, for there is a lot we don't want to be bothered with. The mammalian nervous system, according to the concept of the nineteenth-century English neurologist, John Hughlings Jackson (1835–1911), is organised pyramidally so that mundane behaviour is carried out by spinal and lower brain functions, the cerebral cortex being free for planning, understanding and consciousness. This notion is even built into responsibility in law: an effective defence against murder is that the act occurred as a reflex, or while asleep. If we try to make neural lower-level decisions explicit, behaviour is disrupted and greatly slowed. Try thinking of each step while walking up stairs; progress is painfully slow and running impossible. The same is true for an organization such as an army: if a general had to concern himself (or herself) with peeling potatoes, war would be impossible. On the other hand, it was the making explicit of the routine jobs in field and factory by applying principles of science to everyday life that produced the Industrial Revolution, which in turn changed everyday life practically beyond recognition. Making things explicit takes them from 'intuition' and into the domain of public debate. Socrates did this; but Bacon went further in undermining intuitions with his truth-generating engine, which discovered entirely new facts and organized knowledge in essentially new ways.

The physical sciences made explicit all manner of assumptions, most of which turned out to be wrong. The classical example is Aristotle's, no doubt prehistoric intuition, that heavy objects fall faster than lighter objects in a vacuum. This was shown by Galileo, by argument and experiment, to be incorrect. (The original notion is remarkably resistant to change: flipping through a published draft of the new English Science Curriculum for schools I found this Aristotelean assumption bedded into a question! It was later expunged without comment.) Correspondingly, psychology makes processes of mind and behaviour explicit. Helmholtz did this for perception, as did Freud for emotional life. How successful either was is not the point here: the essential idea is that perceptual processes that had been assumed to be passive and very simple, and emotional processes that had been assumed to be under control of the conscious will, were brought to light as being very different when examined explicitly. What was found was far from acceptable, indeed shocking. Helmholtz's Unconscious Inference for perception and Freud's later Unconscious motives made blame hard to defend, for once behaviour is *explained*, blame seems not to apply. So the science of perception, and much of psychology, appeared to attack the basis of morality.

The physical sciences, with their related technology, also affected morality. As the range of what could be done grew, so guilt grew into areas that had been beyond possible action. Thus, before steam pumps were invented there was no blame attached to insanitary cities; but, once technology made it possible to pump millions of gallons of water every day, then politicians and any others concerned were guilty if the science-based technology was not applied to solve the problem. (No doubt, introducing the profit motive brilliantly achieved progress without too much moral anguish. Or put another way, it automatically rewarded those who did the necessary good.) Making problems explicit and solving them with science introduced irreversible ratchets of change, much of which must be called progress. It has enormously increased freedom of action through travel and communications, improved health (so on average we live twice as long) and potentialities for gaining knowledge. But does the general public understand what science has discovered?

What has happened is that *explicit* knowledge in science, often developed for solving practical problems, returns to *implicit* acceptance and unconsciousness – apart from in a few experts who keep things working, though often without fully knowing *how* they work. This is the dilemma of the public understanding of science. Indeed, it hardly exists, as explicit understanding sinks back to implicitly accepting the wonders of natural and human creation;. The penalty is that very few people can bring their minds to assess problems or invent appropriate solutions, though this need can be vitally important as changes breed new problems which are ever requiring new solutions. This is the worry of politicians who are ignorant of science. It might worry them – but it more than worries us! Possibly fear of explicit thinking stems from the social graces and the diplomatic tact of politics, where smiles hide and even switch off minds.

What of making *psychological* processes explicit? This seems far harder to evaluate. Frankly, this is largely because it is not clear how much true light has been shed on the mind or the soul. At the time of Freud, the unconscious was a deeply mysterious, rather naughty notion. Now, perhaps because of non-conscious computer-mind, consciousness is far more mysterious than anything non-conscious. This is unsatisfactory for considering whether science is good for the soul. But, at least, pyschology has made explicit some of the issues.

If one sees the soul in terms of inertial guardianship of the past, science threatens. If one sees the soul as adventurer in a universe full of rich questions, science is rewarding. In practice, the distinction here is not so sharp, for scientists appreciate the past and live with the music and paintings and architecture of those who reject science's values.

Science is a shared activity which depends on honesty, unlike many of the workings of any society. It counters errors of uncontrolled thought yet is driven by the highest flights of imagination, inspired by often hitherto inconceivable discoveries. Science is tension between imagination and checks from observation. For Bacon, there are in the human soul peculiarly named 'idols of the mind', which produce errors; 'idols of the market', errors due to influence of language; 'idols of the theatre', systems of (misleading) philosophy; 'idols of the tribe', a tendency of the mind to see 'a greater degree of order and equality of things than it really finds'. He sees scientific method as checking such errors and so improving minds.

For him effective science depends on co-operation of divers kinds of minds, not always those with high skills. This is expressed in his last, posthumously published, incomplete book *New Atlantis* (1627). In the first – though imaginary – institute for empirical research of modern times Bacon itemizes the staff:

Three that collect the experiments which are in all books. These we call the Depredators.

We have three that collect the experiments of all mechanical arts; also liberal sciences; and also of practices which are not brought into arts. These we call mystery-men.

We have three that draw the experiments of the former four into titles and tables, to give the better light for the drawing of observations and axioms out of them. These we call compilers.

We have three that bend themselves, looking into the experiments of their fellows, and caste about how to draw out of them things of use and practice of man's life, and knowledge as well for works as for plain demonstration of causes, means of natural divinations, and the easy and clear discovery of the virtues and parts of bodies. These we call Dowrymen or Benefactors.

Then there are those that direct experiments – called Lamps – and three that execute the experiments – called Inoculators. Lastly, apart from novices and apprentices, there are also

Three that raise the former discoveries by experiments into greater observations, axioms and aphorisms. These we call Interpreters of Nature. [And] For every invention of value, we erect a statue to the inventor, and give him liberal and honourable reward.

Not all the contributors to science, however, need be Lamps. Indeed, Bacon saw science as 'levelling mens' whits'. This was a decisive move against the ancient tradition that individual perception and judgement is adequate for seeing any kind of truth. With instruments extending the senses and statistical methods assessing data, mind found its place in science. His account of mind or soul is inconsistent, for sometimes he deduces mind from properties of matter, at other times ascribing the human soul a divine origin (cf. Farrington 1973, p. 171). Certainly, Bacon sees science as good for the soul.

It is often said that science's picture of humanity living on a speck of dust in an infinite void makes us trivial in our own eyes. But surely the truth is, by essentially following Bacon's practical philosophy, that we have at long last attained dignity by sharing observations with *explicit questioning* – so discovering that we have the whit to compass the universe and face up to seeing our place in creation. As we have attained the power to understand and change our world and ourselves, so have our souls grown adult. It is childish to reject science.

Baron Verulum, Viscount St Albans, Keeper of the Great Seal and Lord Chancellor, Sir Francis Bacon, should have the last word. In his essay, 'Of Truth' he says:

The enquiry of truth, which is the love-making, or wooing of it, the knowledge of truth, which is the presence of it, and the belief of truth, which is the enjoying of it, is the sovereign good of human nature.

REFERENCES

Bacon, Francis (1620) *The New Organon*. Fulton H. Anderson (1960) (ed.) (New York: Macmillan/Library of Liberal Arts).

Bacon, Francis (1625) 'Of Truth', in: Arthur Johnson (1974) (ed.) *Essays*. (London: Dent).

Bacon, Francis (1627) *The Advancement of Learning* and *New Atlantis* Arthur Johnson (1974) (ed.) (Oxford: Clarendon).

Farringdon, Benjamin (1973) *Francis Bacon: Philosopher of Industrial Science*. London: Macmillan).

7

CRACKS – OF DOOM AND KUHN

The word 'crack' has a remarkable number of uses and meanings. Collins *Concise Dictionary* lists 31 including: a narrow fissure; to break without separation of the parts; to tell a joke; to force open a safe; to solve a code. Most dramatic is the end of the world – the crack of doom. A crack is a generally unwanted discontinuity: a discrepancy in normal reality which may, however, reveal surprising hidden truths. Cracks can be deeply, sometimes far too deeply, revealing. Exploring cracks can lead to drastic rethinking, even to the collapse of an entire way of seeing, which allows the creation of a new 'Kuhnian' paradigm when an entire science looks and is very different. But cracks are not for everyone. They can be unsightly and dangerous. The owner of a valuable but damaged pot will turn it to the wall to hide the cracks, and a decorator will paper over the cracks.

It is no accident that inventors and scientists are called 'crack-pots'. Cracks are where innovators explore for insights. They are where questions are conceived, to challenge and transform the accepted, so cracks attract not only creatures hiding from the light but also the attention of creative science and art seeking illumination. This is the promise of cracks – yet cracks can reveal faults which spell ruin. So it is hardly surprising that most individuals and organizations do cover over the cracks. To present the bland face of safe success with cracks hidden is the very essence of PR.

An unfortunate side-effect of the current struggle for funds for science is the need for PR, with its crack-hiding promises of success, though the drama of science lies in uncertainty with its possibilities of an unexpected, perhaps far more important success. The great discoveries come by exploring cracks in the structures of assumptions and theories, and between theory and data. A downside of the fascination with cracks in knowledge is that scientists tend to ignore things that work without difficulties or problems and so may not see the pleasures of a trouble-free life. Indeed, normal lifestyles and values may be actively rejected for, though smooth, polished surfaces may be beautiful and safe, they hide what is interesting for science. Yet it is hardly surprising that cracks are generally unwelcome, being signs of danger through revealing unwelcome truths such as the insecurity of the foundation of one's house or the insecurity of a loan. There are many protections from seeing cracks, from decorating to PR.

A subtle protection against academic crack-finding is the use of the word 'merely'. To those of us with pretensions to being 'academics' no phrase is more annoying than calling ideas and discoveries '*merely* academic'. The reply should be that things get interesting when they are not '*merely* practical'. But, unfortunately, this does not have quite the same force. It has to be admitted that practical issues are important, and indeed throughout history science and art have flourished through the leisure bought by the wealth of practical manufacture, trade and commerce. Yet wealth, so necessary for science and art, is ultimately created by asking out-of-this-world questions, and seeking answers that seem to have no practical consequence. There is truly a symbiosis between this '*merely*' and '*practical*', for the world of Mammon depends on cracking abstract problems, and the sciences and the arts depend on Mammon for their needs – which is fine, provided Mammon doesn't crack the whip.

The theoretical science that explores deep cracks in knowledge has transformed our world and our perceptions. It has turned out to be practical, beyond belief. Cracks are signs of danger, protective refuges and enchanted caverns promising unknown wonders. So there are many ways of living with cracks. With such thoughts in mind I suggest a psychological dichotomy, which may run deeper than some well-known psychological dichotomies such as Extrovert and Introvert. It divides people into those who *explore* cracks and those who *cover* cracks. Doesn't this divide humanity?

Professions and businesses have the difficult task of combining these two opposed strategies, for they must present a bland *public* face, without a cracked smile, while at the same time seeing cracks as vitally important signs of danger indicating what decisions need to be made. This double dealing with cracks is very clear to architects, who must attract funding with promises of safe success, but when cracks appear they must diagnose their cause and deal with them, learning from structural cracks inner problems and how repair may be achieved. Similarly, if less literally, the same is so for doctors, financiers and politicians. The opposed needs to hide and yet to see cracks is central for professions dealing with the public, which wants assurance rather than doubt yet must be protected from fear. So, professions and businesses have to combine public crack-hiding with private crack-looking. This duality is most profound in religions, where the deepest unknowns – infinite cracks in our knowledge – are traded for promises of certain eternity.

Living by seeing cracks and living by hiding cracks are so different that very few people can do both, so there are separate specialists in hiding and in seeing cracks. There are the professional problem-solvers, who live with discrepancies, and their opposite numbers the professional PRers, for whom smooth surfaces reflect secure success. The two views are extremely different. For anti-crackers, cracks spell failure through collapse. For crackers, they promise success through deeper insights. These are so different that crackers and anti-crackers find co-operation almost impossible. Crackers see the anti-crackers as bland: anti-crackers see crackers as dangerous. In fact, both are important, for questions lead to truth, yet unquestioning confidence is essential for action; and both are dangerous, for questioning can destroy, yet not questioning rejects intelligence.

Crack-covering surfaces make the structures of reality invisible. But the ultimate hiding is the gloss put on surfaces to make invisible the covering that hides the cracks. This final gloss destroys all perception, so we fail to control the world beyond the mirror of pretence. Is this gloss which hides the covering of cracks the reason why we have so many private and public disasters, so many economic slumps and wars? It is the bland leading the blind.

REFERENCE

Kuhn, Thomas S. (1962, revised 1970) *The Structure of Scientific Revolutions*. (Chicago: Chicago University Press).

8

AT FIRST SIGHT

What would an adult who had been blind all his life be able to see, if the cause of his blindness was suddenly removed? This question was asked by several empiricist philosophers. John Locke considered the possibilities of such a case in 1690, following the question posed in a letter from his friend William Molyneux:

> Suppose a man born blind, and now adult, and taught by his touch to distinguish between a cube and a sphere of the same metal. Suppose then the cube and the sphere were placed on a table, and the blind man made to see: query, whether by his sight, before he touched them, could he distinguish and tell which was the globe and which the cube? . . . The acute and judicious proposer answers: not. For though he has obtained the experience of how the globe, how the cube, affects his touch, yet he has not yet attained the experience that what affects his touch so or so, must affect his sight so or so . . .

Locke comments in the *Essay concerning Human Understanding* (1690, Book II, Ch. 9, Sect. 8):

> I agree with this thinking gentleman, whom I am pleased to call my friend, in his answer to this problem: and am of the opinion that the blind man, at first, would not be able with certainty to say which was the globe, which the cube . . .

René Descartes, in a passage in the *Dioptrics* (1637), considers how a blind man might build up a perceptual world by tapping around him with a stick. He first considers a sighted person using a stick in darkness. Descartes must surely have tried this for himself, and perhaps actually tested blind people. He says of this experiment:

> without long practice this kind of sensation is rather confused and dim; but if you take men born blind, who have made use

47

of such sensations all their life, you will find they feel things with perfect exactness that one might almost say that they see with their hands . . .

Descartes goes on to suggest that normal vision resembles a blind man exploring and building up his sense world by successive probes with a stick.

George Berkeley, in *A New Theory of Vision* (1709, Sect. lxxxv), stresses the importance of touch for seeing by considering that a microscope, by so changing the scale of things that touch no longer corresponds to vision, is of little use; and so if our eyes were

> turned into the nature of microscopes, we should not be much benefitted by the change . . . and (we would be) left only with the empty amusement of seeing, without any other benefit arising from it.

Berkeley goes on to say (Sect. XCV) that we should expect a blind man who recovered sight not to know visually whether anything was:

> high or low, erect or inverted . . . for the objects to which he had hitherto used to apply the terms up and down, high and low, were such as only affected or were in some way perceived by touch; but the proper objects of vision make a new set of ideas, perfectly distinct and different from the former, and which can in no sort make themselves perceived by touch.

These remained interesting speculations until in 1728 an unusually expert and thoughtful surgeon, William Cheselden, reported such a case. Cheseldon was distinguished for new methods of cataract operation and for joining the barber surgeons to the physicians, and he attended Sir Isaac Newton in his last illness (Cope, 1953). Cheselden gave sight to a boy aged thirteen or fourteen, born with highly opaque cataracts:

> When he first saw, he was so far from making any judgement of distances, that he thought all objects whatever touched his eyes (as he expressed it) as what he felt did his skin, and thought no object so agreeable as those which were smooth and regular, though he could form no judgement of their shape, or guess what it was in any object that was pleasing to him: he knew not the shape of anything, nor any one thing from another, however different in shape or magnitude; but upon being told what things were, whose form he knew before from feeling, he would carefully observe, that he might know them again; and (as he said) at first learned to know, and again forgot a thousand things in a day. One particular only, though it might appear trifling,

I will relate: Having often forgot which was the cat, and which the dog, he was ashamed to ask; but catching the cat, which he knew by feeling, he was observed to look at her steadfastly and then, setting her down said, 'So, puss, I shall know you another time.' He was very much surprised, that those things which he had liked best, did not appear most agreeable to his eyes, expecting those persons would appear to be most beautiful that he loved most, and such things to be most agreeable to his sight, that were so to his taste. We thought he soon knew what pictures represented, which were shewed to him, but we found afterwards we were mistaken; for about two months after he was couched, he discovered at once they represented solid bodies, when to that time he considered them only as party-coloured planes, or surfaces diversified with variety of paint; but even then he was no less surprised, expecting the pictures would feel like the things they represented, and was amazed when he found those parts, which by their light and shadow appeared now round and uneven, felt only flat like the rest, and asked which was the lying sense, feeling or seeing?

Being shewn his father's picture in a locket at his mother's watch, and told what it was, he acknowledged the likeness, but was vastly surprised; asking, how it could be, that a large face could be expressed in so little room, saying, it should have seemed as impossible for him, as to put a bushel of anything into a pint. At first he could bear but very little light, and the things he saw, he thought extremely large; but upon seeing things larger, those first seen he conceived less, never being able to imagine any lines beyond the bounds he saw; the room he was in, he said, he knew to be but part of the house, yet he could not conceive that the whole house could look bigger. Before he was couched, he expected little advantage from seeing, worth undergoing an operation for, except reading and writing; for he said, he thought he could have no more pleasure in walking abroad than he had in the garden, which he could do safely and readily. And even blindness, he observed, had this advantage that he could go anywhere in the dark, much better than those who can see; and after he had seen, he did not soon lose this quality, nor desire a light to go about the house in the night. He said, every new object was a new delight; and the pleasure was so great, that he wanted words to express it; but his gratitude to his operator he could not conceal, never seeing him for some time without tears of joy in his eyes, and other marks of affection ... A year after first seeing, being carried upon Epsom Downs, and observing a large prospect, he was exceedingly delighted with it, and called it a new kind of seeing. And now being couched in his other eye, he says that objects at first appeared large to this eye, but not so large as they did at first to the other; and looking upon the same object with both eyes, he thought it looked about twice as large as with the first couched eye only, but not double, that we can in any way discover.

Evidently, the sensory worlds of touch and vision were not so separate, as at least Berkeley imagined they would be, and visual perception developed remarkably rapidly. This was discussed in terms of the Cheselden case by the materialist philosopher Julien Offray de la Mettrie in his dangerously challenging book, *Natural History of the Soul* (1745), where he argues that only education received through the senses makes man and gives him what we call a soul, while no development of the mind outwards ever takes place. (There is a good discussion of de la Mettrie's book in Langer 1925.) A few years later, in his better-known *Man A Machine*, de la Mettrie states:

Nothing, as anyone can see, is so simple as the mechanism of our education. Everything may be reduced to sounds or words that pass from the mouth of one through the ears of another into his brain. At the same moment, he perceives through his eyes the shape of the bodies of which these words are arbitrary signs.

The findings of the Cheselden case (which, though by no means the first, is the first to be at all adequately reported) are confirmed by some later cases; though in others the development of perception is painfully slow. R. Latta described a case of a successful operation for congenital cataract in 1904, which was broadly similar, with almost immediately useful vision. But very often the eye takes a long time to settle down after a cataract operation, which may explain why so many of the historical cases described by M. von Senden (1932) showed such slow development. This is a controversial matter. The Canadian psychologist Donald Hebb in *The Organization of Behaviour* (1949), attributed the general slowness to see after operation as evidence that a very great deal of learning is needed. This, indeed, is now generally accepted but it remains a question how far previously gained knowledge, from exploratory touch and the other senses and from the reports of sighted people, helps new-found vision.

The case of a man who received corneal grafts when aged 52 (Gregory and Wallace 1963), has the advantage over the previous cases that a good retinal image was immediately available. This was so because corneal grafts disturb the eye far less than do cataract operations. In this case, our patient, S.B. could see virtually immediately things he already knew by touch, though for objects or features where touch had not been available, a long, slow, learning process was required. In fact, he never become perceptually normal. It was striking that he had immediate visual perception for things that must have been learned, while he was blind, and that he could not have known innately. Thus, from extensive experience of feeling the hands of his pocket watch he was able, immediately, to tell the time visually. Perhaps even more striking, as a boy at the school for the blind, S.B. had been taught to recognize by touch capital letters which were inscribed on special wooden plates the blind children felt by running their fingers along the outlines of the letters. They were taught capital letters in this way as this knowledge was useful for reading street names, brass plates and so on. It turned out that after the operation S.B. could immediately read capital letters visually though not lower-case letters, which he had not been taught by touch while blind. It took six months or so to learn to see these. The general finding of this case was the dramatic transfer of knowledge from touch to vision. So, S.B. was not like a baby learning to see. He already knew a great deal from touch – this knowledge was available for his newly functioning vision.

Figure 8.1 Drawing of a bus by S.B., 48 days after the operation

(a)

Figure 8.2 Drawing by S.B. six months after the operation

(b)

Figure 8.3 Drawing by S.B. one year after the operation

Many instances of lack of knowledge from earlier touch were striking. He had difficulties with shadows. When walking on steps on a sunny day he would quite often stand on the shadow, sometimes falling. He was remarkably good at judging horizontal though not vertical distances. Thus, while still in the hospital, he could give the distance from him of chairs or tables almost normally, but when looking down from the window (and blind people have little experience of vertical distances) he thought the ground was within touching distance though the ward was several storeys high. When he was shown various distortion illusions, we found that he was hardly affected by them: to him they were almost undistorted. And he did not experience the usual spontaneous depth-reversals of the Necker cube (see Fig. 27.2, p. 254), which appeared to him flat. Indeed, as in the Cheselden case, he had great difficulty seeing objects in pictures. Cartoons of faces meant nothing to him. He also found some things he loved ugly (including his wife, and himself) and he was frequently upset by the blemishes and imperfections of the visible world. He was fascinated by mirrors; they remained wonderful to the end of his life. However, as happened in most of the published cases, S.B. became severely depressed. Evidently, he felt more handicapped with his vision than when he had been blind.

A dramatic and revealing episode occurred when he was first shown a lathe, in a glass case in the London Science Museum, shortly after he left hospital. He had a long-standing interest in tools, and he particularly wanted to be able to use a lathe. We led him to the glass case and asked him to tell us what was in it. He was quite unable to say anything about it, except he thought the nearest part was a handle. (He pointed to the handle of the transverse feed.) He complained that he could not see the cutting edge, or the metal being worked, or anything else about it, and he appeared rather agitated. We then asked the museum attendant for the case to be opened, and S.B. was allowed to touch the lathe. The result was startling: he ran his hands deftly over the machine, touching first the transverse feed handle, and confidently naming it 'a handle', and then on to the saddle, the bed and the headstock of the lathe. He ran his hands eagerly over the lathe with his eyes shut. Then he stood back a little, opened his eyes, and said: 'Now that I've felt it, I can see'. He then named many of the parts correctly and explained how they would work, though he could not understand the chain of four gears driving the lead screw.

Many of these observations have been confirmed by Valvo (1971) in his reports of half a dozen cases of recovery from blindness, facilitated by a remarkable operation – the fitting of acrylic lenses to eyes that had never formed completely. Tissue rejection of the artificial lenses was prevented by placing them in a tooth, which was implanted as a buffer in the eye. (One of these Italian patients, wearing a lens in a tooth in his eye, is a philosopher!) It is now possible to implant artificial lenses without tissue rejection, so perhaps more cases of adult recovery from infant blindness will now appear, to answer by observation questions of epistemology raised by the philosophers.

REFERENCES

Berkeley, G. (1709) *A New Theory of Vision*. A.D. Lindsay (1910) (ed.) (London: Everyman's Library).

Cope, Z. (1953) *William Cheselden*. (Edinburgh and London: Livingstone).

Descartes, R. (1637) *Discourse on Method*. E.S. Haldane and G.R.T. Ross (1967) (trans.): in *The Philosophical Works of Descartes*, 2 vols. (Cambridge: Cambridge University Press).

Descartes, R. (1637) *Optics*. Paul J. Olscamp (1965) (trans.) in: *Discourse on Methods, Optics, Geometry and Meteorology*. (Indianapolis: Library of Liberal Arts; Bobbs-Merril); pp. 65–173.

Gregory, R.L. and Wallace, J.G. (1963) *Recovery from Early Blindness: A Case Study*. Experimental Psychology Monograph No. 2. (Cambridge: Heffer). Reprinted in: Gregory, R.L. (1974) *Concepts and Mechanisms of Perception*. (London: Duckworth), pp. 65–129.

Hebb, D.O. (1949) *The Organization of Behaviour*. (London: Wiley)

Latta, R. (1904) 'Notes on a Successful Operation for Congenital Cataract in an Adult', *British Journal of Psychology*, I, 135–50.

Lange, F.A. (1925) *The History of Materialism* (Boston: Houghton Mifflin).

Locke, J. (1690) *Essay concerning Human Understanding* (P.H. Nidditch, 1975, ed.). (Oxford: Oxford University Press).

Mettrie, J.O. de la (1748) *L'Homme Machine*. G.C. Bussey (1953) (trans.) in: *Man A Machine*. (Illinois: Open Court).

Senden, H. von (1932) *Raum-und Gestaltauffasung bei operierten Blindgeborenen*. Peter Heath (1960) (trans.) *Space and Sight*. (London: Methuen).

Valvo, A. (1971) *Sight Restoration after Long-Term Blindness: The Problems and Behaviour Patterns of Visual Rehabilitation*. (New York: American Foundation for the Blind).

9

AT FIRST BLUSH

What a pain embarrassment is. I had an aunt by marriage whose maiden name was Barrass. Would you believe it – her parents christened her Mamie. So all through school she was M. Barrass.

With embarrassment goes blushing. Why do we blush? Blushing and embarrassment occur in social situations. This is discussed most cogently by Charles Darwin in his great book *Expression of the Emotions in Man and Animals* (1872). Darwin thinks blushing is a public social-warning signal that the person blushing has committed a crime, or has violated the rules or mores of the group in some way, and at least for the moment is not to be trusted. For Darwin, 'Blushing is the most peculiar and most human of all expressions'. It is involuntary, and attempts to control it if anything increase blushing by concentrating attention to it, as the blush is itself embarrassing. Darwin points out that young children do not blush for shame: that blushing does not start before the child has understanding of rules of behaviour and their social significance:

> The mental powers of infants are not yet sufficiently developed to allow of their blushing. Hence, also, it is that idiots rarely blush.

And blushing is not found in primates; presumably because, though they have rules for behaviour, they cannot assess significance and consequences as humans can.

Darwin wanted to see how blushing was related to embarrassment in women, who blush more than men. As he regarded it as a social signal, he was interested to discover whether the blushing occurs in places normally hidden by clothes. But being too embarrassed to try the experiment himself, he got his doctor friends 'who necessarily had frequent opportunities for observation' to see how far the blush spread down below the neckline. It generally didn't. Whether this was because the visibility-limit was set thousands of years ago by the dress style of cave ladies, or whether it was set by individual experience to conform to their Victorian neckline, is an unanswered question.

Charles Darwin asked whether blushing and embarrassment could be reversible. He referred to the observation that, when patients are given nitrate of amyl, they blush in the same regions as when embarrassed.

> The patients are at first pleasantly stimulated; but, as blushing increases, they become confused and bewildered. One woman to whom the vapour had been administered asserted that as soon as she grew hot, she grew *muddled*.

This confusion, this mental muddle, is a most curious feature of embarrassment. Presumably switching off the will of unreliable individuals – with loss of ability to think deviously or act dangerously – serves to protect the group thus threatened from within.

We might expect more and more subtle forms of embarrassment with increasingly sophisticated societies, as there are more rules to violate. What could create more embarrassments than the structure of English society? Charles Dickens, in 1836, described the English sense of clinging ridiculously to a rung of the social ladder, being supported by the security of looking down on the rungs below and occasionally rewarded by attention from above. In *Pickwick Papers* (Chapter 1) members of the Pickwick Club, Mr Tracy Tupman and Mr Winkle, attend a charity ball in Rochester, where there is a dockyard, servicing ships of the Royal Navy. They are introduced by a local stranger:

> 'Wait a minute,' said the stranger, 'fun presently – nobs not come yet – queer place – Dock-yard people of upper rank don't know Dock-yard people of lower rank – Dock-yard people of lower rank don't know small gentry – small gentry don't know tradespeople – Commissioner don't know anybody.'

Now an embarrassment:

> 'Who's that little boy with the light hair and pink eyes, in a fancy dress?' inquired Mr. Tupman.
> 'Hush, pray – pink eyes – fancy dress – little boy – nonsense – Ensign 97th – Honourable Wilmot Snipe – great family – Snipes – very.'

Then:

> While the aristocracy of the place – The Bulders, the Clubbers, and Snipes – were thus preserving their dignity at the upper end of the room, the other classes of society were imitating their

example in other parts of it . . . The solicitors' wives, and the wine-merchant's wife, headed another grade (the brewer's wife visited the Bulders); and Mrs Tomlinson, the post-office keeper, seemed by mutual consent to have been chosen the leader of the trade party.

In such a structured society as ours one only has to hesitate on a significant name or speak in a wrong tone of voice (over-confident, too condescending or whatever) and immediately there is embarrassment. Here I shall confess to some embarrassing experiences. Making them public is, however, suspect – like advertising a blush. I am reminded of a French guidebook (I think to Dijon) which recounts the story of a medieval nun who felt such guilt she arranged to be publicly whipped by a monk every Saturday morning in the market place. After some months, she came to realize that she enjoyed it. So she had her punishment stopped – as a penance!

One can be embarrassed not only by oneself but by others, especially as a child by one's parents. My father was an astronomer, Director of an observatory, nothing embarrassing in that. But he was decidedly eccentric. As he often deviated from the mores of society, I suffered frequent embarrassment. At an international Astronomical Convention (note the word!), held in Paris in very hot weather, my father took his clothes off and swam in the national shrine of Napoleon's Carp Pond at the Palace of Fontainebleau. He was surprised to be arrested. My mother, with her much better French, bailed him out with excuses. There were small headlines commenting on foreign professors. No doubt children find their parents embarrassing, as children are at pains (literally) to discover and absorb the conventions of their society so they can grow up to be accepted and live at ease in the adult world. Childish conventionality may be boring, but how else could it be?

For me, embarrassment is most often associated with being stupid, especially in situations involving superiors and especially those one most likes and respects. An episode I shall never forget concerned two of the nicest people I ever knew: the Master of my Cambridge college, Sir Frank Lee, and the Master's wife, Catherine, Lady Lee. It is a pleasant Cambridge custom for the newly appointed Master of a College and his wife to have their residence, the Master's Lodge, redecorated to their taste. I was invited, while the Junior Fellow, to the honour of lunch at the Master's Lodge. It was still being decorated. Being shown the drawing room – which was one half blue, the other half brown – incredibly ineptly I said to Lady Lee: 'Oh great, you're getting rid of that awful brown.' But that was the *new* paint. What could one say? I still don't know, now. This had a happy ending as they thought it very funny.

Humour seems to be closely linked to embarrassment. Even odder, humour can both cause and can ease its pain.

In this country, for some people the focus of mores – conferring immensely powerful social significance – is the royal family. Most people can be transformed, even overwhelmed, by the presence of royalty. There are stories of brave men collapsing into confusion when spoken to or being honoured with a royal decoration. At the key point of the ceremony in Buckingham Palace, a man being honoured walks up to the Queen, bows, receives his decoration, and after a few words bows again, finally walking backwards from the royal presence. Ladies, of course, curtsey. An experienced journalist confessed that when he was honoured he was so nervous he became fundamentally muddled: he curtsied!

There is the story of the small town mayor who was invited to luncheon with King George V. The King offered the mayor a cigar: 'No thanks, Sire – I only smoke on special occasions.' How did he live with this memory? At least he is not forgotten by us.

A few years ago I received a royal invitation to an evening reception at Buckingham Palace: a rare event indeed, *very* special, a royal command. No excuse, except severe illness, could possibly be adequate not to turn up, or be late for the Great Occasion. And who would not want to look their best and behave at their best? Well, I sent my dress suit to the cleaners, had a haircut, and turned up at my club in London in good time to change. After a long hot bath, I took the dinner jacket out of its plastic bag. It was then disaster struck. The trousers *were not mine*! They came down, or rather up to my knees. The cleaners had switched my trousers with another's.

What could I do? I checked out the club – the members, the waiters – but no go, nothing suitable. I shot round to the large hotel on the corner – no go there. I rang round the tailors in nearby Oxford Street – just closed. So I was stuck, standing in the hall of the club, with no trousers.

As the clock ticked round to the time of the royal reception, with nothing less than panic the brain started to run at maximum speed. 'Who,' I asked myself, 'Do I know in London who is my height, who might have an evening dress suit, might be willing to lend it?' I am over 6 feet 2 inches tall so the choice was not large. Finally, I had it: Jonathan Miller. He was my height, no doubt had been to lots of royal occasions and so would appreciate the situation. Should I ring him direct? No, I decided, first-hand diplomacy was needed. So I phoned a mutual friend, the publisher Colin Haycraft who lives just opposite. His dinner suit would not fit me but Colin saw the situation in a flash, offering to go across and ask if I could borrow Jonathan's. Ten minutes later the club phone rang – Jonathan was out – going to America the next morning – needing it – his wife (very reasonably) wasn't keen to lend it anyway. Colin rang off. What now? The phone rang again – it was Colin – all well – dress suit coming round in a taxi.

The clock was very nearly at zero hour. The taxi arrived with a very ancient, though elegant dinner suit that must have belonged to Jonathan's grandfather. It had huge buttons and a kind of distinguished green sheen. Now the real problem: Jonathan is my height, but about half the circumference around the middle. In fact, he is trim and dapper. It was almost impossible to get it on but – after a struggle – not quite impossible. So I turned up at Buckingham Palace, at the last possible moment, wearing Jonathan's grandfather's dinner suit.

It was indeed the most delightful occasion. There were all sorts of interesting people from a broad spectrum. The Palace had superb pictures and lots of fascinating objcts to look at. But as the fine central rooms had enormous gilded mirrors, it was impossible to avoid seeing myself, everywhere: huge buttons, threatening to come unstitched from a greenish evening suit from a past age, all too clearly on me, here and now, with an embarrassing future surely about to happen.

There is no doubt we try to avoid embarrassments. But as they live far longer in the memory than in the short time of their occurrence, (sometimes I think they never get erased), we steer our lives to avoid embarrassments. This extends to editing ourselves. If we are embarrassed by some kinds of ignorance, we edit the text of 'what really matters'. I am pathologically poor at languages, so when I visit non-English speaking countries I am reduced to a mumbling idiot. My protection is to pretend it doesn't *really* matter; that because one is good at some other things, this total incompetence will be accepted and forgotten. Of course, it isn't.

Very common is the attitude to science that says it is no disgrace to be ignorant of how the universe ticks, and how technologies work. So most people are not embarrassed by scientific solecisms, even so extreme they pass over into being funny which, funnily enough, is just what happens with extreme embarrassment, no doubt as a divine protection.

The bottom line is that as embarrassment is multiplied by increases of social sophistication, which in this country is waning, it is now increased by the new expectations of literacy in languages and science. So – life will go on being blush-making.

REFERENCES

Darwin, Charles (1872) *Expressions of the Emotions in Man and Animals.* (London: John Murray). Reprinted 1965 (University of Chicago Press: Phoenix Books).

Ekman, Paul (ed.) (1973) *Darwin and Facial Expression: A Century of Research in Review.* (New York: Academic Press).

10

HI-FALOOTIN-FI: SOUND SAGA

Getting on for a thousand moons ago I would listen to 'Children's Hour' with a temperamental crystal set. The crystal looked like a piece of coke. To make it work, one explored the crystal with a delicate 'cat's whisker' – magic! – voices and music would crackle through the earphones. This was an advanced wireless, for there was also a brightly glowing valve ('tube' in American) on its heavy insulated board supporting thick wires, going dead straight and at right angles, exactly like the circuit diagram drawn with a ruler. There were rotary switches with large brass studs, and coils perfectly wound on shell-acked cardboard cylinders. The capacitors ('condensors') looked like dusty bars of chocolate. The aerial was a hundred feet or more in length, stretching down the garden.

The first loudspeaker I remember was flat and pleated like a large paper flower. This was another magic – a talking flower. Then a little later wirelesses came in boxes, the sound coming out of a large hole surrounded by wooden sun-rays. Grown-ups talked about which box gave the best 'tone', like violins or cellos. There was heated rivalry with one-up-manship on whose box had the best tone. Then 'baffles' came in: large wooden panels which helped to avoid 'boxiness'. My father, who always had to be two or three up in any one-up-manship game, went for an infinite baffle (no doubt infinity appealed to him, as he was an astronomer and astronomers are frequently baffled) by knocking a hole in a wall and mounting a huge speaker between two rooms. The house shook with the massive bass. Bass was difficult to achieve at that time so this was a great success, as was all too evident to the neighbours. It is said that walls have ears but ours had raucous voices, for at that time 'mains hum' was an unsolved problem. To be technical for a moment, my father adopted a revolutionary DC coupled amplifier circuit, as he believed (and this is still controversial) that frequency phase-shifts associated with the usual AC coupling are musically bad. But this was before separate cathodes had been invented for output valves so the filaments provided the electrons directly,

61

which gave his system a terrifying hum or rather a roar that dominated any music and gave one a hadache. But as the bass was so good, my father was deaf to criticism.

At school we had a club for building shortwave radios. We wound our own coils, learned about HT batteries and grid bias, and we wired up triodes for AF and pentodes for RF amplifiers. The hardest job was cutting holes in the chassis for valve holders. We never had the right tools and one always wanted to add another valve, which ruined the layout. But it was truly wonderful to hear distant countries on a set one had made oneself from bits of wire and a few basic components. Our one-up-manship was in the tuning dials. They had an aristocracy of gears and friction rollers, and release and drive mechanisms, preferably with white scales engraved on black. There was no notion of hi-fi. We did not listen to music. Our wirelesses were for catching far-off voices, across oceans of stormy static. Isn't it odd that we still speak of 'tone' controls? Isn't it even odder that with transisters we have returned to the (then totally mysterious) physics of crystals and cat's whiskers?

Recorded music with quality came after the Second World War. I associate it with the Leak valve amplifier with its huge transformers and its pre-amp. with quite new controls for upping and downing bass and treble. I built something similar in my digs at Cambridge, but was caught by the landlady with wires and soldering irons all over the sitting room and a muddle of bits and pieces hidden in the sideboard. I was never forgiven.

Hi-fi was in. This was the beginning of tape recorders and LP records and stero. Doesn't stereo work surprisingly well, as quite unnaturally both ears hear both speakers? Not surprisingly, earphones, which now are again quite popular (backward time travel!), work better for stereo than do speakers; except that the sound can be heard weirdly inside one's head. A test record of ping-pong makes the ball bounce around in one's skull, especially if one moves one's head a little, when the usual phase changes between the ears do not occur, as the earphones move with the head. I first heard stereo sound and a stereo tape recorder when still a student with a friend, John Brown (now a Professor of Psychology and a leading expert on memory). He also remembers this experience, which triggered in him a lifelong love of recording music at the highest quality.

To those of us who made our own early valve amplifiers, hi-fi (though I don't think the word then existed) simply meant reducing harmonic distortions to make the sound realistic. There were public tests for realism, with string quartets hidden behind curtains so that comparisons could be made between the live and recorded music. This is exactly the logic of the Turing Test, for judging whether a computer has human-like intelligence. The human and computer are hidden behind a curtain and they are questioned with various problems. If the answers are so similar that one is confused whether the person or the computer answered, then one can say that the computer has human-like intelligence (or vice versa.) A snag is that when a simple calculation problem is set, this gives the game away – the computer is far too good at arithmetic! Musicians might object to extending the test in their direction; for the live concert remains a special experience, just as talking intimately to people we can see is special.

My attempts at producing real live music were humilating. I started learning the piano but we had an automatic player piano, worked with long paper rolls with punched holes, which I would play instead of practising. Then I learned the trumpet, which was disastrous. My father being an astronomer would work all night, but as I would practice the trumpet in the early morning its and my popularity hit rock bottom. My school had great musical talent but they were short of a trumpet player in the orchestra (which was why I took it on) and we competed for the title of Best School Orchestra in the South of England. We went from heat to heat, right to the final concert in Queen's Hall in London. (Later this was bombed during the War. I went to its very last concert and heard Elgar's *Dream of Gerontius*.) Unfortunately for my playing the trumpet, I had great dificulty counting the bars of rest between passages and tended to come in early or late, which is hard for the listener to miss. Also it was very easy to come in with an A instead of an E, or vice versa, as both notes have the first two pistons pressed down with a only a small difference of lip. I would get this and counting bars wrong far too often. So – ultimate humiliation! – for the final concert my friends in the orchestra asked me not actually to play. I didn't play a note. We won the competition.

For sound reproduction there is always some limiting factor. The main problems then were the speakers and their enclosures. Some were massively heavy, built with bricks or largely filled with sand, and there were all manner of boxes and pipes and exponential horns and electrostatic marvels. The variety was at least half the fun. The whole thing was part-science, part-occult – a rich recipe for cults.

The first record I bought at the age of twelve was from the HMV shop on Oxford Street in London. It took a long time to choose. How was I to get best value for my pocket money? Clearly, by finding the record with the greatest number of instruments, playing as loudly as possible. At that time one could spend hours in record shops trying them out. The choice was not too hard: the Overture to Wagner's *Der Meistersinger*. Hearing it now takes me straight back to that day searching for the best buy. Then records were only 78s. The small 45s and the first $33\frac{1}{3}$ LPs came much later. I had a memorable $33\frac{1}{3}$ birthday, with LP records for presents. Then ($11\frac{2}{3}$ years later) a 45 record birthday; 78 remains for the future. I shall ask for historical 78 discs of *Der Meistersinger*.

Recently I decided to upgrade my stereo system. But how should the choice be made? With such a wide variety available, it is impossible to try out all of them. So I got a couple of issues of an impressive hi-fi magazine giving detailed tests and comparisons of turntables, tape decks, CD players, tuners and amplifiers – the lot. There were long lists of assessments of available units, rated from 'Poor' to 'Excellent', with comments and prices. The assessments were of two kinds: objective laboratory tests, and subjective sound tests based on panels of practised listeners. Agreements between the objective and subjective ratings were high. Though not in complete agreement, they seldom differed by more than one or two categories: 'Average +' and 'Good' was an almost maximum difference. 'Poor' only occurred once, for the speakers. The subjective comments had remarkably rich variety. The description of one of the expensive speakers was 'An aggressive, messy sounding design whose uncouthness undermines the positive level of detail'. Strong stuff. But what would an inexpensive speaker be like? And why were there no 'Poor', cheap speakers? The choice of speakers was not going to be easy. There were comments such as 'A very subtle and musical performer', or, of a small model, 'Most things to most men, this compact is unlikely to disappoint with its "ballsy" character though lacking weight . . . a bit'. For the amplifiers, there were comments such as 'Rich, deep and captivatingly musical', and 'A subtle, civilized pre-amp though a little lacking in resolution and detail; suited to some tastes but not top-drawer'. Does the electronics of amplifiers really contribute so much to a performance? Certainly this is a long way from our struggles years ago simply to reduce harmonic distortion.

These comments may represent all sort of subtle technical matters such as frequency-phase shifts, simultaneous or staggered arrival of different frequencies at transients, dynamic speaker damping by very low impedance drivers and heaven knows what else. Perhaps they tell us how subtle – both tolerant and demanding – is the ear.

Like pictures presenting large objects on small canvases, hi-fi may present a whole orchestra, a vast opera, in a sitting-room. How could this be realistic? Indeed, to imagine such realities is to experience nightmares. Like a picture's double reality, of a small flat surface presenting huge objects in quite another space, so for hi-fi where one is aware both of the source of the simulation (or stimulation) while at the same time experiencing quite another sound reality. Again like a picture, hi-fi can evoke moments of hyper-reality: a pluck of a string, more poignant than the original.

For choosing my new hi-fi, was it useful to select from these Objective Laboratory Tests and Expert Comments? Looking through the long lists of products to choose from one was of course attracted to assessments of 'Very good' and 'Excellent'. One was also attracted to comments like 'Smooth; good dynamic range' and 'True audiophile sound quality'. But it soon appeared there was a fatal snag. The same assessments – 'Good' and 'Average' and so on – turned up all through the huge price range. But surely the words of the assessments couldn't mean the same for components of very different costs? If they did mean the same irrespective of price, there would be no point spending more than the minimum on an item with an 'Excellent' or 'Good +' rating. But if, as must surely be the case, there is more quality for more outlay, some kind of scaling-constraint is necessary for telling one, for example, which low-priced 'Excellent' component corresponds to a higher priced alternative rated 'Poor'. Rational judgement is not possible without this missing scaling factor for relating quality to price.

The same problem arises for different kinds of equipment which have the same price. Although so-called midis are supposed to sound less good than full sized hi-fi's, this is not reflected in the corresponding ratings. The snag here is that although 'Average' or 'Good' midis are said to give less good performances than full hi-fi's, we are not told what the difference is for the same assessment word ('Poor' or 'Good' or whatever) at different prices – so rational comparison between costs and kinds is not possible here either.

With increasing price does performance increase on a logarithmic function, or what? In practice this is important, for any component can be the weak link; so having got onto this steeply rising price curve, it can be very expensive to match further components of the system. To complicate all this, as my friend John Brown pointed out, quality may not always increase with cost, for some low-cost units may have surprisingly high quality as they are sold in large quantities and so are produced more cheaply. They may have more money poured into their design and testing than is possible for up-market specialist models. So the cost–quality curve may not be smooth, or monotonic.

And what is a 'Best buy'? Best for *whom*? Shouldn't the potential buyers have categories?

These carefully set out comparisons in the hi-fi journal did nevertheless, rightly or wrongly, serve to rule out all but a few options. But then an even odder doubt struck. There was another list, which I at first failed to notice, that had the same kind of objective and subjective assessments – for wires, for connecting the speakers to their amplifiers. These were called interconnect cables, and one learned they are very important. For these passive copper wires there were such comments as: 'Faint audible boom was audible at very low frequencies, but otherwise this cable sounded remarkably neutral.' And, 'Sounding "bigger" and faintly richer than [another wire], slightly grainy at the top end.' And for another, 'Bass is solid and punchy, counterposed by slightly overblown midband which tends to make vocalists larger-than-life.' But could mere passive copper connection cables really do all this? No doubt we used to under-estimate their importance; for us, over 500 moons ago, more or less any bit of wire would do. But it does seem odd that the comments for wires are richer and more varied than for the active amplifiers and speakers. One would think that wires must contribute far less to 'tone', or character of sound than the main dynamic components. Or are these now so good that the connecting wires are the limiting factor that makes the essential difference? This is quite hard to believe; and it would suggest that the other components are all much the same, which they are claimed not to be.

All this made me wonder, as a problem for psycho-physics, how would one test wires or anything else for sounding 'bigger' or 'punchy' or 'overblown'? Testing minimal loudness differences, or making colour matches in a laboratory is not altogether easy but making 'absolute' judgements is far harder, if only because the subjects in the experiment get bored and their criteria drift.

What turntable, CD player, or amplifier, or speaker is each of these connecting cables tested with? With what sort of music? In what mood the listeners? These considerations apply to us listening at home to our hi-fi's. Just as sometimes one wants tinkly harpischord, at another time a full orchestra belting its heart out, so one might want different 'tone' from the speakers according to one's mood. In recent up-market hi-fi's the 'tone controls' have gone. It is assumed that the 'source' is pure and perfect, and that we the listeners are moodless.

How should we choose a hi-fi? They all look much alike: almost identical black boxes with square edges and sharp corners, hiding function and individuality. Though this is a subjective judgement, to me they look rather ugly. I don't like the fashion of black boxes with black switches and knobs: it is almost impossible to find the controls without a strong light and a magnifying glass. Surely this is designer mania, masking function to produce inconvenience.

Is choosing a hi-fi beyond science? Perhaps it is. Is this why there is this mystique (as it seems to be) for very special Tuners and Decks, Amplifiers and Speakers, and very special Cables? Is this why just two or three manufacturer's names are spoken of with no less than religious awe – ownership conferring Fellowship of this Hi-Falootin magic circle?

Today – taking care to get the incredibly thick pure copper connecting cables recommended for the deeply sonorous though texturally neutral speakers – I bought my new hi-fi. It sounds excellent.

11

SENSES OF HUMOUR

How the phrase 'sense of humour' came to be and just what it means I am not at all sure. Presumably it derives from the ancient notion of humours of matter and body and mind; but these do not include being funny. The two meanings, funny-amusing and funny-peculiar, is even odder.

From prehistoric times, the humours were four opposed essences of matter: Hot and Cold, Wet and Dry. These were linked to the four substances: Earth, Air, Fire, Water. Water was wet and cold; Air wet and hot; Fire hot and dry; Earth dry and cold. This conception of all matter was combined with the Hippocratic notion of medicine, holding that the body is made of the four humours: blood (*sanguis*), phlegm (*pituita*), yellow bile (*chole*), black bile (*melanchole*). But, like the agents of alchemy, they were not always thought of as straightforward substances but could be 'philosophical', having mental and sometimes magic qualities. Related to these fluid humours, 'catarrh' was supposed by Aristotle to flow from the brain and 'rheumatism' (from the Greek *rheuma*, flow or stream) was an upset of the balance of the four humours. So dieting was then, as now, advocated both for physiological and for more philosophical or mystical reasons.

Aristotle's notions of the humours, going back to prehistory, were combined with medicine in the way shown in Fig. 11.1.

The humours dominated medicine and psychology from the fifth century BC (Hippocrates, *c.* 460?–377 or 359 BC) and they were central in Galen's (Claudius Galenus, *c.* AD 130–201) medical writings, of the first century AD. They remained important into the seventeenth century, with echoes still remaining in modern psychiatry. The ancient notion of the humours has not died in normal language, for we still speak of our temperaments as 'phlegmatic', 'sanguine' or 'melancholy', and people can have 'spleen'. A person's 'temperament' originally meant the balance of the four humours. For Hippocrates, imbalance was disease: for us it is ill-temper.

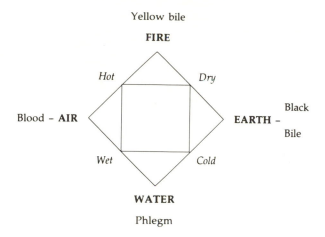

Figure 11.1 Aristotle's Qualities, Elements and Humours. (After Singer and Underwood, 1962, *A Short History of Medicine*, p. 46.)

One of the cardinal humours, the black bile, does not physiologically exist. Whether this should cheer up melancholics is a moot point.

One can be in a 'good humour' or an 'ill humour' and one can be 'out of humour'; but how do these relate to the humour of amusement? What is amusement? Was there a *muse* of humour? What indeed does 'sense of humour' mean? Is it supposed to be a perceptual sense like touch or vision, telling us that some things are really funny? Or, rather, is it supposed, to be an internal mental ability to weigh up and appreciate a situation, like common sense, or a sense of duty? How is humour related to wit? Wit is more pointed, sharper, more cortical than humour; yet both seem to refer to comment rather than to reality. For an example from the Age of Elegance and, we may say, Wit, quoted by Russell (1940):

> The Prince Regent was out walking in Portsmouth when he saw an acquaintance, one Jack Towers. The Prince called out: 'Hullo, Towers! I hear you are the greatest blackguard in the place.' Towers answered, bowing, 'I hope your Royal Highness has not come here to take away my reputation.'

There is a pleasure seeing the point of this joke, based on a situation, that is not unlike the pleasure of suddenly solving a puzzle or making a small discovery by one's own wits.

Humour and invention do not seem far apart and limericks are witty inventions of humour. Of all the many kinds of written humour limericks are the neatest, and puns (though why?) evoke the loudest groans:

Puns have two evil Ends:
Sometimes they gain us Foes,
Sometimes they make us lose
   Our Friends.

Limericks can be usefully memorable. An American teacher, Harvey Carter, is credited with the following limerick to help his students remember *pi*:

'Tis a favourite project of mine
A new value of pi to assign,
   I would fix it at 3
   For its simpler, you see,
Than 3 point 14159.

Einstein's Theory of Relativity owns several limericks. Or rather, they are owned and treasured by those with an inkling of what they mean. Here the humour is in the medium – not the message – for these same statements can be found in 'dry as dust' physics books, where they may be interesting or boring according to taste but are not funny. As limericks, however, provided one knows what they mean, the same ideas appear as funny:

There was a young lady named Bright
Whose speed was far faster than light;
   She went out one day,
   In a relative way,
And returned the previous night.

This one is rather more subtle:

To her friends said the Bright one in chatter,
'I have learned something new about matter:
   My speed was so great,
   Much increased was my weight,
Yet I failed to become any fatter!'

And on the same theme:

A fencing instructor named Fisk
In duels was terribly brisk.
   So fast was his action
   The Fitzgerald contraction
Foreshortened his foil to a disk.

Of course, limericks appeal to medical students and they can be more than risqué. Again form matters; but medicine can be funny in almost any form. Is it an intrinsically humorous subject? Perhaps it evokes all emotions and responses! Here is a mild example of a limerick commenting on the favourite subject of limericks:

The limerick packs laughs anatomical
Into space that is quite economical.
  But the good ones I've seen
  So seldom are clean
And the clean ones so seldom are comical.

More typical (for the definitive collection of blue verse, see Whitworth 1990) is this one:

Word has come down from the Dean
That by use of a teaching machine
  Old Oedipus Rex
  Could have learned about sex
Without ever disturbing the Queen.

Is humour always our invention – or can the universe be funny? We would all agree that the universe is funny-peculiar, for truth is even odder than fiction. But is the universe funny-humorous? Both these very different kinds of funny can belong to descriptions, quite apart from the facts or whatever they describe. This reflects a similarity of humour to beauty for a painting. Or a prose or poetic description may have beauty whatever it represents or describes. So the medium is not the message.

Is humour, like beauty, in the eye of the beholder? Or rather, how do they get into the eye – received from outside or created from within the mind? In other words, are things themselves funny or is it our imaginations that make them so? We have just the same doubt here about beauty, and for that matter ugliness, as we do about humour. Ruskin called Wordsworth's view of beauty as existing objectively in nature, the 'pathetic fallacy'. Presumably it is as intellectually pathetic to call nature ugly, or frightening, or interesting. It is an even more jaundiced (though perhaps correct) view, that nothing can be objectively funny; yet all these, it would seem, are in perception rather than in what we perceive.

Philosophers have written far more about beauty than about humour; yet humour is just as important, for humour presents at least as many questions for our place in the universe. The French philosopher Henry Bergson (1859–1941), in his interesting book *Laughter* (1911), suggested that the only funny things in nature have human associations. He thought that landscapes cannot be funny unless they suggest the human (especially, at least for men, the female) form; that one may laugh at an animal, but only when it looks (ridiculously) human. For Bergson the universe is not funny except for our role in it. Our role may be beyond a joke.

71

Figure 11.2 Switches of perception can be amusing

It is possible to have a sick joke on the saddest, most tragic topics, or happenings. Though death is tragic, the story of the school boy whose life was set by hatred of his head master is rather funny. His hatred built up through his school years – until he saw only one possible profession – to be an undertaker. Biding his time, he bought one Rolls Royce car, then another, another and another, until in a few years he owned twenty-seven, black, shiny, valuable Rolls Royces. Then his moment came – the head master died. His pupil buried him. This was his last undertaking. Selling the Rolls Royces, he retired with laughter in his eyes. Is this funny? I am not so sure.

Science is not noted for its humour, yet jokes are to be found in almost any scientific journal or book. Although statistics is regarded as the most boring subject it has (though it often hides) some of the best jokes. A standard work on Scientific Tables has the footnote 'Corrections to the Random Number Table'. A recent newspaper item on a village crime, reported this excuse for lack of police support: 'There are only 2½ policeman available – two were off sick'. Yesterday I was reading about an experimental study on whether moderate consumption of alcohol reduces heart disease. The result was positive for England and for various other European countries. But this glad result could not be confirmed for France. Why not? It wasn't possible to find a French control group for comparison who did not drink wine every day! Funny things keep happening. In the Bristol Exploratory, our hands-on science centre, we had a travelling exhibition throughout one summer of almost life-sized model dinosaurs, which moved and called to each other with their electronic voices. The exhibition was called LIVING DINOSAURS. At the end of the summer they were collected, for another exhibition, in huge refrigerated lorries!

As any lecturer knows, jokes are sensitive touchstones for testing whether the audience is awake and following, or even ahead of what he or she is trying to say. For students and colleagues these jokes are 'in-group' so they are barred, through the barrier of boredom by incomprehension, from the media. Lots of people might switch off. Are people switched on to science by television or radio? At least in this country there is no media soap opera with a scientist in the cast, with significant issues for discussion or science gossip. This omission from the media is very likely the fault of scientists. It seems that scientists are not attractive enough for the public to include them in their world. What is surely needed is lightness of touch without being arrogant or condescending or trivial. The media danger is the stereotype of the mad professor. This misses the point – because it is laughing *at* rather than *with*.

It is a sad fact – though fortunately with notable exceptions – that scientists are most easily accepted on the media by cartooning their work and hiding its significance, even to playing the fool. Yet it is wrong to say that to be funny one must be foolish or, indeed, that foolishness is particularly funny. On the contrary, foolishness is embarrassing. The point is that *sense*, when shared, can be extremely funny. There is a curious hang-up to admitting this significant truth. For humour to be shared, there must be mutual understanding – which is needed for laughing with though not for laughing at. To laugh with is to demonstrate membership of a club, but laughing at is a response of ignorance, and it may be an aggressive attack. So laughter can be threatening. The downside of humour is that laughter can be a weapon imposing power through assumed superiority. This is also the downside of science.

For some reason (presumably there is a reason), combining seriousness with humour is easier in live lectures than on television, which tends to be either funny or serious but seldom both. The difficulty is to use humour as a condiment, without allowing it to swamp the serious import; for as a condiment humour can bring out the flavour of a thought, though with too much the meat of the matter is lost to taste and made trivial. As it is, the media have a sadly restricted range of humour. In a serious lecture, a touch of humour relieves the tension and can free the mind for a moment, to come back to reconsider afresh. We may look to the day when television will present ideas and discoveries and funny aspects of science as a matter of course – offering wider experience for us all to share. Then life should be richer and a lot more interesting. But for science presented on the media, both seriousness and humour seem to be intimidating. Perhaps humour is too public a test of understanding; for it is all too obvious when a joke, and therefore the point, has not been appreciated – as response to humour is visible and audible. It may be a quickening of the expression, or even a groan that gives the game away; but best is a smile, a spontaneous laugh, and a return joke – as humour is a social game to be shared. But this is an interactive game. The limitation of television and radio (except for phone-ins) is that they are but one-way – the audience cannot answer, or laugh back or in any way contribute – as they are not interactive. Hence the importance of live lectures and discussions, and also live theatre where an audience can contribute laughter and applause to show its pleasure, or displeasure, with the sense or nonsense on offer.

There are public and there are private jokes. In laboratories, just as elsewhere, there are private and even some secret jokes. In my Cambridge laboratory, we had a long-standing private secret that started with a hyacinth in a glass jar suspended on a string. We added a second hyacinth just below it: this was our lowercinth. Finally there was a third glass jar, way above the others: our synthesis. It must be admitted that half the fun of this was that the joke was unknown to our visitors. They simply saw three hyacinths in glass jars. Like gossip, once such jokes go public they lost much of their point.

Jokes can be bizarre and science can be bizarre. It does not of course follow that jokes are science, or that sciences are jokes. What does follow, though, is doubt as to whether humour is a helpful guide for scientists, or for the public trying to evaluate what they say. In normal life, humour can balance common sense by pointing out absurdities, which is a powerful way to avoid error. This can work for some science; but the most interesting sciences depart so far from common sense that they look counter-intuitive and even absurd. In challenging belief, the most exciting science departs form normal guides for sense and so is very hard to distinguish from nonsense. Are the 'paradoxes' of quantum mechanics nonsense? Can reality be nonsensical? However this may be, such interesting nonsensical humour is a special kind of philosophical nonsense, such as that in *Alice in Wonderland* and *Through the Looking Glass*. Yet science is itself a far more incredible wonderland than Alice's. Science goes beyond the limits of sanity, as judged by common sense tempered with worldly humour. We do not at all expect answers to questions such as what is the nature and role of consciousness, or the origin of the universe, to be intuitively reasonable. Indeed, we would be disappointed to find that the universe is encompassed by our common sense, where humour has its place.

Like any other institutions universities have their own classical stories. A famous Cambridge example is Professor J.J. Thomson covering the blackboard with mathematics during a lecture. He suddenly stopped, looked at the complicated squiggles for several moments, then said, 'Well, of course it's obvious . . . ' He left the stage and went into his private room behind, where he wrote mathematics on its blackboard for half an hour. Returning to his by now restive audience he told them: 'Yes – it *is* obvious'. Amid the laughter the Professor continued his lecture.

REFERENCES

Baring-Gould, W.S. (1968) *The Lure of the Limerick*. (London: Granada Publishing).

Bergson, Henry (1911) *Laughter: An Essay on the Meaning of the Comic (Le Rire)* C. Brereton and F. Rothwell (trans.) (London: Macmillan).

Gregory, Richard L. (1986) 'Laughing Matter', in: *Odd Perceptions*. (London: Routledge), pp. 7–15.

Monk, Ray (190) *Ludwig Wittgenstein: The Duty of Genius*. (London: Vintage), pp. 529–33.

Redfern, Walter (1984) *Puns*. (Oxford: Blackwell).

Russell, Leonard (1940) (ed.) *English Wits*. (London: Hutchinson), Introduction, p. x.

Singer, Charles and Underwood, Ashworth E. (1962) *A Short History of Medicine*. (Oxford: Clarendon).

Whitworth, John (1990) (ed.) *The Faber Book of Blue Verse*. (London: Faber & Faber).

12

ZAP!

Staying for nearly two months over one summer with friend Stuart Anstis in San Diego, we had a wonderful time experimenting with his computer graphics, discussing everything from after-effects of movement to the Greek philosopher Zeno, who proved that movement is impossible. We did experiments in the lab with Rama (V.S. Ramachandran), and I gave a summer school course on the History of Psychology. As usual, the teacher learned far more than his pupils. They already knew they didn't know very much – I learned that I didn't. Giving a summer school in California is truly both privilege and pleasure. (Except that I had the wrong kind of Visa, so I didn't get paid!)

It was not all work. We explored the desert, having fun with Rama and his family. We had all sorts of parties and discussions with the remarkably interesting people in this favoured, delightful place where the weather is always wonderful and colleagues combine getting on with their work and each other while having a lot of fun. We didn't work and socialize all the time. Some times, during the evening, we would look at television.

Like most of us, Stuart has a remote control for his TV. His has about twenty pre-tuned buttons. One can sample the offerings very fast and indeed one did for, quite frankly, there was not a lot one actually wanted to see. This reaction could be an example of cultural fixation on the BBC; or it could be that the BBC is actually very good. In any case, I confess to finding that the BBC programmes (and replays were surprisingly frequent) were, apart from a few notable exceptions, by far the best on offer. Unlike here in Britain, television is not a major component of American life, yet there is an awful lot of it. Twenty or so choices (it may be more) would be a lot of choice indeed if they were significantly different, but they aren't. One sees more or less the same quiz show, the same situation comedy, the same police drama, on almost all the channels.

What struck me, was how often this same scene occurred: a gun is pointed at someone – zap! – dead. Playing with the remote control buttons, in one hour I counted sixteen zaps. This did not seem exceptional. If these zaps had come as the culmination of some great build-up of dramatic tension they may have been effective but, as it was, they had about as much significance as someone blowing their nose.

For many dramas, as the plot thickens the cast must be thinned. This is like taking the pieces off the board in drafts (checkers), or removing pawns, knights, bishops, castles or the Queen in chess as they are captured. The act of removal for drafts or chess is a deft flick of the wrist and twitch of the fingers, which goes almost unnoticed. The worry is this: pushing the remote control button to zap a TV channel is just the same act as zapping a life with a gun. Zapping TV is so automatic, so easy, so clearly related to each transitory dislike or mood or petty annoyance. Zap! – it's gone! – programme or person.

Looking at several books on TV violence and experiments on the effects of television, especially on children, I have not yet come across this exact point: that TV life-or-death by remote control – carried out many times every day by children with a deft flick of the finger – is remarkably like the power of the gun. Has murder by guns increased since the invention of TV remote controls? How one would set about demonstrating a causal connection I have no idea. But is specific evidence for forming this connection necessary when we know the immense power of Pavlovian conditioning?

My first boss at Cambridge, Norman Mackworth, had a young daughter who kept goldfish in a large tank in the sitting room. Mac would give the fish a pinch of food every evening when he came home from a hard day at the MRC Applied Psychology Unit. As he opened the door the fish would rise to the surface, with jaws agape, waiting to be fed. Then Mac found himself feeding the fish at all hours. He had only to give them a glancing look from his armchair and there he was, getting up and finding the fish food and feeding them yet again. The fish had conditioned him!

It is so easy for day-to-day, routine events to form conditioned reflexes. We know this from the work of Pavlov, Skinner, and many others. We know this so well we can be essentially certain that zapping TV images with remote controls will associate with zapping people with guns. It would not be so bad if guns were a rarity on TV, used only for self-defence or in war. This repeated, by-the-minute flick of the wrist and press of the button – zap! yet again – is the danger we should consider.

The worlds of film and television have gun terminology. They shoot a scene. A subject is in mid-shot, or near-shot, or out of range. Human passions have 'explosive' violence. They frame their scenes, and they have projects in their sights. Wouldn't it be amusing to reverse the situation on TV?

A man looms through the fog. (Mid-shot)
A *remote control* appears. (Near-shot)
Zap! – the man falls.

This would be funny because the gun connection is already formed deep within our nervous system. So the switch of gun to remote control would have immediate meaning for the laugh-centre of the cortex.

This zapping business occurred to me a few months ago in California, but only last week it was reinforced in London by virtual reality. Howard Rheingold, the author of the recent book *Virtual Reality* (1991) was in London giving lectures. I was invited to do a TV interview with him. This took a whole day, as we visited two virtual reality set-ups in London and we tried it out in the studio. These were virtual reality games. What were the games? You wouldn't believe it – they were zapping men from other worlds.

Why is zapping so popular? I haven't the remotest idea.

REFERENCES

Adler, R., Lesser, G.S. Meringoff, L.K., Robertson, T.S., Rossiter, J.R. and Ward, S. *The Effects of Television Advertising on Children: Review and Recommendations*. (Lexington, Mass.: Lexington).

Barlow, G. and Hill, A. (1985) (eds) *Video Violence and Children*. (London: Hodder and Stoughton).

Cullingford, C. (1984) *Children and Television*. (Aldershot, Hampshire: Gower).

Davies, M.M. (1989) *Television is Good for Your Kids*. (London: Shipman).

Dorr, A. (1986) *Television and Children: A Special Medium for a Special Audience*, Vol. 14. (London: Sage).

Rheingold, H. (1991) *Virtual Reality: The Technology of Computer-Generated Artificial Worlds*. (New York: Summit).

13

VIRTUALLY REAL

How do we know that what we see or touch or hear or taste is really there? How can we know that anything in our perception is real? This must be about the oldest question in philosophy and it has received many answers.

If we never experienced illusions the answer might be clear and obvious – that what we experience is real. But we are as sure as anything that we are often fooled by our senses, and that we dream. Occasionally, we confuse dreams with reality. But to say that reality is a dream or that all experience is illusion is to say nothing, for illusions and dreams require some kind of reality to give them or any discrepancies from truth a meaning.

Dreams and many perceptual illusions are fictions generated by the brain or the organs of sense, for most of us especially by the eyes.

After-images, following stimulation by intense light, are effectively pictures stuck on the retinas, but they appear to us as objects in the outside world. Helmholtz (1866) described why retinal after-images are seen as external objects though they are in the eyes ('entopic'), with his general principle applying to all retinal images:

> Such objects are always imagined as being present in the outside world as would have been there in order to produce that same impression on the nervous mechanism, the eyes being used under ordinary normal conditions . . .

As after-images are 'projected' into external space and seen as though they are normal objects, it can be exceedingly hard to tell after-images from objects. The only definite difference is that after-images move with the eyes, whereas the real world appears fixed even when the eyes move. At first sight, even second sight, this is quite paradoxical for it is real-time optical images of the world, and not frozen after-images, that move across the retinas when the eyes move. After-images are like photographs stuck to the eyes and moving with them, which is quite different from normal vision. Yet normally the world remains

79

still as we move our eyes – and after-images, quite differently, move with the eyes.

The point is that the world is perceptually stabilised against the motion of the retinal image with eye movements, we believe by cancellation of the 'image–retina' movement signal against the command signal to move the eyes. But for after-images there is no image–retina motion signal as they are fixed to the retinas. So the command signal to move the eyes is not countered by motion across the retinas – so we see our brain-commands to move the eyes in the motion of the after-image (Gregory 1966, p. 99–101). The same happens if, for some reason, the eyes can't rotate. Then when the eyes are willed to move, but cannot obey, the world swings round in the direction they should have turned.

Much that we see is not 'out there' but comes from inside us. We create much of our seeming reality. It is hard to distinguish what we receive from the senses and what our brain and senses create.

As after-images can be confused with reality they are dangerous. I well remember, while driving at night in New Mexico, confusing brilliant after-images from lightning with reality. This was while working in an observatory at Cloudcroft, testing a telescope camera designed to minimize atmospheric disturbance of astronomical images. After the wonderful clarity of the New Mexico night sky, just before dawn a violent storm of lightning and thunder would shatter the heavens. Several times, driving down the mountainside late at night, we had the truly frightening double reality of the road suddenly transmuted by a blinding flash into an identical illusion. The copy would separate from the reality, and move slowly into the trees, as our eyes moved. Which visual road moved was the test for reality. But there is scarcely time to sort this out driving down a mountain road in a storm at night!

Each eye has a huge blind region where the optic nerve leaves the retina. This blind spot is near the edge of clear vision, about 15° away from the fovea, and is as large as the eye's image of thirty moons. It is a simple matter to 'see' your local blindness. Hold the page about 6 inches from your eyes, and look with the left eye at the * and the @ disappears as it falls on the blind spot. At a critical distance (try moving the page backwards and forwards slowly) the @ will disappear when you look at the * with your left eye. It disappears when its image lands on the blind spot of your left eye.

@   *

But, and this is an intriguing question, why don't you 'see' your blind spots, as great black patches, hovering around near the edge of your sight? Why don't you see them now, on the page as you read? Are the blind regions so familiar that they are ignored, much as the ticking of a clock is ignored? Or more extreme, as these regions of the retinas have been blind from birth, are they simply not represented in the visual 'projection areas' of the brain? Or very different: does the brain create what 'ought' to be there – to fill the blind regions with visual fictions? A new experiment (Ramachandran and Gregory 1991) suggests that this is so – that unknowingly we create our own realities in the blind regions of our eyes. If this is the right way of looking at it, in this experiment we can actually see what our brain creates.

This is easy to do with an Amiga home computer, using the paint program. A pattern is drawn on the screen, with a coin-sized blank region. A dot is placed some distance away. When this is fixated without moving the eyes, after about ten seconds the blank region disappears. This is an artificial blind spot. As it can be near the centre of vision, it is easy to see what happens. The question is: when it disappears is it being passively ignored, or has the brain actively filled it in, with the surrounding pattern?

The next step is to substitute the pattern, with its blank region, for a completely blank screen. (This is easy to do with an Amiga computer, by pressing the 'J' key.) The blank screen should have the same brightness and colour as the initial patterned screen, and contain nothing but a fixation dot in the same position, so the eyes don't have to move. What happens when the blank screen is switched on? A rough copy of the pattern is seen where the pattern was blank! Evidently, the brain has created a bit of the pattern to fill in the blank region. We now see what our brain has created. It will even create patterns of dynamic twinkle or visual 'noise.' This is quite unlike the much more familiar after-image, following looking at a bright light, seen most dramatically as a compelling virtual reality with lightning on a dark night. (See also 'What Are Perceptions Made of?)

After-images are just one of many visual fictions that merge with reality. Everyday perceptions are largely fictional, but usually these fictions do not mislead and are useful for giving continuity to the fragmentary sampling of reality by the senses. But just what is fiction and what is fact is important for survival: fictions of the senses can lead to disaster.

Do we test for reality – all the time – everyday? The philosopher John Stuart Mill made the interesting suggestion that we recognise objects as external things because they can disappear. He defined objects (Mill 1865) as 'permanent possibilities of sensation'. He based this notion on two postulates of mind. First, that the mind is capable of expectation, second, on the power of association of ideas. That is, phenomena which occur together or are in close association are 'thought together' to form what he called an 'indissoluble association.'

In this way, objects are created from the bits and pieces of sensory stimuli.

Very like Helmholtz's celebrated later notion of perceptions as 'unconscious inferences', though much less well known, Mill said that: 'We see, and cannot help seeing, what we have learnt to infer, even when we know that the inference is erroneous'. Mill gives the example:

> I see a piece of white paper on a table. I go into another room. If the phenomenon always followed me, or if, when it did not follow me, I believed it to disappear *e rerum natura*, I should not believe it to be an external object.

He points out that these associations for seeing objects are called up so rapidly and are so powerful that they seem intuitive, though they are based on experience.

Mill surely pushed this too far when he tried to explain deductive certainties as generalisations of instances. For him, it is certain that $2+3=5$ because as children we played with bricks and found by experience – by induction from many instances – that this is so. But attempts to equate deduction with induction (and attempts to 'justify' inductive inference or try to make inductions, like deductions, certainly true) are no longer accepted. It seems better to think of induction as lying within scientific method, rather than as a branch of logic.

These issues are controversial. The philosopher Sir Karl Popper (Popper 1972) takes the very extreme view that there are no inductions; that induction is no more than (in his words and with his italics) *'optical illusion'*. How, though, one would run one's life (or a railway) if this were so, is far from clear. Without inductions (even though they are often hard to justify), we would have no expectation of trains arriving, or the sun rising, or that these words will have any meaning. In normal life, if not for philosophers, we live by inductive expectations in a mental virtual reality of the expected future. Reality hits us when we are surprised.

Film-makers depend on the powers of perception to create sense from bits and pieces of sampled scenes. It is surprising that we accept pictures which are absurdly large or ridiculously small, and with the tricks of cutting which show impossibly fast – indeed, often instantaneous – changes of scale and viewpoint. Sometimes, we the observers travel faster than light, yet in cinema or television we accept these impossibilities as normal.

How do we appreciate the endings and beginnings and changes of scenes? How do we know that shots belong to the same scene, even though different objects are revealed? In real life we have to move our eyes and bodies to achieve location changes; yet, watching television, we are instantly transported by changes of retinal images to another place, to another country, to the moon, even to some physically impossible world.

Film and video editing and dubbing are intuitive arts, carried out with great skill yet, apparently, with few explicit rules or theory. As Jonathan Miller and some others, especially Julian Hochberg (Hochberg 1978, 1987) appreciate, there is much to be learned here. So it is surprising that the perceptual skills of the audience, as well as techniques of film and video editing, are not studied more fully. Evidently, sounds can help to establish continuity though silent films can still be followed: it is interesting to switch off TV sound. Making home movies, or videos, it would be interesting to add mismatched sound and see whether this upsets visual continuity. Background music not only sets mood – it helps to determine continuity of scene. I am not aware that these very interesting perceptual issues have been adequately studied and reported. Surely there is scope here for research projects linking technologies of representation with intriguing perceptual issues, raising also some challenging questions for philosophy. For example, is it possible to test John Stuart Mill's idea of our acceptance of reality by using techniques of cinema and television?

Emerging as it were in mid-shot, is the new technology of Virtual Reality. How is this different from film and TV? It differs in two ways: it provides 3-D stereo vision with small cathode-ray tubes, one for each eye, in the goggles of a helmet. Much more important – VR allows sophisticated interaction. Interaction is achieved by storing a full, three-dimensional, 'solid' world. This world may be real or imaginary. It may be bizarre, impossible, even violating the basic laws of physics. One can walk around in the computer-world, one's position being continuously monitored from a little aerial on the helmet. One can 'touch' and one can 'pick up' objects with the DataGloves, which have many small sensors detecting movements of the fingers. The whole system of 3-D goggles, DataGloves and computer is known as the 'reality engine'. The explorer of virtual reality is a *cybernaut*.

It is even possible to introduce another person into the computer world: a teacher, a friend, a lover. In the future it will be possible to pick a book from a library shelf and open it and read it just as in 'real' reality. However, at present, computer memory and processing speeds are too limited and virtual reality is often sketchy and is rather jerky for fast movements. But because of the perceptual significance of interaction the experience is nevertheless compellingly vivid.

I experienced VR for the fist time at the NASA/Ames Laboratories, in California in 1988. This was also the first VR experience of Howard Rheingold. In his book *Virtual Reality* (Rheingold 1991) he describes this experience (p. 132):

I found myself floating inside a luminous wire-frame depiction of a space shuttle. Precisely disparate images presented to each of my eyes combined to create a near-perfect three-dimensional stereogram, a close to 3-D image. Stereographic enthusiasts would approve the qualifiers: computation-intensive 'shaded polygons' (the building blocks of high resolution computer graphic models) and other techniques to present secondary depth cues could produce a more perfect three-dimensional image than wire-frame.

Rheingold puts his finger on the reason why this rather early, quite crude, visual presentation was so effective (p. 132):

When a cybernaut shifts his gaze or waves her hand, the reality engine weaves the data stream from the cybernaut's sensors together with updated depictions of the digitized virtual world into the whole cloth of a three-dimensional simulation. The computer engine, however, contributes only part of the VR system. Cyberspace is a cooperative production of the microchip-based reality engine sitting on the floor of the laboratory and the neural engine riding in my cranium.

Cooperation with the neural cranium engine is indeed vital for all perception. The cooperation is greatly enhanced by hand–eye interaction – for real and for virtual reality.

VR technology has developed fast in the last few years. Wire frames are now filled with surface texture to increase 'reality' and each increase in computer power speeds the essential interactive changes. A significant addition is force feedback to DataGloves, so one can *feel* the effects of touching and handling virtual objects. This has been applied to the world of atoms by Frederick Brooks at the University of North Carolina, which is a major centre for VR research, with his students and colleagues (Brooks 1975, 1977; Brooks *et al*. 1990). They have been simulating protein structures in VR for over twenty years, ever since the late 1960s. They include DataGlove feedback, so that atomic forces can be felt. This helps difficult chemical problem-solving for discovering 'keys' and 'locks' in large molecules for creating designer-drugs for medicine. The promise of VR is now open to all scientists and designers, dreamers and inventors. It may become the next psychedelic drug for taking ourselves out of ourselves by taking us out of the world.

Reality engines are becoming more powerful and they are coming down in price. This is helped, just as for the early history of cinema and television, by the entertainment appeal of VR. Like cinema and TV, VR also has applications for education. This should be important, because interaction is so necessary for discovering and understanding real reality. This has been claimed by educationalists at least since John Dewey's aphorism 'Learning is doing'. It is the essential philosophy of recent hands-on science centres, including the Exploratorium in San Francisco and the Exploratory here in Bristol, England.

The uses of VR are legion. Skills from surgery to singing may be practised and improved. Implications of theories and hypotheses may be experienced and tested out in (a curious kind of) practice. On the other side, crimes may be planned and it could become an alternative, opting-out life-style. This, though, could be turned to discovering new conceptual universes with alternative laws. What would it be like to live in an non-Euclidean world, to approach the speed of light, or experience quantum reality at first hand?

Much as novels present alternative lives, more vividly will VR allow us to live in entirely different surroundings with a new or even with no body. Not only other personalities, but our own pasts as well as our potential futures may be captured for eternity. Virtual Reality should turn the silver screen to gold.

REFERENCES

Brooks, F.P. (1975) *The Mythical Man-Moth: Essays in Software Engineering*. (Reading, Mass: Addison Wesley).

Brooks, F.P. (1977) 'The Computer Scientist as Toolsmith: Studies in Interactive Computer Graphics', *Information Processing 77*, B. Gilchrist (ed.) (Amsterdam: North-Holland) pp. 625-34.

Brooks, F.P. Ouh-Young, Batter, J.J. and Kilpatric, P.J. (1990) 'Project GROPE – Haptic Displays for Scientific Visualisation, *ACM Computer Graphics*, 24, 4, pp. 177-85.

Gregory, R.L. (1966) *Eye and Brain*. (London: Weidenfeld and Nicholson). Fourth edition 1990.

Hemholtz, H. von (1866) 'Concerning the Perceptions in General'. *Treatise on Physiological Optics*. Vol. III, 3rd edn., J.P.C. Southall (trans.), *Optical Society of America*, New York, 1925, Section 26. Reprinted 1962, (New York: Dover).

Hochberg, J. (1978) 'The Perception of Motion Pictures', in: *Handbook of Perception*, E.C. Carterette and M.P. Friedman (eds). (New York: Academic Press).

Hochberg, J. (1987) 'Perception of Motion Pictures', in: *The Oxford Companion to the Mind*, R.L. Gregory (ed.) (Oxford: Oxford University Press), pp. 604-8.

Mill, J.S. (1865) *Examination of Sir William Hamilton's Philosophy*.

Popper, K.R. (1972) *Objective Knowledge*. (Oxford: Oxford University Press).

Ramachrandran, V.S. and Gregory, R.L. (1991) 'Perceptual Filling In of Artificially Induced Scotomas in Human Vision', *Nature* 350, 6320, 699-702.

Rheingold, H. (1991) *Virtual Reality: The Technology of Computer-Generated Artificial Worlds – And how it Promises and Threatens to Transform Business and Society*. (New York: Summit).

14

QUESTIONS OF QUANTA AND QUALIA

We cannot define truth in science until we move from fact to law. And within the body of laws in turn, what impresses us as truth is the orderly coherence of the pieces. They fit together like the characters in a great novel, or like the words in a poem. Indeed, we should keep that last analogy by us always. For science is language and, like a language, it defines its parts by the way they make up a meaning. Every word in the sentence has some uncertainty of definition, and yet the sentence defines its own meaning and that of its words conclusively. It is the eternal unity and coherence of science which gives it truth, and which make it a better system of prediction than any less orderly language.

Jacob Bronowski (1953) *The Common Sense of Science*

Following the amazing success of mathematical physics from the insights of Galileo and Newton inspired by the stars, four centuries ago, the observer has been almost entirely ignored by the physical sciences. This is so even though Galileo and Newton were extremely interested in how we see things, and why we have what are now sometimes called 'qualia' – sensations of consciousness, such as colours – which for them and indeed for us are now highly mysterious. Later, qualia and consciousness became taboo topics in science (including psychology!), perhaps because questions of consciousness did not fit well with mechanical accounts of physics, or with analogies from physics and current technologies to mind. Now, mechanical accounts have broadened to allow concepts of intention, purpose and intelligence for manmade machines. Since de la Mettrie's book *Man a Machine* (1748), it is hardly possible to say that we are not machines – except for consciousness.

From being rejected, the observer – us – has a place in the new physics of this century, in relativity and quantum mechanics. The role of the observer surfaced in Positivist philosophies, as what is accepted as having *meaning* is limited to what can be *observed*. This is a basis of the language-based philosophy of Logical Positivism, early this century, which owed much to the Austrian physicist Ernst Mach (1838–1916), who tried (unsuccessfully) to base all of physics on how things appear in human sensory perception. Mach also wrote an important and interesting book on perception, translated as *The Analysis of Sensations* (from the German of 1886). He did not at all reject perception as important for physics; neither did the psychologist William James's philosophy of Pragmatism (1907), which claimed that meaning comes from use.

Mach's Operationalism is generally acknowledged as important to Einstein's thinking. This notion of Operationalism from sensory experience is clearly discussed by the American philosopher Percy Bridgman, who wrote in his *Logic of Modern Physics* (1927, p. 102):

> In origin the concept [of force] doubtless arises from the muscular sensations of resistance experienced from external forces. This crude concept may at once be put on a quantitative basis by substituting a spring balance for our muscles . . .
>
> In origin [thermodynamics] was without question physiological, in much the same way as mechanical concept of force was physiological.

The notion is that hands-on and eyes-on experience sets up the first crude concepts, which may then be refined by science. The 'raw' experience remains important. This way of thinking is seen most dramatically in Einstein's famous rejection of universal simultaneity, on the ground that as light has a finite velocity, observers at different distances would have different time shifts. Einstein wrote (1936):

> I believe that the first step in the setting of a 'real external world' is the formation of the concept of bodily [physical] objects of various kinds. Out of the multitude of our sense experiences we take, mentally and arbitrarily, certain repeatedly occurring complexes of sense impressions (partly in conjunction with sense impressions which are interpreted as signs for sense experiences of others), and we attribute to them a meaning – the meaning of the bodily object. Considered logically this concept is not identical with the totality of sense impressions referred to; but is an arbitrary creation of the human (or animal) mind. On the other hand, the concept owes its meaning and its justification exclusively to the totality of sense impressions which we associate with it.

How observations and measurements are made is central both to relativity and quantum physics. Einstein continually refers to our use of rulers and beams of light and clocks as measuring rods of space and time for giving meaning to concepts of space and time.

The quantum mechanicians refer to particle counters and inter-ference patterns as tantalising signs that can only be read from mental models of what might be out there. It is a question for both, what reality there is out there, beyond observations. The psychological school of Behaviourism of that time, following J.B. Watson (1918–58) and B.F. Skinner (1904–90), carried Operationalism to the extreme of altogether denying subjective experience – qualia – consciousness. There is something paradoxical about this, however, for the physicists wanted to build physical reality on just what the Behaviourists were denying – sensations! Watson (1913, 1924) and Skinner (1938) maintained that effects of sensory stimulation could only be described in terms of resulting behaviour. So (and even more paradoxical, as behaviourist psychology was seeking scientific respectability) the Behaviourists denied the sensations the Operationalists accepted as basic for physics.

Is Behaviourism's denial of sensations, of qualia, scientifically respectable or is it a cop-out? It might be compared to an electrical engineer prepared only to discuss pointer readings of his voltmeters, and so on, not what the readings mean. This looks frankly ridiculous if one wants to know what is wrong with one's TV, for the pointer readings are pointless if one does not know what the meter is connected to. On this analogy we may see certain kinds of behaviour (laughing, weeping, moaning, sighing, wincing) as pointing to inner sensations. But the meter readings and the behavioural signs may be in error. For example, the needle might have stuck, and the person might be acting. Behaviourism holds that behaviour *always* lies when it con-notes sensations. This is like a voltmeter that *never* registers voltages. The difference is that a 'lying' meter would soon lead to wrong diag-noses for ailing TVs. It is not clear (except for psychotherapists?) what lying behaviour leads to. Our whole social and personal life depends on the assumption that behaviour (including speech) does not always lie. Thus if a physicist claims to have observed something, we generally accept what he says, while realising that there may be errors or illu-sions that need to be checked by other observations or instruments.

The extreme form of Operationalism is Phenomenalism. This asserts that nothing can be said of reality beyond appearances. So it is Physics-Behaviourism. As the rules work, but there is no intuitive mental model of understanding, this might apply to quantum mechanics. The leader of the Copenhagen interpretation of quantum mechanics, the Danish physicist Niels Bohr (1885–1962), took this Physics-Behaviourism view. He urged that *nothing can be said of reality apart from observations*. The prob-lem for quantum mechanics is that the observations suggest a reality so bizarre there seems no safe ground beyond observations; so bizarre, the very nature of measurement and observation is questioned. This questioning is quite similar for psychology and for quantum physics.

Whether any further similarities link them should, however, be viewed with caution. As is said in 'What Are Perceptions Made Of?' (p. 107), to suggest that consciousness is to be explained in terms of quantum physics may look too like this (silly) syllogism:

Quanta are mysterious,
Consciousness is mysterious
   therefore
Consciousness is Quanta.

As it stands, this is not at all a strong argument, but could it lead to important insights?

Though classical physics exorcised mind from the universe, could recent physics provide key ideas for understanding mind in brains? This is suggested by the distinguished mathematician and astrophysicist Roger Penrose in *The Emperor's New Mind* (1988). In the section 'Beyond quantum theory' (pp. 402–4) he asks:

Is our world governed by the rules of classical and quantum theory, as these rules are presently understood, really adequate for the description of brains and minds? There is certainly a puzzle for any 'ordinary' quantum description of our brains, since the action of 'observation' is taken to be an essential ingredient of the valid interpretation of conventional quantum theory. Is the brain to be regarded as 'observing itself' whenever a thought or perception emerges into conscious awareness? The conventional theory leaves us with no clear rule as to how quantum mechanics could take this into account, and thereby apply to the brain as a whole.

As Roger Penrose says, quantum physics is needed to explain properties of matter, including why the teeth of the cogs of mechanical calculating machines (invented by Pascal in 1642) remain fixed and so effective. This is attributed to the discrete energy states (especially electron orbits of atoms) which is central to quantum mechanics, but not explained in classical physics. And, of course, the working of microchips, transistors and so on of electronic computers depend very directly on quantum principles.

But one does not need to refer to quantum principles of matter to explain how a mechanical calculator works. What matters are the numbers of teeth, which are engaged, and so on. Why the teeth themselves remain in place, from second to second and year to year is not a necessary part of a description for understanding how the mechanism works and what it does. What is essential is to understand the procedures carried out by the machine, procedures of multiplication, integrating and so on, to appreciate what the machine is doing and how it works at this conceptual level. *Cognitive* concepts are much more important here than knowledge of why brass and steel have their properties. Thus, Charles Babbage's pioneer mechanical computer of the 1820s, which presaged modern programmed electronic computers, can be adequately described in terms of its mechanical properties and the programs it carries out. Quantum properties can be ignored.

Is this true also for modern electronic computers, whose components depend on certain specially selected quantum properties of matter? To explain the 'hardware' of Pascal's or Babbage's computers, quantum effects were not at all known to their inventors and can be ignored by us; but quantum physics *is* essential for designing and understanding the microchips which are the heart of electronic computers. The question for us is: can we ignore, as for mechanical computers, intimate properties of matter for understanding brain/mind? Or should we, as for electronic computers, make use of basic (quantum) physics of matter for understanding how brains work and so how brains are related to minds?

Roger Penrose takes the latter view. This is opposed to the more extreme aspirations of artificial intelligence ('hard AI'), which aims to explain mind in terms of cognitive procedures which might be carried out by alternative physical means. The American philosopher John Searle (1984), who takes a similar view to Roger Penrose, has lampooned this by suggesting that hard AI is as silly as making a mindful brain out of 'old beer cans'. But is this essentially silly? If beer cans could be arranged to carry out cognitive processes, store information and so on – why not? Is it essentially different from making a calculator with metal or wooden wheels; or neural nets from rubber bands?

What matters is where the essential action lies. Consider a game of billiards: without quantum principles the balls would not hold together, or be elastic. But considering the game, the physics of the balls and so on does not need to be known and is not referred to. The commentator does not launch into a lecture on physics: he or she comments on strategy, and relies on the audience knowing the rules of the game, and that the points are scored or lost according to which balls do or don't drop into the pockets. The rules of the game and the scoring *have nothing to do with physics*. This is just how we may see cognitive brain processes: the physics and physiology are important – essential – but do not capture the essentials of the 'game' of thinking and seeing. Whether we concentrate on the cognitive rules and data on the other hand, or, look for answers of mind in physics or physiology, are very diferent ways of looking at brain and mind. Both are important, but for many questions only one is relevant: the other can generally be ignored. This is indeed a non-vicious dualism. For a given question, *either* brain physics and physiology are important *or* cognitive processes carried out by physiology provide the key. Ultimately though, the two views should be fused – like the two eyes giving binocular depth from their different points of view – not disparate or rivalling, as at present.

Whether either or both combined can account for consciousness – and where consciousness's importance lies – seems untouched, invisible for either view and we do not yet have an adequate synthesis to see conceptually how we see qualia in consciousness.

John Searle and Roger Penrose plump for answers in the substance of the brain. Searle thinks that there is something unique in brain-substance; Penrose thinks that there is some to-be-discovered quantal principle which will explain all. He would need to say why brains, but not tables or chairs, are intelligent and conscious. What is so special about brains? Roger Penrose is more interested at this point in consciousness than intelligence; it is consciousness he looks for in quantum physics. He does not think that the inspirations and insights of mathematicians are given (like a game) by the rules or algorithms used for carrying out mathematics. In short: how the algorithms are selected or invented is for Penrose quite different from how they are used. He looks to quantum physics, both for consciousness and the 'hunches' intuition.

Here I am all too aware of my limitations, but let's try to pursue the quantal tack.

FROM QUANTA TO QUALIA

The German physicist Max Planck (1858–1947) derived the notion from the behaviour of 'black body' radiators and absorbers of light, that energy changes in discrete jumps. This radical idea that energy comes in packets – in *quanta* – was conceived by him in 1901. Neils Bohr explained the lines in the spectrum of hydrogen from a model of the atom in which there is a central heavy nucleus with much lighter electrons circling in orbits. If this was just like the solar system, the electrons would not have discrete orbits and they would collapse into the nucleus. The key idea is that electrons jump into larger, higher energy orbits when the atom receives extra energy – as when light shines on it – and may then collapse back into a smaller, lower energy orbit – when it gives out light. This is clearest for a phosphor that absorbs and gives out visible light, or the phosphor of a TV screen that accepts energy from the electron beam and emits visible light. Brighter-than-white soap powders convert ultraviolet into blue light in this way. What is so different from classical physics is that these transformations always take place in jumps of energy. When many atoms are involved, the jumps smooth into continuous changes and may be ignored. But to explain many phenomena (including the retinal receptors of eyes), one must consider the discrete energy steps central to quantum physics.

Einstein used the quantum concept in 1905 to explain the photo-electric effect, that electrons are not 'boiled' off metals according to the strength or intensity of light, but are only removed from the metal by light which is above a critical frequency (or corresponding short wavelength). It is the *energy* in each quantum (or for light, 'photon') that is crucial; not the *amount* of light or number of photons. The steps or discreteness of energy was entirely unexpected in classical physics and it came as a great surprise early this century. It was even odder, as shown by the British physicist Paul Dirac (born in Bristol in 1902) that light has the dual properties of waves and particles; for in a given detecting or observing situation, light *either* displays wave or particle properties, never both at once.

Things get even more bizarre in the simple situation of light or electrons passing through a pair of closely spaced slits or holes (exactly as in Thomas Young's experiment of 150 years ago, which first clearly demonstrated interference of light and so showed that light is made of waves) to produce an interference pattern – even with *electrons*, which were thought of as *particles*. The most odd thing is, that even when there are so few electrons or photons per second that virtually never will more than one pass simultaneously through the slits, an interference pattern still appears. It may take days or months to produce it on a photographic plate; but why should an interference pattern appear when only a single 'particle' passes through at a given time? Can a particle interfere with itself?

A strange thing happens when any attempt is made to discover which slit a given photon is entering, or has entered, as it passes to the photographic plate (or counters or whatever kind of detector that may be used to identify them). When information is available to detect which slit is being (or has been) entered – the interference pattern disappears! Is it that, as energy is needed to record what is happening, this somehow disturbs the situation so that the diffraction pattern is lost? Or is it that the needed *information* destroys what is being observed?

The famous lack of precision as to what can be observed is described by the Uncertainty Principle, conceived by the German physicist Werner Heisenberg (1901–76). This is that, at the microscopic scale, both motion and position cannot be precisely detected or measured: there is a trade-off between precision of measuring position and velocity such that, as the one is measured more accurately, the other can be known only with a lower precision. Heisenberg concluded that because light is energy packets of quanta, and energy is needed to make a measurement or detect a position or velocity, there is an absolute limit to precision as energy and information are granular. For large objects this may be ignored, but it is so important for the microscopic objects of quanta that their status as 'objects' has to be in some kind of doubt. As they display what for macroscopic objects is very odd, even paradoxical behaviour, their 'objectness' is in doubt just because they are so different from familiar-to-normal-perception macroscopic objects. Let's look at one of these strange and even paradoxical properties of photons and electrons.

One would think that if one of the slits of the interference experiment were blocked, this would have the same effect as only one photon at a time passing through a slit. But we are told this is not so. It is as though a photon 'knows' the other slit is open – for with only one slit there is no diffraction pattern, yet with *single photons* and both slits open there are diffraction patterns. A way out of this conundrum (Davies and Brown 1986 pp. 8–9; Feynman 1985) is to suppose that quantum particles do not have well-defined paths in space. It is at least convenient to think of each particle as possessing an infinity of different paths, each of which contributes to its behaviour. These paths, or routes, thread through both slits in the screen and encode information in each. The suggestion is that this is how a particle can keep track of what is happening throughout an extended region of space. The finding (following John Wheeler's suggestion of a 'delayed choice' experiment) that even when the electrons have gone through the apparatus, determining *where they had gone* destroys the interference pattern, looks like an effect *backwards in time*. So even the usual assumption that time must travel forward is challenged! It is, however, generally stressed that this is very limited backwards-time travel and cannot be used to alter the past (Gribbin 1992).

What happens over large separations between the detectors? This was the question of the famous imaginary Einstein–Podolsky–Rosen (EPR) experiment. The idea is to split a single particle into two equal parts: A and B. The Uncertainty Principle should prevent us from knowing both the position and the momentum of A or B at the same time. Yet, because of Newton's law of action and reaction (conservation of momentum), a measurement of A's momentum can be used to deduce B's momentum. And as A and B will move the same distance at a moment in time after the split, a measurement of A's position should give B's position. The point is that because of the symmetry of A and B, an observer on, say, A could know the momentum or velocity of B. But this implies it *has* a definite velocity and momentum. So it must be an objectively 'real' particle. In a celebrated debate,

Einstein used this situation to challenge Niels Bohr, who replied that the particles are not 'real' until they are observed. Bohr suggested that the other particle is an inseparable part of the quantum system. But what if the particles are allowed to separate by a great distance? How could they still cooperate even though signals cannot travel (as relativity theory says) faster than light? Einstein described this as 'ghostly action at a distance'. It *appears* like this, given reality for each individual particle. But for Bohr the reality is that the particles never separate, as our familiar objects would separate in such a situation. Recently, just half a century after it was conceived, this action-at-a-distance (or alternatively, continuity through separation) has been experimentally established by the French physicist, the late Alain Aspect, using oppositely polarized photons from a common source. Could this be related to extended memory in the brain? Should psychologists take this physics seriously?

A central puzzle is that *observation seems to set reality*. This would hardly arise if the uncertainty was thought of as observational uncertainty; but there are strong reasons for believing that the uncertainty is in the external world, before an observation is made, and that the observation 'collapses' the wave function of probability into a particular reality. One reason for accepting this is that the diffraction patterns occur and remain on the photographic plate for all to see long after the experiment. Another reason is that measurement in one place affects distant states of affairs. What then, in this ultimate sense, is an observation? And what is the observer – the photographic plate, the eye and brain looking at it – or what?

An observation requires a detector (a counter, an eye or whatever) but these are made of matter, and so have the same kind of quantum properties as what is being detected. John von Neumann (1903–57), a Hungarian-American mathematician, co-inventor with Alan Turing of the digital computer, described this as an unending chain of measuring devices, each detecting the preceding member of the series, none able to bring the series to an end by 'collapsing' the wave packet. Though the buck stops at the President's desk – what observation can collapse the possibilities of the wave packet into a single event, that can then pass as a fact into history? What could be so special about perception? Especially as the physiological senses and all instruments are physically based, and are subject to quantal laws?

Here, *consciousness* has been invoked. This has been discussed in various terms (Penrose 1990, Zohar 1990), but it is not at all clear that (or how) consciousness can collapse probability packages into particular realities. This suggestion goes much further than saying 'Where there are no ears, the falling tree makes no sound', for it suggests that without ears, eyes and cognitive conscious brains there would be no tree! This is what, though for different reasons, Bishop George Berkeley (1685–1753) said in *Treatise Concerning the Principles of Human Knowledge* (1710) and in the three *Dialogues between Hylas and Philonous* (1713).

In the *Principles*, Berkeley wrote (XLV):

> The objects of sense exist only when they are perceived: the trees therefore are in the garden, or the chairs in the parlour, no longer than while there is somebody by to perceive them. Upon *shutting my eyes*, all the furniture in the room is reduced to nothing, and barely upon opening them it is again created.

Quantum physics also holds this; except that continuous perception is not needed to maintain reality, as a single act of perception is supposed to collapse the possibilities into a permanent reality.

It is a serious problem that eyes and ears and fingers and brains are subject to quantal effects, just like the objects they perceive. So how can they collapse the wave packet of probabilities into more or less permanent reality? What is so special about (physiological or technological) *detectors* that they can create realities, though they are themselves made of the same stuff as the reality they detect? This is where consciousness has been invoked. It was suggested by the mathematical-physicist and philosopher Eugene Wigner (1961) that, although the eye and the entire nervous system of the human observer are subject to quantum principles, his *consciousness might lie outside physics* to be the final stopping place where reality is set.

Even if we suppose that consciousness (though brain-based) is independent of physics, there are bizarre consequences. We would have to suppose that wave packets were not collapsed in all the history of the universe before there were conscious creatures. Yet surely most of what goes on is never observed, yet passes as causal events into history and sets up the future.

Perception (not mere detection) would need some cognitive abilities; so a mouse might do, but not a plant, or an amoeba, or an insect. (A vegetarian friend has suggested that inability, or ability, to collapse wave packets would be the rational divide for what can, or cannot, be eaten without guilt!)

HALF-ENTER – SCHRÖDINGER'S CAT

As early as 1935, the Austrian physicist Erwin Schrödinger (1887–1961) suggested the much-discussed paradox known as 'Schrödinger's cat'. A cat is prisoner in a box, with a gun aimed at its head. There is also a Geiger counter, with a very small radioactive source, so small that in, say, an hour there is an equal chance of one atom decaying or none decaying. Then there is a mechanism to fire the gun from a quantum of energy. If a particle is emitted it fires the gun and the cat is dead. The point is that the gun amplifies the single radiated quantum to produce a macroscopic event that we can easily observe. Now to our macroscopic common sense, according to whether an atom decayed or not, the cat must be either dead or alive. But on the quantum paradigm, this is not *determined* until the cat is *observed*. Before the observation it is curiously half-dead and half-alive. It should be in this suspended, between dead-and-alive condition, until someone (or a fly? or a camera?) looks in the box.

What would the cat think about it? Well, the cat could be replaced by a person. If the box is opened and 'Wigner's friend' is still alive, we could ask him what it felt like. Although similar situations should frequently occur, no one on record has reported this half-dead, half-alive state. We may safely assume it does not actually happen; yet according to (most versions of) quantum mechanics it should happen.

Are the two very different 'realities' of how the macroscopic world appears to us and what appears from quantum experiments, twin peaks of a mainly hidden iceberg? Is there a hidden linking reality, which once discovered will reconcile what seem to be paradoxes in nature? This is the approach of the English physicist, the late David Bohm (1980), with what he calls the 'Implicate order' submerged beneath our sensed reality.

Isn't there another way of looking at Schrödinger's cat? The cat is a large macroscopic object made of a vast number of atoms. Why should the collapsing wave packet from perceiving the cat correspond to an *entire object*? Indeed, what is an object in perception is very often arbitrary and ambiguous. Is this book one object? Are its leaves, its words, its letters objects? A book might be rendered half nonsense with a few changes to its words or letters. Is a cat obviously one object, or are the whiskers, the eyes, the ears, the tail of a cat objects? Certainly we can see them (or much smaller parts, such as individual brain cells) as objects in their own right. What is supposed to 'collapse'? Does it depend on what is being seen as *an* object? Could just one whisker become 'real', when only it is seen as an object?

It is a contingent fact about the cat-object, that cats can't be half alive and half dead – but what has this got to do with atomic wave packets? Isn't there a philosophical mistake here, in expecting uncertainty of *micro*scopic wave packets to apply to uncertainty of large *macro*scopic objects? If this is a mistake, it could be mistaken to suppose that the observation of large objects collapses microscopic wave packets, or vice versa. For what is detected when perceiving a cat is a tiny sample of all its atoms. The perception is a hypothesis based on this sample. Are detected samples, or rather the perceptual hypothesis that this is a cat, supposed to collapse the wave packets? Surely 'aliveness' and 'deadness' refer to the perceptual-hypothesis cat, not to detected atomic events.

Atoms are not alive or dead – but cats do flip from alive to dead.

Let's look again at *detection*. In one sense, a detector (an eye, a photocell, a Geiger counter) is affected and produces effects just like any other physical system. Where it differs is that it *signals data*. It is its use that makes it special, and this is given by what it is connected to and what this does. A special characteristic of detecting is that the effect may be delayed for a long time. Thus, cosmic rays from millions of years ago may be detected now from traces left in mica found in ancient rocks. Here a perfectly normal physical event becomes a detection when it is used by a brain. But it is hard to believe that this observation sets reality backwards, by millions of years!

What happens to wave packets of visually ambiguous objects, such as duck-rabbits? (See Fig. 14.1.) Physically, they may be part-duck and part-rabbit: perceptually they flip from totally duck to totally rabbit, and back again for as long as they are observed. If reality is set by cognitive perception, what is set should depend on which of alternative perceptions is selected. So on this account, we should be able to flip realities – to change the real future with perceptual illusions. Is this too bizarre? How do we know, when quanta and qualia are beyond common sense?

All we have done is to raise questions. But only the curved hooks of question-marks are capable of catching answers.

Figure 14.1 Jastrow's Duck-Rabbit. Although the picture doesn't change, the perception changes from duck to rabbit and from rabbit to duck. Wittgenstein calls this an 'aspect change'. We may think of it as alternative perceptual hypotheses. These are entertained in turn, as there is no deciding evidence for whether this is, or is most like, a duck or a rabbit.

MEASURING QUALIA

Sometimes we need to measure qualia. Estimates of pain are made on a bearability scale of, say, nought to ten, when patients are asked to imagine extreme or no pain, to set the limits of the scale. Does it make sense to ask 'How much pain?' without reference to some physical scale of measurement? What would this be? It has been suggested that subjective scales of qualia derive from interactive experience, from infancy and onwards, with experiments with various kinds of objects. How far subjective scales of sensation depend on experiencing objects is a very interesting question which is open to experiment.

For ten years while at the University of Cambridge I ran a practical class for philosophy students, in which we would try to tie down words and concepts with simple experimental situations. The idea was to try to avoid the circularities of language by looking for operational definitions. One of the simple philosophical experiments consisted of three lights: one dim, another bright, the third adjustable in brightness. The aim was to adjust this middle light to set it half way in brightness between the dim light and the bright light. The question was: 'What does it *mean* to say it is half way in brightness between the other lights?' This leads to: 'What *kind* of scale applies to sensations?' And: 'Can sensation scales be compared with physical scales?' We would, of course, discuss Weber's and Fechner's attempt to measure sensation objectively (Boring 1942).

Although we still seem to be unclear just how to interpret their ideas and experimental results, without any doubt their approach has fundamental importance for considering sensation, and it is perhaps the only starting point. A key notion is to measure just-noticeable-differences (jnds) of brightness or whatever and count the number of jnd steps between two values. This is a beautiful idea, but it is still unclear how jnds should be added for measuring large differences of sensation. Adding inches works fine for length measurements because an inch is the same wherever it is; but this is only so for linear scales and we can hardly assume that sensations lie on a linear scale. Weber's Law says that jnds get proportionally larger with increase in stimulus intensity (for brightness, weight and more approximately for loudness) so it seems that sensations lie on a roughly logarithmic scale, but this is not a simple matter.

Questions of how to measure sensations bridge psychology and physics: they are truly psycho-physical questions. Suggested answers may come from physics as much as from psychology. It was the Harvard physicist and philosopher of science Percy Bridgman (1882–1961) who introduced Operationalism into the psychology of perception. In 1927 he asked: 'What is length?'and answered that it depends on what operations we carry out to measure length, saying: 'The concept is synonymous with the corresponding set of operations'. This was in the spirit of Einstein's relativity. Speaking of simultaneity of flashes of lightning, Einstein wrote (1916):

> The concept [of simultaneity] does not exist for the physicist until he has the possibility of discovering whether or not it is fulfilled in an actual case. We thus require a definition of simultaneity such that this definition supplies us with the method by means of which, in the present case, he can decide by experiment whether or not both the lightning strokes occurred simultaneously.

This operational requirement led to considerations of how events could be simultaneous for widely separated observers, as light travels at a finite speed. This prevailing operationalism in physics led the Harvard psychologist S.S. Stevens (1906–73) to adopt 'An operational base of psychology' (Stevens 1935).

There have been several attempts to measure qualia and value judgements on psychological scales related to physical scales. Stevens got his subjects to assign numerals (from a previously agreed range of numbers) to experienced brightness, or weight or loudness or whatever, as he presented physical values. This gave two columns of numbers: one for sensations, the other physical values on a physically defined scale such as for weight or length, etc. Here is an example where assigned numbers are related to physical magnitudes of weight:

Psychological weight	Physical weight
10	100
9	88
8	76
7	62
6	50
5	41
4	31
3	22
2	15
1	7

Such data, using these kinds of procedures or operations, gave Stevens a plotted slope in which the experience increased in estimated subjective intensity more or less steeply as the physical stimulus intensity was increased. In general, he obtained a Power Law relating physical magnitude with sensation.

Where R is the response, S the Stimulus, and k and n are constants:

$$R = kS^n$$

Stevens found that the value of the exponent n (the slope of the plotted curve) is different for each of the modalities of the senses. For brightness (Brils) it is 0.3–0.5; for loudness (in Sones) it is 0.3; for subjective duration (Chrons) it is 1.05. The physical stimuli for these are respectively: light intensity – as measured with some kind of photometer; sound intensity – an amplitude of pressure changes of the air at the ear; duration – as clock time. It has been objected that the results depend greatly on the instructions given to the subjects, and also on the range of numbers allowed and various other experimental problems. Stevens defended his position – that he really was measuring sensations – by saying that *all* measures and scales depend upon assumptions which are hard to justify, and may be arbitrary and may lead to circularity. What you get depends on the operations adopted, and so ambiguity in the whole of science may only be pushed back a step and never avoided.

Such methods have been applied to measuring not only sensations but also value judgements, beauty, and even moral values. Economics depends ultimately on our judgements of values and costs. Can economics be based on measures of qualia?

The Cambridge psychologist Christopher Poulton (Poulton 1987) has pointed out several technical difficulties in Stevens' approach, if one expects truly 'objective' answers. A very interesting question he raises is whether we build our scales of sensations from infancy through experience of objects, using operational procedures of which we may be, and indeed are, totally unaware. Christopher Poulton is surely right to emphasize the importance of building internal sensory scales by experience of the object world. This notion is philosophically interesting and it has practical consequences. What of stimulus magnitudes that do not have familiar physical units? For these, Poulton concludes, people only perceive *differences* in magnitudes and cannot perceive *ratios* of magnitudes directly. There is the technical reason for this, that ratios require a zero at the sensory threshold, which units of discriminability do not have; but there may be the deeper reason that internal ratio scales depend deeply on related experience of the object world, while differences are detected without need of internal scales.

Is it only the perceived, or assumed, object-significance of qualia that matter to us? This can hardly be so for we derive pleasure from sounds of music, tastes of food, colours of paintings, flowers and the blue of the sky. Perhaps, indeed, qualia are the source of all pleasures – including even of thinking, for there are qualia associated with thinking – and there are qualia of nostalgia, regret and so on associated with memories. Do we have qualia in imagination? Can we call up in imagination full-fledged sensations, of red or of pain? When I look at a red patch, shut my eyes and try to call it up in memory, it is so much fainter it hardly deserves the term 'quale'. Yet one can make a shot at matching colours by memory. Is this done by *naming* colours? Probably not, for the names given to colours of paint are not specific and can seem inappropriate.

This question of memory qualia surely has immediate significance for everyone – especially for those of us who study perception and for artists – as considerable time elapses between observing and representing, or measuring, what is seen. It would be interesting to know how errors of matching qualia-memories increase with lapsed time. Ideally, we should know this to validate any day-to-day observation, and even more so for science and art. Yet, as we have said, we no longer think of qualia as the data of perception. The brain's data are neural signals, especially action potentials in afferent nerve fibres. The brain's memory data are no doubt physical changes which we do not sense and have not yet been identified experimentally. As we are often unaware of perception and we act much of the time on the basis of memories that we do not recall in consciousness, it is very hard to see what qualia do. If they serve to communicate to others our internal states and needs, isn't it odd that philosophers emphasize the essential *privacy* of sensation and yet try to make sensation the basis of *objective* knowledge? It is hard to make sense of sensation, as we are flip-books of ambiguities. Is there any way of avoiding ambiguities of words such as 'see', 'perception' and 'quale'?

There is little or no evidence for 'purity' of any sensations. The well-known size–weight illusion is a beautiful demonstration, showing that even the apparently simple sensation of weight is not pure: it is compounded of not only skin and muscular signals from lifting, but also assumptions or inferences of density of the substance of which the object is made. For a smaller weight is experienced as heavier: its size may be given by its visual appearance to affect its apparent weight, or by any other modality, or even none when there is an assumed size. Helen Ross (while my graduate student at Cambridge) designed and carried out several experiments on the size–weight illusion which still seem to me important. She found that *discrimination* for weight changed as a function of *apparent* weight. Thus, differences in weight of small objects which – by the size–weight illusion – felt heavier than larger objects of the same scale weight, required a greater difference in weight to be discriminated as heavier or lighter. Isn't that an interesting finding? We were even more surprised to find that large, very surprisingly light weights are also difficult to discriminate.

The more surprising the weights – heavy or light – the harder they are to distinguish. It is hardly surprising that Helen went on to work on effects of weightlessness in space with shuttle crews! It seemed to us that weight is not signalled directly from (afferent) signals from the joints and muscles but that these might be compared against an internal 'guestimate' set up by the size of the weights. To an engineer this might well suggest a Wheatstone Bridge circuit – which also works over a wide range, and also has a loss of sensitivity when its internal guestimate is too great or too small. This engineering analogy makes sense, yet the idea fell flat on its face: it was never taken up or shot down. It is odd what attracts attention – sometimes even odder, what is ignored.

REFERENCES

Berkeley, Bishop George (1710, 1713) *Treatise Concerning the Principles of Human Knowledge* and *Dialogues between Hylas and Philonous*. G.J. Warnock (ed.) (1962). (London: Collins/Fontana).

Bohm, D. (1980) *Wholeness and the Implicate Order*. (London: Routledge & Kegan Paul.

Boring, E.G. (1942) *Sensation and Perception in the History of Experimental Psychology*. (New York: Appleton-Century-Crofts).

Bridgman, Percy (1927, reprinted 1980) *The Logic of Modern Physics*. (Salem, N.H.: Ayer).

Davies, P.C.W. and Brown, J.R. (1986) (eds) *The Ghost in the Atom*. (Cambridge: Cambridge University Press).

Dirac, P.A.M. (1982, 4th edn) *The Principles of Quantum Mechanics*. (Oxford: Oxford University Press).

Einstein, A. (1936) 'Physics and Reality', *Journal of the Franklin Institute*, 221, 313–47.

Feynman, R. (1985) *QED: The Strange Theory of Light and Matter*. (Princeton NJ: Princeton University Press).

Gamow, G. (1966) *Thirty Years that Shook Physics: The Story of Quantum Theory*. (New York: Dover).

Gribbin, J. (1984) *In Search of Schrödinger's Cat: Quantum Physics and Reality*. (London: Corgi).

Gribbin, J. (1992) *In Search of the Edge of Time*. (London: Bantam).

James, William (1907) *Pragmatism: A New Name for Some Old Ideas*. (New York: Longmans, Green).

Mach, Ernst (1886) *Die Analyse der Empfinderengen, funfte vermehrte Auflage* (Jena). C.M. Williams and S. Waterlow (1897) (trans.) *The analysis of Sensations*. (New York: Dover).

Mettrie, Julian Offray de la (1748) *Man a Machine*. G.C. Bussey (1953) (trans.) (Illinois: Open Court, La Salle).

Penrose, R. (1990) *The Emperor's New Mind*. (Cambridge: Cambridge University Press).

Popper, K.R. and Eccles, J.C. (1977) *The Self and its Brain*. (Berlin: Springer).

Poulton, C. (1987) 'Quantifying Judgements', in: R.L. Gregory (ed.), *The Oxford Companion to the Mind*. (Oxford: Oxford University Press).

Searle, J. (1984) *Mind, Brains and Science*. (London: BBC Publications).

Skinner, B.F. (1938) *The Behaviour of Organisms*. (New York: Appleton-Century-Crofts).

Stevens, S.S. (1951, 1958) (ed.) *Handbook of Experimental Psychology*. (New York: Wiley. London: Chapman and Hall), pp. 1–49.

Watson, J.B. (1913) 'Psychology as the Behaviourist Views It', *Psychological Review*, 20, 158–77.

Watson, J.B. (1924) *Behaviourism*. (Chicago: Chicago University Press).

Wigner, Eugene (1961) in: I.J. Good (ed.) *The Scientist Speculates*. (London: Heinemann). And in: W.J. Moore and M. Scriven (1967) (eds) *Symmetries and Reflections: Scientific Essays of Eugene P. Wigner*. (Westpoint, Conn.: Greenwood).

Zohar, Danah (1990) *The Quantum Self: Human Nature and Consciousness Defined by the New Physics*. (New York: William Morrow).

15

WHAT ARE PERCEPTIONS MADE OF?

> Now in so far as it is recognized that the constituents of the environment are not present inside the body in the same way as they are present outside it, to that extent they are bound, the moment they are inside it, to become something essentially different from the environment.
>
> Ernst Mach (1886) *The Analysis of Sensations*

If you ask brain scientists 'What are *perceptions* made of?' they will scratch their heads. If you ask physicists 'What is *matter* made of?' they will scratch their heads and say it is a silly question. Yet such questions are mental (and dinner money) meals for philosophers. Following years of thought a philosopher may decree that they are meaningless – not on the menu – but this will be claimed, perhaps rightly, as *discovery*, for an important way of answering a question is to show that it has no meaning. The Verification Principle of the Logical Positivists (Ayer 1936) claimed that questions lacking any conceivable test, by observation or experiment, of suggested answers are strictly meaningless. Thus not very long ago it was claimed that to ask whether there are mountains on the back of the moon is meaningless – until a Russian rocket photographed it, finding mountains! Technology keeps pushing back the frontiers of what cannot be asked as new techniques extend observations and experiments for testing suggested answers.

The requirement that every 'atomic' statement needs to be verified empirically has now been relaxed, allowing occasional tests of hypotheses to be adequate. This is like a bridge requiring only occasional supports. But some kind of structure – physical or logical – is required. So we may think of a theory of mind as a structure allowing only occasional observations to have meaning.

Can the science of perception find ways of giving meaning to the question 'What are perceptions made of?' Since most people would say that perceptions are made of sensations (now often called qualia) this can turn into 'What are qualia?' or, 'What is consciousness?' (See 'Questions of Quanta and Qualia', p. 86).

Mind has often been identified with consciousness – so unconscious thoughts or unconscious perception seemed impossible. Freud's notion of the Unconscious Mind (and earlier, Helmholtz's notion that perceptions are Unconscious Inferences) came as an unwelcome, hard-to-accept shock. Now the table has turned and it is consciousness that seems hard to explain, or even to accept, as we lack observational evidence for sensations in other people or in animals.

The most basic decision to make is whether brains are *receivers* or *creators* of thoughts and consciousness. My prejudices strongly favour the latter answer, which is almost universally held in the brain sciences though it counters most religious beliefs. Survival after death has seemed to need a mind-substance to continue after the physical brain is no more. This is the pre-computer age assumption; now we are familiar with software immortality, given by the copying of disks. The disks do not have to survive for their 'minds' to survive.

Why do we accept that brains are creators rather than receivers? If paranormal evidence of telepathy were stronger, we might change our minds. Positive evidence that mind is brain-based comes from the effects of brain damage. If you damage a radio receiver, you do not generate quite new bizarre programs, yet this is just what happens with brain damage. The losses and fantastic creations which ensue most strongly suggest that the brain creates not only dreams of imagination but also much that we accept as reality. This does not mean that brain-creations are false, but that what we see can never be taken at face value. Thus you see a sunset as red – in consciousness – but the red is in yourself, not in the sky.

ACCOUNTS OF CONSCIOUSNESS

There are many philosophical accounts of consciousness. I will start by admitting a series of negative reactions (no doubt in part prejudices) to almost all of these various accounts. The first to come to mind is René Descartes's extraordinarily famous 'I think, therefore I am.' What does it mean? As the 'I' is in the definiens and in the definiendum, it is taut-ologous. Why is it necessary that because there is thought there is an 'I' to have the thought? It suggests that 'I' is a substance, but is this necessarily so? Does a thinking, problem-solving computer have to have an 'I'? This is a matter for debate. For us, or for computers, 'I think, therefore I am' is not an analytic, necessarily true statement; it can be questioned. We do not have to assume an 'I', or consciousness, when there is problem-solving or thinking. It is a very real question how far machines can be intelligent without consciousness. Philosophers would like to answer this philosophically: scientists look at it as an empirical question. There are tantalising difficulties for both.

The Identity Theory (Armstrong 1968) that mind is just another *aspect* of matter is interesting. A favourite analogy-example is 'Lightning is electricity'. Yes, but this is hardly sufficient to account for lightning: why it occurs only in certain conditions, what makes the noise of the thunder, etc., etc. This requires an elaborate conceptual model, with electricity an important part, but that would not be sufficient. So electricity and lightning are not identical. Or at least, there is lots of electricity that is not lightning, so it is not helpful simply to say that they are identical. To say that mind or consciousness is identical with brain substance does not tell us what is special about either, and so this is not helpful. It is, however, at least for me, rather helpful to say that ultimately *matter is just as mysterious as mind*. If a physicist is asked 'What is matter – what are electrons made of?' he soon runs out of steam. It gets like: the earth stands on an elephant, the elephant stands on a giant cat, the cat stands on a mat, which is on a tortoise – and so on for ever.

Psychologists quite often see consciousness as a supervisor. My prejudice (and I confess here to several prejudices) against consciousness as supervisor, overseeing the work of the higher nervous system, comes from doubting whether a computer would need consciousness over-and-above its programs (or adaptive nets) to perform intelligently. If I couldn't see from its electronics and programs and so on how it did certain difficult tasks, I would assume (and my lack of programming skills makes this an easy assumption) that there must be procedures operating that I don't happen to understand but which, with further technical know-how, I might understand. It is very far from clear what would push one into believing it needed a meta-neural, or meta-computer conscious supervisor, over and above the physics and software. Hierarchies of supervision within a computer are commonplace. And what would the non-computer hardware and non-computer software supervisor be 'made of'?

Can the Turing Test help? Alan Turing (1912–54) suggested that a machine's 'intelligence' could be assessed by comparing its responses to questions with those of a human being, both being hidden behind a curtain and printing their answers on a teletype (Turing 1950). Turing explicitly said that the machine can only to be compared with human *performance*, including verbal performance, and this is not a test for *consciousness* in man or machine for consciousness is not clearly related to performance. It could only be a test if we knew what consciousness *does*. This assumes that awareness has causal effects on behaviour. But does, for example, showing that some tasks are performed better when mental images are reported justify this step?

We cannot say simply that the matter of physics is conscious without either accepting that *all* matter is conscious (and so tables and chairs are conscious) or at least outlining what kinds or arrangements of matter are conscious. The physiologist is likely to say, not that special kinds of matter are necessary, but rather that some very common substances (such as calcium) do the trick *when organised in certain ways*. It is the task of the physiologist to discover these organizations, which is neural-engineering. But this comes back to the difficulty of seeing how essentially engineering concepts can account for consciousness.

To suggest that certain properties of matter, such as curious features of quantum physics, are responsible does not allow us to say why brains are conscious but not tables or chairs. There is a danger that something like this unhelpful syllogism is operating:

Consciousness is mysterious
Quantum mechanics is mysterious
   therefore
Consciousness is quantum mechanics.

For we do not want to say that all matter is conscious, yet all matter is subject to sub-atomic physics. What we want to know is what is so special about brains.

What *is* so special about brains? Is it language? Can one really believe that there is no consciousness, no awareness, in non-linguistic animals? Can one really believe that consciousness started in man with the voice of Homer (Julian Jaynes 1976)? This seems to be pushing regard for the classics too far.

Most suspicious, to me, is the notion that there is some special substance in the brain that imbues consciousness. The American philosopher John Searle (Searle 1984) lampoons the converse view, that ordinary matter might (in some circumstances) be conscious, by asking 'Could old beer cans be conscious?' But there is no claim that old beer cans are appropriate components for a physiological brain or a computer. OK – beer cans are not sufficiently like brain cells – but so what? If one can't get a circuit to work with the available components, this is no argument for saying that no generally available components, or materials, can do the job.

It does not follow from anything we know, or from any argument so far stated, that brain cells have to be made of some unique-to-brains consciousness-substance. This claim is, indeed, a return to the bad old idea of Vitalism, which precluded scientific explanation, as with its supposed special substance having just the properties to be explained it excluded analogies by claiming uniqueness. To assume that the question is outside science in this way is to make the same kind of non-helpful step backwards as saying that life is explained by postulating a 'life substance'.

Provided it is not defined in terms of mystery, I find it helpful to consider *emergence*. When, for example, atoms of oxygen and hydrogen combine, the resulting water is extremely different from these gases. This is not some magic genie in the bottle: the molecule is a new shape, with different properties. We get emergence simply piling up bricks – a tower or an arch are quite different from jumbled bricks. Couldn't consciousness be an emergent property of physiological activity? This would not prevent it having causal effects; water can put out fires, created and maintained by hydrogen and oxygen, or of course other kinds of fire. There seems no reason why emergent consciousness should not affect the brain processes creating it. An orchestra makes music which we may say 'emerges' from the instruments. Music is not a thing or a substance yet it affects the musicians producing it.

One of my teachers at Cambridge (I just missed Wittgenstein) was the philosopher John Wisdom, whose wonderfully quixotic lectures and his essays 'Other Minds' (which sometimes give the essential bottom-line idea in a footnote) fascinated us (Wisdom 1952). What John Wisdom was trying to do was to anaesthetise us, his students – to make painful questions go away like tooth ache does with the administration of nitrous oxide. This he did with analogies, continuing for a term or more, such as comparing evidence for another's sensations with seeing the glow of a fire over the horizon. Questions of what we can and cannot know or say live on in his students' minds over forty years later – so the anaesthetic didn't work! Or rather, it had only short-term effects on some of us. But perhaps we had not learned how to inhale.

One of Wisdom's most telling questions was 'Suppose someone had an operation, and the anaesthetic (perhaps indeed all anaesthetics) did not stop pain – but only prevented the *memory* of the pain lasting until after the operation. Would this be an acceptable anaesthetic?' Presumably one could push this to the length of a whole lifetime. John Wisdom's anaesthetic treatment is closely related to his hero Wittgenstein's account of consciousness, which associates sensation-statements with observable behaviour. For Wittgenstein, as for Wisdom, it is meaningless to speak of sensations apart from their associated behaviours, such as squirming or moaning when in pain. This is because of the demand for some way of verifying that there are sensations in another person. One might say that this demand from Logical Positivism – though it was abandoned by Ayer (Ayer 1946, Introduction) as unworkable as there are many examples of statements that do have accepted meaning yet are unverifiable – has prevented many philosophers from accepting 'pure' sensations in others dissociated from behaviour, though we do not demand behavioural evidence for our own consciousness.

ACCOUNTS OF PERCEPTION

Consciousness is often associated with perception. Yet, just as for thinking, we can conceive that animals or machines might perceive without being conscious. We do not, indeed, seem to be conscious of all we perceive. We often behave appropriately without being aware of what we are seeing, or doing.

Each of the many accounts of perception has been closely linked to a theory of knowledge. Some notable Greek philosophers – Pythagorus, Plato and, more geometrically, Euclid – thought that visual perceptions are given by invisible rays shooting out of the eyes, like fingers, to explore and touch objects. This notion had the snag that near and very distant objects, including stars, both appear together as soon as the eyes are opened, though the rays were supposed to shoot from the eyes at less than infinite speed. This theory did not at all suggest what perceptions are made of – though it was appreciated that it would be circular to suppose (to take the original example) that the sound of a bell is *made* of the sound of a bell. Realizing this was a major conceptual breakthrough by Theophrastus (*c.* 372–286), who criticised Empedocles for saying that perceptions are internal copies of external objects:

> . . . with regard to hearing, it is strange of [Empedocles] to imagine that he has really explained how creatures hear, when he has ascribed the process to internal sounds and assumed that the ear produces a sound within, like a bell. By means of this internal sound we might hear sounds without, but how should we hear this internal sound itself? The old problem still confronts us.

Other philosophers, very differently, thought that visual perceptions are surfaces of objects, and so made of whatever objects are made of. This idea had the obvious snag that, unlike touch, eyes can sense very distant objects. How could surfaces of distant objects enter the eyes? This 'naive realism' had a hard time accounting for basic perceptual experiences such as the changing shapes of tilted coins viewed from various distances and positions. Democritus suggested the notion that objects radiate 'shells' or 'husks', spreading out like ripples from stones dropped in a pond but keeping their shapes, as simulacra of objects. On this account, we see distant objects through mysterious intermediate entities, neither objects nor images, that came to be known as 'sense-data', lying between the world of objects and our perceptions. This notion was popular through the Middle Ages, surviving right up to this century as the sense-data of the Empiricist philosophers, even to the quite recent Cambridge philosopher C.D. Broad (1929) and the Oxford philosopher H.H. Price (1932).

All the ancient and many far more modern accounts of perception were fundamentally erroneous because they lacked appreciation of a critical fact – that the world of objects is optically imaged in the eyes. It is a strange quirk of the history of science that the Greeks had no notion of optical images. When retinal images were – at last! – appreciated by the astronomer Johann Kepler (1571–1630) early in the seventeenth century, this *scientific* discovery fundamentally affected the *philosophy* of perception. It was now clear that objects are imaged in eyes as optical perspective projections, changing according to distances and orientations. So many ancient philosophical questions disappeared as they received answers from science. This did, however, raise new questions of 'What are perceptions made of?' For sensations are not what enter the eyes: they are not surfaces of objects, nor retinal images.

The alternative pre-modern science account that vision is given touch – like by probing rays which shoot out from the eyes – promised reliable knowledge of distances and shapes of external objects; but it gave no suggestion of what perceptions might be made of. What it did do, and this was important, was to suggest that perceptions are some kind of internal *representations* which would in many ways be very different from the objects they represent. Thus, the perceptual world of sensation was separated, and accepted as very different, from the world of matter. As Theophrastus said when he objected to Empedocles explaining how creatures hear by means of the ear itself producing sound, 'How should we hear this internal sound itself? The old problem still confronts us'. Similarly for the retinal images of the eyes, we must avoid the infinite regression of eyes looking at images in eyes looking at images in eyes . . . which gets nowhere.

But what are these inner representations of object-reality? Are they what perceptions are made of? Or should we ask, 'What are the representations made of? (Somehow, this seems less important: does it really matter whether a symphony is recorded on a record, a tape or on a CD?)

The Empiricist philosophers of the eighteenth and nineteenth centuries thought of perceptions as made of sensations. With the influence of modern physiology, we are now drawn to regarding neural activity as the basis of perceptions. Sensations are no longer seen as the data on which perceptions are based, or what perceptions are made of.

We know that sensations are not raw data of perception, for we know that even apparently simple sensations are cooked and flavoured by what they might signify. As shown very clearly in examples of visual ambiguity, the same object, with unchanging retinal images and unchanging neural signals, can give alternative very different

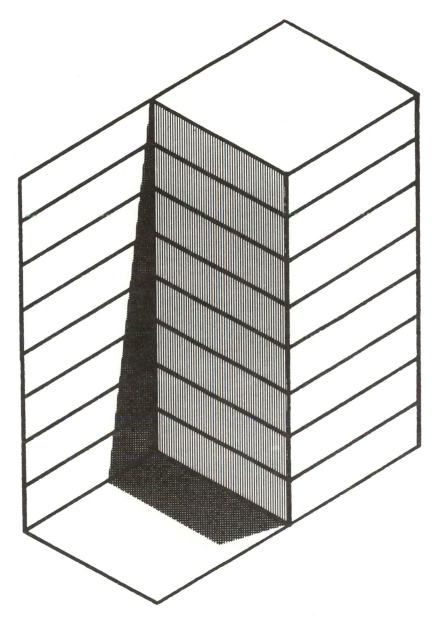

Figure 15.1 Mach's flipping corner figure. The shadow can be seen as being in an inner corner or an outer corner. The figure flips in depth. For most observers, the dark region changes brightness according to whether the corner is 'in' or 'out'. It looks lighter when in, as this is a plausible shadow. Shadows tend to be perceptually ignored as they are not useful objects. Thus, sensations can be affected 'downwards' from knowledge or assumptions.

perceptions. This is important evidence against 'direct' (Gibson 1950) theories, and also against sensations being raw, uninterpreted data. It is an important fact for science and philosophy that perceptions, including simple sensations, can change according to interpretations of what object is seen, though the eyes' images remain unchanged.

A nice example of this was pointed out by the Austrian physicist Ernst Mach (1838–1916). (See Fig. 15.1) The apparent brightness of a shadow seen on, or in, a corner (such as a bent card) changes when the corner reverses perceptually in depth (Mach 1897). While seen as an inner corner, the shadow looks lighter than when it appears as an outer corner – though there is no physical change of luminance to the eyes. Whether it appears light or dark depends on whether it is seen as a shadow or as a mark on the wall or on the bent card. This change of sensation may be attributed to brightness constancy, as shadows tend to be visually ignored. This works 'downwards' from the prevailing object perception, changing with the alternative perceptions of the corner – and so whether most probably it is or it isn't a shadow – though the stimulus to the eye and its signals to the brain remain unchanged. So, we learn that brightness sensation is affected by *interpretations* of neural signals, according to what kind of object is seen, correctly or incorrectly. As the brightness sensation changes with these perceptual flips, sensations cannot be raw, uninterpreted data of perception as the Empiricist philosophers and some recent psychologists supposed. This simple demonstration seems to show very clearly that the philosophers were wrong. But is it the business of philosophers to find truth through demonstrations of phenomena? Surely this is science's task!

Here, a simple observation has immediate philosophical significance. But – like any word, or sentence, or any perception – this observation itself needs to be interpreted. Are we certain of the significance of this flipping phenomenon? I have just made several assumptions: that perceptions quite indirectly represent the world of objects; that there are 'bottom-up', i.e. neural signals which have to be interpreted. I also assumed that perceptions are essentially predictive hypotheses, and that there can be alternative perceptual hypotheses selected from 'top-down', i.e. stored knowledge, derived from past experience. More specifically, we learn that knowledge of shadows can (top-down) affect brightness constancy. But like any other experiment, this beautiful observation does not give raw data from which conclusions necessarily follow. There might always be other interpretations, other 'meanings', of any experiment or observation – for all observations, not only the flips of 'perceptual ambiguities', are inherently ambiguous.

For discussing these matters we need exceptionally well chosen words, for there are very confusing ambiguities of language and concepts for discussing and thinking about perception, especially 'seeing' as experience and 'seeing' as understanding. It is sometimes possible for both meanings of 'see' to apply, as when we see a joke in a cartoon. And of course the meaning of a word can change with context – flip-change with meanings of the sentence in which it lies. Thus, 'ring' and 'bell' have entirely different meanings, in: 'Winter's blue men ring the church bells,' and 'Spring's blue bells ring the church'. Here 'ring' and 'bell' take on meanings according to the sense of the sentence.

We may believe that ambiguity between 'seeing' for the eyes and 'seeing' with knowledge lies deep within processes of perception and understanding. Indeed, this ambiguity is so deep it is almost impossible to express it without using ambiguous words. If we describe it as a distinction between *sensation* and *sense*, this is ambiguous, as 'sensation' and 'sense' each have these two meanings. Equally, 'senseless' can mean 'stupid through lack of understanding', or lack of sensation, as in 'knocked senseless'. (The first is top-down, the second is bottom-up senseless.)

Perhaps all alternatives are just as ambiguous: 'appears', 'appreciation', 'apprehension', 'discern', 'impression', 'aware', 'conscious of', 'discriminate', 'respond', 'view'. These all have this same in-built ambiguity of 'sensation' and 'sense' or, for that matter, 'sense' and 'sensibility'. Verbal and conceptual ambiguities are very important concerns of philosophers. Sensibly, the Oxford linguistic philosopher J.L. Austin (1962) used the unusual and so perhaps not philosophically contaminated word 'sensibilia' to refer to sensations. The word 'quale' is, however, now in favour.

ENTER QUALIA

'Quale' is now used to attempt to convey the notion of pure sensation. The word itself is not new. In Old English it could mean torment or torture. A quale-house was a house of torture; a quale-sithe was death from pestilence. But more basically it meant the quality of a thing. It was thus used in 1675 (according to the *Oxford English Dictionary* by Croft in *Naked Truth*): 'The *quid*, the *quale*, the *quantum*, and suchlike quacksalving forms'. This specifies the *what*, the *quality*, and the *quantity* of something. In his translation of Plato's *Republic* the classical scholar Benjamin Jowett (1875, 2nd edition, I, 270), gives: 'When I do not know the "quid" of anything how can I know the "quale"?' Here again, quale means the quality of an object, and it does not refer especially to sensation. Its meaning of pure sensation, without reference to objects or anything else, is a later invention of philosophers who are beset by the ambiguity of the words that are the tools and the materials of their trade. The deep problem, surely, is that words can be ambiguous because our notions are ambiguous – and we do not always know how to cure conceptal ambiguity. Philosophers' methods include using hopefully unambiguous words and imposing hopefully disambiguating definitions. But is it possible to find 'pure' words, or to define words to anchor thoughts or perceptions securely on facts to get our bearings without ambiguity? This is best done by pointing to shared objects, sometimes leading to formal operational definitions. Thus, we agree on colour names even though our sensations of colours may be very different. The particular difficulty about words such as 'see' is that they do not refer to common shared objects. They are 'subjective', which seems to preclude operational definitions. Because of this, though they seem to be the most certain things we know for ourselves, they may be denied, as in Behaviourism.

Rather than doubt our own qualia, we usually accept them as uniquely certain. There are, however, philosophical exceptions to this. The American philosopher Paul Churchland (a friend) in his very useful introductory book on philosophy of mind, *Matter and Consciousness* (1984), in discussing the doctrine of Behaviourism which tries to deny sensations or qualia, writes (p. 24):

> To have a pain, for example, seems to be not merely a matter of being inclined to moan, to wince, to take aspirin, and so on. Pains also have an intrinsic qualitative nature (a horrible one) that is revealed in introspection, and any theory of mind that ignores or denies such *qualia* is simply derelict in its duty.

And later (p. 75), Churchland describes the most generally held traditional view of perception and mind that:

> Our perception of the external world is always mediated by sensations or impressions of some kind, and the external world is thus known only indirectly and problematically. With introspection, however, our knowledge is immediate and direct. One does not introspectively apprehend a sensation by way of a sensation of that sensation, or apprehend an impression by way of an impression of that impression. As a result, one cannot be the victim of a false impression (of an impression), or a misleading sensation (of a sensation). Therefore, once one is considering the states of one's own mind, the distinction between appearance and reality disappears entirely. The mind is transparent to itself, and things in the mind are, necessarily, exactly what they 'seem' to be. It does not make any sense to say, for example, 'It seemed to me that I was in considerable pain, but I was mistaken.' Accordingly, one's candid introspective judgements about

114

one's own mental states – or about one's own *sensations*, anyway – are incorrigible and infallible: it is logically impossible that
they be mistaken. The mind knows itself first, in a unique way,
and far better than it can ever know the external world.

Paul Churchland was forced to use ambiguous words for what
he was at pains to express most clearly – 'sensations', 'apprehend',
'impression'; nevertheless, we do understand him. (And did you
notice that my use of 'at pains' just above is similarly ambiguous?)
Perhaps this passage from Paul Churchland's book is not difficult to
understand even though – through no fault of his – each well-chosen
key word is crucially ambiguous, because we accept this argument
as sound and its conclusion true. But Churchland goes on to deny
its truth! As we should expect, these doubting arguments are much
harder to read. Churchland goes on to disagree with the commonly
held notion that sensations are certain – that, for example, one
cannot be mistaken that oneself is in pain. He holds that the meanings
of words such as 'pain' are not limited by associations with an inner
state or quale – as empirical discovery from childhood of conditions
in which qualia appear are important for their classification and
naming. And they are not simple, or unitary, as there are many kinds
of red, or of pain, as we discover in various situations. Paul Churchland suggests that, rather than being certain, self-knowledge is unlikely
to be as reliable as perception of the external world; for as self-
knowledge was less important for the evolution of the brain it was
not so important for survival. This would be questioned by Nicholas
Humphrey (1983), who suggests that self-knowledge is biologically
important for appreciating by analogy from ourselves the needs of
friends and intentions of enemies.

Another of Churchland's arguments (p. 76) is that: 'The distinction
between appearance and reality must collapse in the case of sensations, since our apprehension of them is not mediated by anything
that might misrepresent them.' Dramatically again, Churchland then
denies the implied conclusion that the appearance and reality of qualia
must be identical. He points out that misrepresentation by an intermediary is not the only way that errors can occur – for the sensation
of pain may be produced by non-pain-inducing stimuli, or may
occur by suggestion, or with nothing to be corrigible about, as in a
dream. But here, in trying to understand, I for one cannot escape the
inherent ambiguity of the words that have to be used. Writing science
is far easier! Normally we are less bothered by ambiguities, as in science
we have operationally defined experiments and shared assumptions
or 'paradigms'. Given basic shared assumptions, disagreements are
generally clear and, remarkably enough, are often quickly resolved

across all cultural or other boundaries. Philosopher's language as it struggles to avoid ambiguity can appear almost absurdly convoluted to scientists who do not have to grapple with these difficulties. But what are the issues here, over sensations or qualia? Can these be questions for science? Perhaps it is philosophy's job to find out, and to interrogate science. Much of science has grown from hard-to-ask philosopher's questions.

Paul Churchland's questioning of the certainty of sensations may be doubting their significance. We often want to know, and may need to know urgently, whether a pain is signalling damage requiring action; whether baring of the teeth is a smile of welcome or a threat; whether the apparently approaching lights are really those of a car driving towards us on the wrong side of the road. But is it only the object-sources of qualia that matter to us? This can hardly be so, for we derive great pleasure from sounds of music, tastes of food, colours of paintings, and flowers, and the infinite blue of the sky. Perhaps indeed qualia are the source of *all* pleasures, including even thinking, for there are qualia associated with thinking. And there are qualia of nostalgia, regret and so on associated with memories.

Do we have qualia in imagination – in mental images? Can we call up in imagination full-fledged sensations of red, or pain? When I look at a red patch, shut my eyes and try to remember it, my mental 'image' hardly deserves the vivid term quale. Yet one can make a shot at matching colours by memory. Is this done by naming colours? Probably not, for the names given to colours of paint and so on are not specific and can seem inappropriate. Why, at least for most of us, are remembered qualia so lacklustre? It may be because qualia are of individual things, but in imagination we generalise from experience. Thus we only see *a* triangle, but we can conceive general properties of *many* triangles – as triangularity. These general descriptions may be stored as rules. This is Emmanuel Kant's account in *Critique of Pure Reason* (1781):

> It is schemata, not images of objects, which underlie our pure sensible concepts. No image could ever be adequate to the concept of a triangle in general. ... Still less is an object of experience [a thing seen] or its image ever adequate to the empirical concept; ... The concept *dog* signifies a rule according to which my imagination can delineate the figure of a four-footed animal in a general manner, without limitation to any single determinate figure such as experience [a quale], or any possible image that I can represent *in concreto*, actually presents.

This question of lacklustre qualia of memory has practical significance for those of us who study perception, or who paint, or decorate a home – for considerable time may elapse between seeing and comparing colours. It would be interesting to know just how errors and uncertainty for qualia change with elapsed time. Ideally, we should know this to validate any observation in science or for normal life, for at least a few seconds separates perceptions and judgements. As we have said, we no longer think of qualia as the *data* of perception: the data are neural signals, such as action potentials in nerve fibres. Yet, ability to store present perceptions as data for later recall seems a primary role of qualia. They do seem to allow us to deal with the world by brain-created virtual realities from the immediate past; yet, very often, we are unaware of perception and much of the time we act on the basis of memories that are not recalled in consciousness. So it is very hard to see what qualia are necessary for.

If private qualia are necessary for communicating to others our internal states and needs (by describing an internal theatre?) isn't it odd that philosophers and some physicists, such as Ernst Mach, emphasize the essential privacy of sensation – yet try to make sensations the basis of objective knowledge?

The American philosopher of mind Daniel Dennett (a friend) asks: 'Are qualia brain pigments, or figments?' This is to question, in the spirit of behaviourism, whether there are qualia of sensation or at least whether they have any significance. Dennett has written extensively on philosophy of mind and qualia (*Brainstorms* (1978); *Consciousness Explained* (1991)). He also analyses the status of sensations in his essay 'Quining Qualia' (Dennett 1988), which was presented in a memorable symposium on consciousness held on Lake Como. His verb, 'to quine' refers to the American logician Willard Van Orman Quine (cf. Quine 1960) whose position is defined neatly in Dennett's satirical dictionary of eponyms, *Philosophical Lexicon* (1987) as: 'To deny resolutely the existence or importance of something real or significant'.

Dennett sets out, not entirely to deny consciousness, but to suggest that 'Conscious experience has no properties that are special in any of the ways qualia have been supposed to be special'. This because the properties of qualia are 'so unlike the properties traditionally imputed to consciousness that it would be grossly misleading to call any of them the long-sought qualia.' The 'long-sought' refers to the ancient notion that qualia are attached to objects – or at least are very closely related to the world of objects. Dennett tackles the problem with an ingenious series of 'intuition pumps', especially through experiments involving such situations or conceivable possibilities as replacing human wine-tasters with a wine-tasting machine – and the 'inverted spectrum' in which an individual's colours are supposed to be reversed so she would see red at the short wavelength blue end of the spectrum and green at the longwave red end. Would she know she was different from us? How could she know? Dennett also looks at experimental findings such as the effects of some substances (indeed, most substances) on taste, especially the curious property of phenol-thio-urea which tastes bitter to three-quarters of us but has no taste for the others; and the effects of turning everything upside down with inverting goggles, as was actually done by G.M. Stratton (1897) and repeated several times since, with the finding that almost complete adaptation occurs after several days, especially following active interaction with objects. The adaptation is both behavioural and perceptual; though perhaps things continue not to look quite right.

What Dennett succeeds in doing is breaking away from accepted usage of words as the criterion for philosophical respectability towards empirical science, even when the proposed experiment cannot actually be carried out. This half-way between pure speculation and empirical testing may well be a necessary step towards experiments right through the history and, no doubt, the future of science.

Dennett rejects the 'Cartesian theatre' of an inner world of qualia. For him an account of consciousness is successful in so far as it escapes Dualism. But why does an inner 'theatre' of qualia imply, or require, dualism? Isn't this Cartesian Dualism supposing that consciousness is a special substance? Suppose we thought of it rather as an aspect of physical brain activity, something like software processes dependant upon but to be described differently from hardware? Then it is not a 'theatre' with an audience. Indeed, such dualities are very common, for many things have various aspects requiring different descriptions.

For Dennett, although he makes effective use of findings of science, philosophy is essentially putting up metaphors for interpreting phenomena. Thus, in *Consciousness Explained* (1991), in a delightfully under-the-top conclusion:

> All I have done, really, is to replace one family of metaphors and images by another, trading in the Theatre, the Witness, the Central Meaner, the Figment, for Software, Virtual Machines, Multiple Drafts, a pandemonium of Homunculi. It's just a war of metaphors, you say – but metaphors are not 'just' metaphors; metaphors are the tools of thought. No one can think about consciousness without them.

Can science's experiments check and confirm or dispatch philosophical metaphors of consciousness? Dennett's work is full of references to experiments. He would be the first to welcome experiments for checking his metaphors.

In *Consciousness Explained* Dennett considers the surprising phenomenon of sight-without-sensation: 'blind sight', also sensation-without-sight: the apparent filling-in of blind regions of the retinas,

118

known as scotomas. Extensively studied over the last few years by highly respected psychologists, especially Larry Weiskrantz (Weiskrantz 1986, 1988, 1990), blind sight is the ability to respond correctly to, or to name simple visual stimuli – though the subject is adamant that he sees nothing. This occurs for large regions of the visual field following a lesion on one side of the cortex. The most probable explanation is that sub-cortical projections from the eyes are functioning, but do not produce consciousness or qualia. This may be like the vision of much simpler animals whose brains do not have a cortex. Blind sight is a highly suggestive phenomenon that surely will yield up even more secrets as this interesting research develops. It is worth noting that blind sight is surprising because we associate consciousness with seeing – yet it is conciousness that is mysterious!

An almost opposite phenomenon is sensation-without-sight, from insensitive regions of the retina including the enormous blind spot (where the optic nerve leaves the retina) which has no light-sensitive receptors. We are normally entirely unaware of this huge blind area in each eye. When you are reading this page, there is a blind area to the left of where you are looking in your left eye, and to the right of fixation in your right eye – yet with either eye open, you are not aware of a blind region. Either this is ignored, or scotomas are actively filled in.

Dennett thinks, on his theory or metaphor of mind, that they are ignored and not actively filled in. Here, surely, it should be possible to test a key part of the metaphor, by experiment.

In *Consciousness Explained*, Dennett says (p. 345):

> Tacit recognition that there is something fishy about the idea of 'filling in' is nicely manifested in this description of the blind spot by the philosopher C.L. Hardin in his book *Color for Philosophers* (1988, p. 22): 'It covers an area with a 6 degree visual diameter, enough to hold the images of ten full moons placed end to end and yet there is no hole in the corresponding region of the visual field. This is because the eye-brain fills in with whatever is seen in the adjoining regions. If that is blue, it *fills* in blue; if it is plaid, we are aware of no discontinuity in the expanse of plaid'.

Dennett comments:

> Hardin just can't bring himself to say that the brain fills in the plaid, for this suggests, surely, quite a sophisticated bit of 'construction,' like the fancy 'invisible mending' you pay good money for to fill in a hole in your herringbone jacket: all the lines line up, and all the shades of colour match across the boundary

119

between old and new. It seems that filling in blue is one thing – all it would take is a swipe or two with a cerebral paintbrush loaded with the right colour, but filling in plaid is something else, and it is more than he [Hardin] can bring himself to assert.

It is amusing that Dan Dennett calls this 'fishy', for it was while experimenting on fish that my friend and colleague V.S. Ramachandran and I had thought of an experiment to test for active filling-in across the blind spot. Working at the Scripps Oceanographic Institute near San Diego, we were placing flounders on various patterns to see how good they are at copying on their backs for camouflage the colour and patterns of pebbles or sand around them. We suddenly thought – if fish can do it, why not the human eye! So we tried it out on our own eyes. The method was this: we put a pattern on a computer screen, then holding the eye steady on a fixation point, we switched the pattern to a plain surface of the same colour and average brightness. We saw the pattern, crudely present, in the blind spot. But the blind spot, where the optic nerve leaves the eye, is far out in the visual field and hard to 'see'. So we created artificial scotomas in our eyes.

We made these artificial blind regions anywhere we liked, by making a blank region on the patterned field, and staring fixedly at a nearby fixation point on the (Amiga) computer screen. After a few seconds the blank region disappeared (probably by an adaptation effect known since 1804 as the Troxler Effect). When the blank region disappeared the pattern seemed continuous; but was this through active filling-in or through a passive ignoring of the blank region? When we switched to the blank screen, containing nothing but the small dot for keeping the eyes from moving, we saw a crude version of the stripe pattern where the gap had been in the first field, remaining for several seconds. This worked for stripes (and indeed plaids), and even more surprising it worked remarkably well for dynamic twinkle on the first screen, and nothing on the second screen. Evidently the brain is able to fill gaps by creating not only static but also moving patterns. It will not, however, create missing objects, or parts of objects such as missing noses (see 'Conning Cortex', p. 173). This brain activity is quite simple-minded.

We were seeing, for several seconds, 'virtual realities' (cf. 'Virtually Real', p. 80). It is philosophically neat to suppose that blind regions are ignored, but experiment suggests that the brain can actively create what ought to be there. Probably the brain creates virtual reality qualia much of the time.

Dennett, clearly rightly, says that an explanation that includes a description of what has to be explained is not a useful theory: so we should not expect components of the nervous system to be conscious, or have qualia. (And atoms of organisms are not alive, though largish parts can be alive, and so presumably, conscious.) An analogy is liquidity of water: oxygen and hydrogen are not themselves liquid; yet brought together as molecules, they are liquid. So we should not expect liquidity in atoms, or consciousness in the terms of a theory of qualia. But surely an adequate explanation should say why the molecules formed of oxygen and hydrogen have the properties of water. Similarly, we would like to know how it is that combinations of active brain cells are conscious and have qualia. Dennett sets out to persuade us that qualia are not brain *pigments*, but rather figments. This is a move towards demoting and perhaps finally rejecting qualia, in the behaviourist tradition. At least before final exorcism – does this quailing from qualia diminish the problem of consciousness? The alternative view is that qualia are not physically in the world, or *figments* to be rejected, but that qualia are brain-created pigments – phenomena to investigate and explain.

It may well be that *all* perceptions are descriptions. This is the view of Zenon Pylyshyn (1978) as he considers imagery and artificial intelligence. Roger Shepard's experiments on measuring the rate of mental rotation of three-dimensional objects (Shepard and Metzler 1971) would be seen as activating rules for rotation – possibly not entirely different from rotating shapes in computer graphics, where shapes are generated by operating rules and rotated or transformed by modifying rules. Such transformations and rotations can and they indeed do take place 'unseen' within the computer. As for our minds, the operating processes are hidden.

Technology can now produce smell-sensors and colour-detectors which are in some ways comparable to the nose and the eye; so we can begin to carry out experiments on machine-perception. But can such sensing devices ever tell us about qualia? What are the limits of devices for sensing objects? Can new devices push back what seems such ultimate limits to knowledge? I have mentioned the Russian rocket that photographed the unknown and seemingly unknowable back of the moon, and there are many such examples in physics and biology showing that limits to what can be asked and answered are seldom absolute. For a very long time astronomers despaired of finding out what stars are made of. It seemed inconceivable that this would ever be known – it seemed strictly impossible until, in 1814, Joseph Fraunhöfer discovered dark lines in the sun's spectrum. When these were identified with the spectral lines of familiar chemical elements on earth it was suddenly possible to identify the substances of the sun and stars, from fingerprint patterns of their spectral lines.

Are the fingerprints of spectral lines from untouchable stars essentially different from links to other minds – of language and observed behaviour? Astronomers interpret stella spectra from comparisons with spectra from substances we interact with on earth. In other words, the question now is whether experiments can lead to our knowing qualia in other minds somewhat as we know what the stars are made of. Is identifying other's qualia essentially different?

For some time after Fraunhöfer discovered the lines in the sun's spectrum there was doubt as to whether they really did tell us what the sun, and later, stars are made of. Then something dramatic happened. Lines were seen which did not correspond to any known element on earth. What on earth were they? This was a mystery, until in 1895 William Ramsay discovered an unknown gas on earth that gave the same spectral lines. The new gas was named helium from Helios, the sun. Discovered on the sun before it was known on earth, its properties turned out to be remarkable in many ways. It was the first element to be created artificially by nuclear disintegration. This extra-terrestrial discovery of helium confirmed the spectral link between the matter of earth and that of the stars. Could there be somewhat similar, powerful predictions for relating our experiences to qualia of other minds – even to cognitive machines?

The snag is, so far as we can see, language and behaviour cannot do quite the same for qualia as helium did for spectral lines. First, because we know (from illusions, and effects of coloured light, and so on) that our own qualia are not simply or directly related to objects we share. Secondly, because we can lie about qualia. Even the 'Ouch!' when someone hits their thumb with a hammer may be false. Actors can pretend to hurt themselves and feel pain or love or fear, but spectral lines cannot pretend or lie (though they may appear abnormal in special situations). Paul Churchland persuades us that our own qualia are not reliable. Daniel Dennett is saying that if we believe qualia are telling us what the world is like in sensory respects, then all qualia lie all the time. Nevertheless, there is good and there is bad cooking, and interesting and boring music, as experienced. So, after all, do qualia have some part to play, though they are unreliable actors?

Is it certainty of the presence of sensations that is in question – or is it causes, effects or references of sensations that is being questioned? What have references to an object, or to anything else, got to do with whether there is a sensation of some kind? Or is the question-point rather: Could I *name* a sensation, if it had no reference? We may have sense without sensation; but can we have sensations (qualia) without some sense of what they mean? If possible at all, this must surely depend on how terms are defined. If defined by reference to other words, we can hardly expect a secure anchorage to know our bearings in the world beyond language. If the definitions are by reference to shared facts we might expect anchorage, provided the accepted facts are not too theory-laden. This is the importance of operationally defined experiments and generally accepted methods and units of measurement: they might provide anchoring facts. Theory-laden facts flip conceptually when alternative theories (or paradigms) are entertained. But what are the equivalent reference facts for sensations? As soon as references are suggested they seem irrelevant for testing whether a sensation or quale is present. Yet we do speak of illusions – departures from the *quid* (the what) or the *quantum* (the amount) – as phenomena of perception that we can investigate experimentally. Thus, in experiments on distortion illusions, we compare qualia with lengths or curvatures or sizes or distances, or whatever we take to be physical quid and quanta of objects. The measurements refer to comparisons with quid or quanta, and are never measured as pure sensations or isolated qualia. So we arrive and end at the paradox of perception: that we only claim certainty of what we cannot describe or measure. Is this also a paradox of physics?

Although all words and perceptions are inherently ambiguous and are affected by context, we only experience spontaneous changes in rather special cases, such as the Necker Cube (see Fig. 27.2, p. 254) or Jastrow's Duck-Rabbit (see Fig. 14.1, p. 97) when the evidence for alternative perceptual hypotheses is nearly equal. This tells us (if we need telling) that perceptions of the present are intimately linked with the past and to an extent are fixed by the experienced past. With measuring instruments and scientific method we try to break away from the in-built conservatism of perception. But science (we universally believe) does not have qualia.

WHAT IS IT LIKE TO BE A BAT?

Qualia of vision or hearing, touch or taste, and the other major sensory 'modalities' are extremely different. It would seem impossible for someone missing a modality to guess what it would be like to possess it. This is well expressed in a celebrated essay, in which Thomas Nagel (1974) asks 'What is it like to be a bat?' A bat 'sees' with its echo-location apparatus: does it have seeing, or hearing, or any modalities of qualia like ours? How could we ever find out? Is the difficulty so much greater for considering bats as for considering the qualia of our friends?

As we see from the size–weight illusion (see 'Questions of Quanta and Qualia', p. 101), and the shadow on Mach's flipping corner (Fig. 15.1, p. 111), the senses are not separate and their qualia are affected by assumptions about objects. In other words, the modalities of the senses are not separate and they are not isolated from top-down knowledge.

Many sensations are given by physiological mixtures (for example, sensations of damp, stickiness and tickle) though they seem uniquely different sensations. Where do the modalities come from? The philosopher, Immanuel Kant, considered that they are given innately from birth. Very differently, Hermann von Helmholtz thought they are derived from the experience of handling objects.

Physiologically very different channels, such as vision and hearing, are certainly innately different. If the eyes were connected to the auditory brain – we would hear light! But Helmholtz could be right in thinking that experience sets up many qualia modalities. Then the question is: do children brought up in different conditions and learning different skills develop different qualia? If so, this could be why communicating with and understanding other people can be so very difficult. This is a large part of the magic of music. Few of us can enter the minds of painters or musicians any better than we can conceive what it is like to be a bat. Could Beethoven have written the late *Quartets*, when he had lost all hearing, without having intensely vivid memory qualia?

To my mind, rejection of qualia is a philosophical symptom of over-demand for immediate verification. What is striking is that although we cannot experience another's experiences, we are as certain as anything – more certain than of anything else – that other people do have experiences, sensations, qualia. The whole of our lives are based on just this knowledge, or rather this certain-assumption. Codes of behaviour, cooking, music, all social life – these depend not only on our knowing or certain-assuming that others have qualia, but that their qualia are generally similar to ours. We do, however, sometimes get indications of differences (such as others liking Wagner when Wagner gives us a headache) and, somehow, this is particularly strong evidence for their qualia, and in some degree our knowing what they are like. There is a great deal in physics, such as what goes on at the centre of the sun, that cannot be immediately verified; but this does not stop meaningful speculation, for physicists have powerful conceptual models and analogies for seeing *conceptually* what no one can see *perceptually* – even to meaningful speculations on the origin of the universe billions of years before life.

But still we lack crucial experiments. Perhaps by discovering how anaesthetics work to remove consciousness, we may be able to tease out what is critical for consciousness. Perhaps, much as surprising chemical properties emerge from changed combinations of atoms or molecules, we might be led to see how qualia are created by brain processes.

WHAT *ARE* PERCEPTIONS MADE OF?

The following passage comes from the previous essay 'Questions of Quanta and Qualia', p. 90.

> What matters is where the essential action lies. Consider a game of billiards: without quantum principles the balls would not hold together, or be elastic. But considering the game, the physics of the balls and so on does not need to be known and is not referred to. The commentator does not launch into a lecture on physics: he or she comments on strategy, and relies on the audience knowing the rules of the game; the points scored or lost according to which balls do or don't drop into the pockets. The rules of the game and the scoring *have nothing to do with physics*. This is just how we may see cognitive brain processes: the physics and physiology are important – essential – but do not capture the essentials of the 'game' of thinking and seeing. Whether we concentrate on the cognitive rules and data or, on the other hand, look for answers of mind in physics or physiology, are very different ways of looking at brain and mind. Both are important; but for many questions only one is relevant: the other can generally be ignored. This is indeed a non-vicious dualism. For a given question, *either* brain physics and physiology are important *or* cognitive processes carried out by physiology provide the key. Ultimately though, the two views should be fused – like the two eyes giving binocular depth from their different points of view – not disparate or rivalling, as at present.

Now let's ask, for billiards and for chess, 'Where is the game?' For billiards or for chess (where the physics of the board and the pieces is less important) we cannot in any simple way equate the game with the balls or the pieces – because they are only significant for following rules and satisfying, or failing to satisfy, intentions. Without the rules and the intentions there would be no game. And yet for billiards (or snooker) the balls and the table and the cue and so on are essential. Very good chess players can play the game in their heads. Presumably, patterns of firing of brain cells substitute for the board and the pieces. Chess pieces are strictly called 'men', but it is an ancient confusion to think of people in the mind. The mind is perhaps better conceived as games played by brain cells: games depending on physics and physiology to work, but depending on rules and scored points for meaning. On this account, the rules of games and cognitive rules for seeing and thinking are very different from rules or laws of physics, and cannot be reduced to physics. Perceptions live within yet lie separated from physics, in this brain-game that is ourselves.

REFERENCES

Armstrong, D.M. (1968) *A Materialist Theory of Mind*. (London: Routledge & Kegan Paul).

Austin, J.L. (1962) *Sense and Sensibilia* (reconstructed from manuscript notes by G.J. Warnock). (Oxford: Clarendon Press).

Ayer, A.J. (1936, revised 1946) *Language, Truth and Logic*. (London: Gollancz).

Ayer, A.J. (1959) (ed.) *Logical Positivism*. (Toronto: Collier Macmillan).

Broad, C.D. (1929) *Mind and its Place in Nature*. (Cambridge: Cambridge University Press).

Bronowski, Jacob (1953) *The Common Sense of Science*. (Cambridge, Mass.: Harvard University Press), p. 70.

Churchland, P.M. (1984) *Matter and Consciousness*. (Cambridge, Mass.: Massachusetts Institute of Technology Press).

Dennett, C.D. (1978) *Brainstorms: Philosophical Essays on Mind and Psychology*. (Cambridge, Mass.: Bradford Books).

Dennett, C.D. (1987) *The Philosophical Lexicon*. (Delaware: American Philosophical Association).

Dennett, C.D. (1988) 'Quining Qualia', in: A.J. Marcell and E. Bisiach (eds) *Consciousness in Contemporary Science*. (Oxford: Clarendon Press), pp. 42–77. Reprinted in: W.G. Lycan (1990) (ed.) *Mind and Cognition: A Reader*. (Oxford: Blackwell), pp. 519–47.

Dennett, C.D. (1991) *Consciousness Explained*. (Boston, Mass.: Little, Brown & Co.).

Fodor, J.A. (1975) *The Language of Thought*. (New York: Thomas Crowell).

Gregory, R.L. (1970) *The Intelligent Eye*. (London: Weidenfeld).

Gregory, R.L. (1984) *Mind in Science*. (London: Weidenfeld).

Gregory, R.L. (1988) 'Consciousness in Science and Philosophy: Conscience and con-science', in: A.J. Marcell, and E. Bisiach (eds) *Consciousness in Contemporary Science*. (Oxford: Clarendon Press), pp. 257–72.

Gibson, J.J. (1950) *The Perception of the Visual World*. (Boston, Mass.: Houghton Mifflin).

Hardin, C.L. (1988) *Color for Philosophers: Unweaving the Rainbow*. (Indianapolis: Hackett).

Humphrey, N. (1983) *Consciousness Regained*. (Oxford: Oxford University Press).

Jaynes, Julian (1976) *The Origin of Consciousness in the Breakdown of the Bicameral Mind*. (Boston, Mass.: Houghton Mifflin).

Kant, Emmanuel (1787) *Critique of Pure Reason*. Norman Kemp Smith (1929) transl. (London: Macmillan).

Mach, E. (1897) *Analysis of Sensation*. English translation, 5th edn. 1959. (New York: Dover).

Nagel, T. (1974) 'What Is It Like To Be a Bat?' *The Philosophical Review*, October. reprinted in: D.R. Hofstadter and D.C. Dennett (1981) *The Mind's Eye*. (New York: Basic Books).

Poulton, E.C. (1987) 'Qualities', in: *The Oxford Companion to the Mind* (R.L. Gregory, ed.). (Oxford: Oxford University Press, pp. 666–70).

Price, H.H. (1932) *Perception*. (London: Methuen).

Pylyshyn, Z. (1978) 'Imagery and Artificial Intelligence', in: C. Wade Savage (ed.) *Minnesota Studies in the Philosophy of Science*, vol. IX. (Minneapolis: University of Minnesota Press).

Quine, W.V.O. (1960) *Word and Object*. (Cambridge, Mass.: Massachusetts Institute of Technology Press).

Ramachrandran, V.S. and Gregory, R.L. (1991) 'Perceptual Filling-in of Artificially Induced Scotomas in Human Vision', *Nature* 350, 6320, 699–702.

Searle, J. (1984) *Mind, Brain and Science*. (London: BBC Publications).

Shepard, R.N. and Metzler, J. (1971) 'Mental Rotation of Three-Dimensional Objects', *Science*, 171, 701–3.

Stevens, S.S. (1935) 'The Operational Basis of Psychology', *American Journal of Psychology*, 47, 323–30.

Stevens, S.S. (1951) 'Mathematics, Measurement and Psychophysics', in: *Handbook of Experimental Psychology*. (New York: Wiley), pp. 1–49.

Stratton, G.M. (1897) 'Upright Vision and the Retinal Image', *Psychological Review*, 4, 182–7.

Turing, Alan (1950) 'Computing Machinery and Intelligence', *Mind*, October 59 (n.s, 236), 433–60.

Weiskrantz, L. (1986) *Blindsight: A Case Study and Implications*. (Oxford: Oxford University Press).

Weiskrantz, L. (1988) 'Some Contributions of Neuropsychology of Vision and Memory to the Problem of Consciousness', in: A.J. Marcell and E. Bisiach (eds) *Consciousness in Contemporary Science*. (Oxford: Clarendon Press), pp. 183–99.

Weiskrantz, L. (1990) 'Outlooks for Blindsight: Explicit Methodologies for Implicit Processes' (The Ferrier Lecture), *Proceedings of the Royal Society of London*, B239, 247–78.

Wisdom, John (1952) *Other Minds*. (Oxford: Blackwell).

16

APPEARANCE AND REALITY
A number of ideas

The fact of illusion and error is in various ways forced early upon the mind; and the ideas by which we try to understand the universe may be considered as attempts to set right our failure .... The world, as so understood [with these ideas], contradicts itself; and is therefore appearance and not reality.

F.H. Bradley (1893) *Appearance and Reality*, p. 1

Philosophy is written in this grand book – I mean the Universe – which stands open to our gaze, but it cannot be understood unless one first learns to comprehend the language in which it is written. It is written in the language of mathematics, and its characters are triangles, circles and other geometrical figures, without which it is humanly impossible to understand a single word of it; without these, one is wandering about in a dark labyrinth.

Galileo Galilei (1632) *Il Saggiatore*

As science gives us ever more surprising knowledge we become less certain of what we know, and perception becomes even odder. The notion that we are born with certain knowledge, and that perception reveals truth, has been eroded over the centuries so now we may well ask, 'What is illusion – what true?' Science does not claim more than hypotheses to describe and explain the seen and unseen world. Much of science saves the appearances by suggesting hypothetical models for restructuring our perceptions. Milton puts this beautifully for astronomy at the time of Copernicus, in *Paradise Lost* (Bk vii, I, 23):

He his fabric of the Heavens
Hath left to their disputes, perhaps to move
His laughter at their quaint opinions wide
Hereafter, when they come to model Heaven
And calculate the stars, how they will yield

The mighty frame, how build, unbuild, contrive
To save appearances, how gird the sphere
With centric and eccentric scribbled o'er,
Cycle and epicycle, orb in orb.

By now we are familiar with accepting accounts of science as hypotheses. It is a less familiar, and indeed a disturbing idea, that our apparently immediate direct knowledge by perception is also questionable hypotheses. This at once suggests that much of perception may be illusion – and it is phenomena of illusions which suggest that perceptions are hypotheses. How do we know when they are in error? We may check one perception against another, or set perceptions against assumed reality (that a straight line appears bent by comparison with a nearby ruler: it may also appear bent in the illusion situation!) but can we seek deeper criteria for deciding between appearance and reality?

It may be suggested that what is accepted as reality or mere appearance depends on accepted accounts of the physical sciences. But as the hypotheses of science change, its prescriptions for true vision change correspondingly. So this divide between appearance and reality shifts and as science has many 'Levels' of description – from surface appearances to concepts that are non-intuitive but remotely related to experience – it is hard to know which account should correspond with appearances. Which accounts should be accepted as references for *reality* from which deviations may be judged *illusory*? Yet we can hardly reject all appearances, for it is by moment-to-moment perception that we live to survive another day, rather than by the weird – even odder – accounts of physics.

This reference-to-physics notion makes philosophers turn to science for what is appearance, what reality. This takes away the philosophers' traditional role as Guardians of Truth. They were, however, seldom consistent guardians (which made philosophy interesting) for they developed various schools of accepted truth: Phenomenalists, accepting only appearances; Materialists, accepting only matter with empiricism their sole route to reality; Idealists, accepting only mind with *a priori* knowledge their reality.

Why is this called 'idealism'? – it should be called 'Idea-ism!' The local dialect of Bristol in England, where this is written, disconcertingly introduces 'L's on the ends of words. Bristol itself appears as Bristol on old maps. In the local dialect, an idea is called an 'ideal' – 'Oh, what a good ideal!' This is confusing (and for a merchant city usually untrue). What Idealist (or Idea-ist) philosophers hold is that all reality is, or at least depends on mind. Bishop Berkeley thought that existence of matter depends on it being perceived; but he did think that matter is different from mind. Other Idealists (Idea-ists) identify matter and mind. As mind is traditionally associated with awareness, or sensation, for them all reality is but appearances. The snag is that this, by a slippery slope, leads to solipsism.

Philosophers in Oxford (which is supposed to have more professional philosophers than did ancient Athens) have grappled with such questions for many years. F.H. Bradley's book *Appearance and Reality* (1893) argued for a monistic unity of things – such that a truth must be the whole truth and, in some sense, all things are one thing in a universal mind. Bradley not only defended *a priori* knowledge but throughout his life he resented and attacked Empiricism as though it were an evil. Thus he served unwittingly to inspire Bertrand Russell, among others, to revolt against Idealism – to accept experimental science as the whole bringer of new knowledge.

It is easy to scoff at 'a truth must be the whole truth' and so on but science, too, seeks unifying accounts. This is puzzling because science also delights in differences, which are just as important as similarities for classifying and explaining.

Moving on from Bradley, rejecting Idealism, Oxford philosophy sought to capture reality in intuitions, expressed in normal language. The assumption was that common intuitions and appearances are true. But then, with the impact of the startling, non-intuitive discoveries of modern science, which were quite different from the normally held beliefs and hard to express in language, common sense had to be rejected. So the bizarre accounts early in this century of Relativity and of Quantum Mechanics had a devastating effect on Oxford philosophy. So (especially Cambridge) scientists became the guardians of the truth.

Science's counter-intuitive discoveries, somewhat paradoxically, cast doubt on Materialism – as the new science re-introduced the observer and the observer's mind was supposed to have a part to play in the physical worlds of Relativity and Quantum Mechanics. Though mind does not seem to have a solo part as some Idea-ists had supposed, as cosmology persuades us that things got on pretty well while the stars were in their infancy, long before perception, or consciousness, entered the scene of the universe.

Perhaps most striking about science is its ability to forge agreements. Of course there are controversies but, unlike any other human endeavour, theories and experiments of science can, almost within minutes, change minds across continents in spite of very different social, racial and political beliefs.

Entirely unlike Common Sense philosophy, it is the *surprising* theories and experiments that are taken seriously as evidence of reality. Similarly, it is surprising perceptions that convince us there is 'something out there'.

Other important bit-players are numbers. Are numbers objects – like tables or stars – or are they ideas in mind? Granted, we cannot see or in any way sense numbers as we can see and sense tables and stars yet, like physical objects, numbers can be surprising and they can force agreements. So numbers are vital for settling issues and differences in science and commerce. It is this that makes them seem objectively real, though unsensed: or, though ideas, do they seem objective because they have such power to change our minds and convince us? We all agree that 1 more than 12 is 13, and that 13 is a prime. We all agree that $\frac{365}{12}$ = 30.416666666. Indeed, such agreements are more complete and compelling than any sensory objects. For many philosophers and scientists, numbers and their properties are more deeply real than matter and nothing like so inconstant or inconsistent as mind. But we soon run into problems. Do we have to say that negative and, worse, that the so-called imaginary numbers ($\sqrt{-1}$) are also objectively 'real'? Descartes rejected imaginary numbers altogether as unreal; but later, they were reified as 'complex' numbers.

The philosopher and historian of mathematics, a close friend of Bertrand Russell, Philip Jourdain (1956) thought of imaginary numbers as useful operators carrying out procedures to make the machine of mathematics work. Comparing this with handling objects of sense, I may tidy my papers but the operations of tidying do not exist in the sense that my papers and my desk exist as objects; yet they do exist, or my papers would not get tidied. Operations exist not as nouns but as adverbs: $\sqrt{-1}$ may be not a noun but rather an adverb in mathematics. But are all numbers adverbs – rather than self-existing nouns? Just as sensed objects can be surprising, so also are many properties and structures of numbers. It is even odder that although numbers are shared and discussed, and surprise us like objects of sense, they do not occupy space. So we cannot see numbers: or can we?

Enter the computer – with graphics.

Computers can now generate wonderful pictures. Computer-generated patterns such as Mandelbrot pictures are, as from another world, disturbingly beautiful (Fig. 16.1). Are they the first picture to give appearances to abstract reality, in a way undreamed of by classical philosophy or science? Do they bridge object-appearance and abstract-reality? There are earlier hints of the powers of pictures to abstract reality, for Plato would have said that geometrical drawings of proofs and principles show mathematical realities. But are not these diagrams guides to how to think rather than pictures of another world of mathematics? Are they not maps to guide the exploring mind rather than windows through which to see abstract reality?

131

Figure 16.1 An example of one of the beautiful computer-generated
Mandelbrot patterns

Figure 16.2 A fractal

There is a hint of visual patterns depicting mathematical properties in graphs. At least, it is very helpful to *see* an exponential or a logarithmic function or whatever plotted as a graph. I cannot think of a probability distribution apart from bell-shaped curves. Somewhat oddly, the development of graphs and their early uses are missing from histories of mathematics. Apart from maps and drawings of movements of the planets and trajectories of cannon balls there seem to be very few hints of graphs before Cartesian geometry. Newton's teacher, Isaac Barrow, devised a graphical form of differential calculus (Boyer 1949) and integration has commonly been done graphically, but graphs do not seem to have been used for showing properties of equations much earlier than a hundred years ago. Graphs are certainly useful for thinking in science and for presenting results. It would be interesting to know how useful they are to pure mathematicians.

Fractals show that certain patterns recur in a surprising range of objects, and remain much the same over an enormous size range. It is interesting that a representation of a coastline does not have a clear length, as the greater the resolution of measurement the longer it gets: so apart from atomic limits, the coastline of a country of finite area is infinite, at the highest resolution, and the patterns of indentations look almost the same over a huge range of magnification. This is not at all like Euclidian geometry with its lines and triangles and circles.

Can fractals allow us to see hidden properties of the familiar objects we perceive through the senses? Now that the computer can transcend ordinary graphs by presenting visually in a few seconds the results of super-human computations, even in real time, it is important to ask, can computer pictures allow us to *see* realities of numbers? Can they not only stimulate our minds but, quite directly, reveal up-to-now hidden features of the abstract though real world of numbers? Fifty years before computer graphics, around 1915, two French mathematicians, Gaston Julia and Pierre Fatou, investigated rates of growth of equations with complex ($a + bi$, where $i = \sqrt{-1}$) numbers. They found that some sets of such numbers, instead of growing to infinity or shrinking to zero, were drawn towards a particular steady state, or to a cycle of values now called attractors. When these numbers are plotted on a graph, with real numbers on one axis and imaginary numbers on the other (an Argand diagram), they produce weird maps as of unknown countries with complicated shorelines and patterns of islands, floating in numbers. When first discovered they were intolerably tedious to produce and investigate, but now anyone can generate them in dramatic colours on a home computer. Benoit Mandelbrot used an Argand diagram to plot what happened when a complex number, c, was multiplied by itself (squared), and added to the original number c. The result Z_1 is squared and added to c, then the second result Z_2 is squared and added to c, and so on. Each point was plotted as black when the number grew, or white if it shrank or remained constant. The resulting wonderful shapes are envelopes of iterations – which computers are very good at doing.

In general, these iterative processes represent limited ranges of positive feedback in non-linear systems. This can apply to population growth, to electronic control and, no doubt, to important brain processes. But what has made these computer-generated pictures take off and become famous is, surely, their immediate visual appeal. The earlier Julia sets did not catch the public eye or mind before they were pictured with imaginative variations and careful choice of colour by computer graphics. Newton invented a related method for finding the roots of an equation $f(x) = 0$ by a dynamic process of iteration where guessed solutions compete. These are useful for discovery and they generate visually interesting computer-graphic patterns.

An interesting question surely is: are these computer-generated numbers so conceptually significant that they allow abstract realities to be seen as objects are seen? If so, are the more *visually* interesting patterns also the more *mathematically* interesting? Is there such a link between beauty and truth?

Do these pictures of mathematics make visible what up to now have been hidden or undiscovered realities? If so, could computer graphics be a tool for exploring claims of mindful Idea-ism – where seeing *a priori* truths is allowed? For Empiricist Materialism, *a priori* knowledge is taboo. We all have to learn the hard way: testing reality by handling objects, to learn to see and understand. Could fractals dip beneath Phenomenalism, and serve to test between Materialism and Idea-ism?

This is an extreme claim! Plato might have accepted it. If Plato was right in saying that mathematical truths exist apart from our minds, we could now at last be seeing what was present but invisible before the technology of computer-graphics. If, on the other hand, numbers with their incredible properties are constructions of the human mind, we are seeing our own inventions, however surprising, projected on computer screens. If this be so, computer pictures are not windows to reality: they are perhaps distorting mirrors of mind.

REFERENCES

Barnes, M. (1988) *Fractals Everywhere*. (San Diego, Calif.: Academic Press).
Boyer, C.B. (1949) *The History of the Calculus and its Conceptual Development*. (New York: Dover).

Bradley, F.H. (1893) *Appearance and Reality: A Metaphysical Essay*. (London: Allen and Unwin).

Jourdain, P.E.B. (1956) *The Nature of Mathematics*, in: J.R. Newman, *The World of Mathematics*, Vol. 1. (New York: Simon and Schuster), pp. 4–72.

Mandelbrot, B.B. (1982) *The Fractal Geometry of Nature*. (San Francisco: W.H. Freeman).

Peitgen, H-O., Richter, P.H. (1986) *The Beauty of Fractals: Images of Complex Dynamical Systems*. (Berlin: Springer-Verlag).

Wollheim, R. (1959) *F.H. Bradley*. (London: Peregrine).

17

MIND IN A BLACK BOX

One supposed fact has from the earliest times misled philosophers and, more recently, many scientists who are concerned with knowing how we see. This 'fact' is that we may see *inwards* to our own processes of vision much as we see *outwards* to perceive the objects of the world. But the fact is that inside is hidden – opaque. We are indeed Black Boxes.

The term 'black box' has various meanings, including the record of an aircraft's life read after its death; but our meaning here is different, and it is somewhat technical. *Collins Concise Dictionary* defines black box as 'A self-contained unit in an electronic or computer system whose circuitry need not be known to understand its function'. This implies that there are 'levels' of function and understanding. I tried to express this, over thirty years ago, in the chapter of a book edited by William Thorpe and Oliver Zangwill, which grew out of a discussion group that ran as a weekly adventure for ten years in Bill Thorpe's rooms in Cambridge and published as *Current Problems in Animal Behaviour* (1961). My point was that – just as for electronic or any other engineering systems – there are levels of description which it is important to distinguish and recognize. Explanations must be at an appropriate level to be useful and not misleading.

The black box is a low-resolution, very general description. The suggested 'levels' for describing and explaining electronics or brains were given in 'The Brain as an Engineering Problem' (Gregory 1961) as:

- **blueprints**: showing the *appearance of components – the anatomy;*
- **circuit diagrams:** showing the *functional properties* of the components – the physiology;
- **block diagrams**: showing the *flow of power or information*. (Or, this might have been put more clearly as *general operating procedures*.)

The book was written before digital computers were at all commonplace and when we were thinking in analogue terms, especially with the control concepts of cybernetics. I shall go on to suggest that

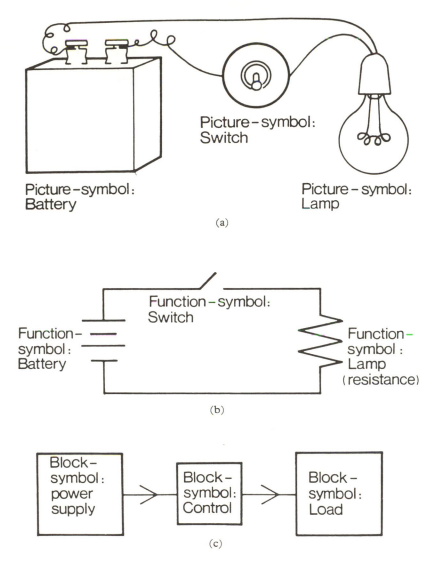

Picture – symbol:
Switch

Picture – symbol:
Battery

Picture – symbol:
Lamp

(a)

Function – symbol:
Switch

Function –
symbol:
Battery

Function –
symbol:
Lamp
(resistance)

(b)

Block –
symbol:
power
supply

Block –
symbol:
Control

Block –
symbol:
Load

(c)

Figure 17.1 The Black Box *(a)* shows a simple blueprint type of diagram.
Pictorial representations of the components are linked with paths of
conductivity (the wires). This may be compared with histological descriptions
of the brain. *(b)* shows a circuit diagram. The symbols show conventional
functional properties of the brain. This may be compared with physiological
descriptions of the brain. *(c)* shows a block diagram. The blocks show the
functional units of the system, indicating the causal processes in terms of the
flow of power or information. This may be compared with cybernetic
descriptions of the brain. (From Gregory 1961.)

the analogue-digital distinction is fundamentally important, but too often confused.

A central point of 'The brain as an engineering problem' was how difficult, indeed impossible, it is to localize brain function or say where processes are going on, without knowledge of what the internal functions are – requiring appropriate levels or kinds of description. This applies to explaining phenomena. For example, to explain perceptual illusions it is important to know whether an illusion (or any malfunction) is due to:

- *failure* of components to carry out functions;
- *inappropriateness* of procedures;
- *inadequacy* of rules of operation.

A black box is literally a working hypothesis. Ideally, it should include all levels of description. When the description is nearly complete it will no longer be black. A strong test for appropriateness and completeness is that it works. But, as there may be alternative possible working systems, this is not quite an infallible test.

Can we expect a machine actually to work as a brain works – actually to see – as we see? So far, artificial intelligence (AI) seeing machines do not work anything like as well as brain-based (BI) perception. So their claim to mirror visual brain function must be weak. What has gone wrong, or rather, not gone entirely right with AI? We are confronted with alternatives:

A black box's

- Components are not *capable* of carrying out the necessary functions;
- Design logic is *conceptually* inadequate;
- Hardware or software is not sufficiently *complete* to work.

Most black box accounts are mere sketches, which could not possibly actually function. Nevertheless, they can be useful for they can suggest the essential components and logic of the system.

IN AND OUTS OF BLACK BOXES

Although any suggestions given here will be far too sketchy actually to work, they may be useful as conceptual magnets for attracting questions which could cast light in the black box of the brain.

Vision has unusual 'engineering' characteristics (even apart from our awareness, our consciousness), for perceptions are far richer than the available signals from the eyes and the other senses. Thus, visual perception has the intelligent characteristics of:

138

- Continuing through data gaps in space or time. Objects may be partly hidden, and we do not look continuously at things, yet perceptually controlled behaviour continues.
- Reading meaning from retinal images. Vision allows appropriate behaviour to non-optical features of the world. We see that wood is hard, and ice-cream cold, from knowledge of materials and objects.
- Predicting into the immediate future. Responding directly to stimuli of the senses is not typical; normally, perceptions and behaviour are appropriate to the source of stimuli – objects.
- Coping with unfamiliar and new kinds of objects and situations. This, and the above features of vision, to my mind indicate that perceptions are creative hypotheses – essentially similar to the predictive hypotheses of science (Gregory 1968, 1970, 1980).

These obviously important features of vision seem to be incompatible with a direct 'pick-up' account of perception (Gibson 1950). Perception is not driven 'bottom-up' from sensory inputs. A large contribution from 'top-down' knowledge seems appropriate for the black box of vision.

Let's try to go further. It is clear that vision is not driven by bottom-up-signals – for we are not slaves to immediate stimuli. It is clear also that vision is not driven by top-down knowledge of objects – for it is possible to see unfamiliar and new objects. The ability to see new objects allows perceptual learning.

Like language, perception very frequently copes with unique situations – we might say by rules, for generating new hypotheses. This strongly suggests that perceptual hypotheses (perceptions) are *generated* by following rules, somewhat analogous to grammar, or syntax, of languages.

Rules such as legal laws allow decisions to be made, for dealing with the present from past experience and to predict the future. Rules derived from the past can lead to errors as situations change. Useful rules must be broader than individual events, and so cannot precisely define them. When inappropriate they can generate systematic errors. For vision this is so for the rules of perspective geometry of retinal images, which allow us to see three-dimensional objects from two-dimensional images. This works fine for normal objects, but queer-shaped objects such as the Ames Demonstrations (see 'Adelbert Ames', p. 238) have shapes that violate assumptions of the parallel sides and right-angular corners of many familair objects. The perspective drawing distortion illusions are probably due to mis-scaling of size and shape and distance when these rules are misapplied to flat surfaces (see: 'Putting Illusions in their Place', p. 259). Their interest, at least for me, is that these phenomena occur not because of limitations of components, of the eye and nervous system, but at the deeper level of the operating procedures. So these phenomena of illusion can illuminate depths of the black box of vision.

If there was a sufficient variety of operating rules to be selected according to every need, illusions such as these could be avoided. But appropriate rules are not available for all situations. This, surely, is like not always having appropriate programs on hand for one's computer. One selects floppy disks, but there are never enough programs to cover all needs. The visual brain has such a shortage of 'floppy disks' that illusions due to inappropriate operating procedures are very common. We may call these, by analogy with inserting floppy disks in to computers, *side-ways* rules.

These are not *bottom-up*, like sensed signals; or *top-down*, like stored object knowledge; but are side-*ways* operating rules for interpreting sensed and stored data, according to need. Let's try to represent this with a simple black box diagram. As it will be only two-dimensional, we may call this the 'flat box' (Fig. 17.2).

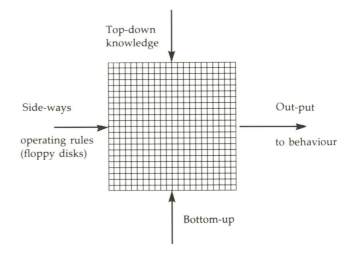

Figure 17.2 The Flat Box. Bottom-up signals from the eyes and other senses are read with top-down object-knowledge, and general rules we may think of as inserted like floppy disks side-ways, as needed

So far we have a flat box with three kinds of input:

- *Bottom-up signals* from the senses;
- *Top-down knowledge* of familiar objects;
- *Side-ways operating rules* – for interpreting or reading sensory signals and stored object knowledge.

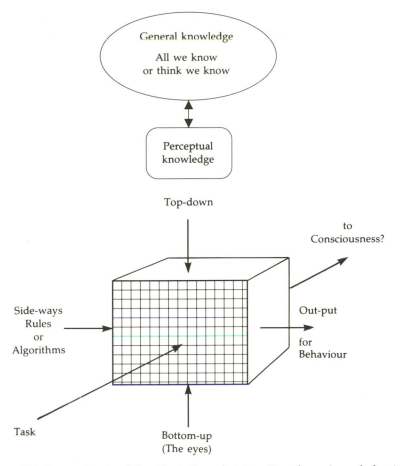

Figure 17.3 Ins and outs of the Black Box of vision. Top-down knowledge is divided into two: general knowledge – all we know or think we know, which includes abstract concepts far beyond perception; and perceptual knowledge – which is limited to what is needed for reading bottom-up signals from the eyes and other senses. (So we can have an illusion, and know it is an illusion.)

Is there a third dimension for the black box of vision? We may add 'the task' for which the box should be working as appropriately as possible, and we may add (mysterious) 'consciousness'.

The store of knowledge for perception is shown as smaller and separate from general conceptual knowledge, for there is strong evidence that perception cannot tap all our conceptual knowledge and understanding. Why are they separate? A reason is that perception must work extremely fast – in a fraction of a second – for survival. But conceptual thinking can be and is much slower. One second is a long time perceptually; but thinking things out may take minutes, or even years. It would take far too long to have to access from our total store of knowledge for perception – which must find answers in a fraction of a second to be useful in real time. So top-down perceptual knowledge is drawn from a highly restricted data-base, and there are only rough and ready checks and corrections, so that illusions are quite common. Conflicts between knowledge and perception can remain unresolved for ever: the eye is fooled every time by illusions we recognise and understand conceptually.

So the black box of vision (there may be many modules) is surrounded by conceptual knowledge which it feeds but slowly. It, in turn, is only slowly and often not at all affected by conceptual knowledge. No doubt, perceptual learning and learning from perception are slow as a great deal of reorganizaton is required in the 'spreadsheet' of the mind to assimilate new data and ideas. So it is hardly surprising that we are not fully consistent in our knowledge and beliefs. Also, the system must be slow (as gaining knowledge in science is slow) because only a few instances are not adequate for safe inductions from experience. Sensory data has a hard time overcoming the inertia of wisdom.

To summarize the ins-and-outs of the proposed black box of vision, we have:

- *Bottom-up* signals from the eyes, and the other sense organs, which are processed by rules for converting the signals into useful data. (This is pre-attentional processing.)
- *Top-down* knowledge, enriching the sensory data and allowing non-optical characteristics of objects to be read from the eyes' signals. (Visual 'clues' are important here, such as reading that a road is slippery from its reflections, or that wood is hard, or a knife dangerously sharp.)
- *Side-ways* operating rules, inserted for processing sensory signals, data and knowledge. (Rules such as perspective apply to virtually all objects. When they are inappropriate they can produce systematic errors such as distortions of shape and size and distance.)
- *Put-in* interrogation, for selecting operating rules according to need. (For the box may carry out different tasks according to need; as different features need to be processed, for example for driving a car, threading a needle, painting a picture, reading, proof reading, or whatever.)
- *Take-out* answers, for contributing to behaviour, and somehow giving awareness – consciousness – in perception.

The trouble for understanding consciousness is that, although bright to perception of external objects, our boxes are black internally. When all is going according to plan there is little or no awareness.

Consciousness seems to be given by *mismatches* between 'take-out' answers and what results in behaviour. For, surely, we are most aware of novelty and surprise.

We have said that, at least for higher organisms, perception is not *driven* from bottom-up signals from the senses – or *driven* from top-down stored knowledge – or *driven* from side-ways operating rules. Visual phenomena of ambiguity are significant here. We come near to seeing our own perceptual systems – inside our black boxes – while perception is actively seeking solutions, sometimes never finding an answer accepted as reality. The same input gives alternative percep-tions, presumably from an ensemble of likely objects or solutions when there is no evidence favouring one possibility. Perception is affected by object-probabilities (clearly seen with the hollow mask that looks like a normal face); but perception is not driven top-down from stored knowledge, or we would be unable to see anything unfamiliar. If this were so, we would be effectively blind and so at great risk in unusual situations – and perceptual learning would be impossible. So there are good reasons for why we can perceive unlikely and even impossible things, even though there is a perceptual bias towards the likely.

For ambiguity – what *initiates* flips beween possibilities? William James (1890) and later Sir Karl Popper and Sir John Eccles (1977) have suggested that though the brain is entirely responsible for creating perceptions, the mind – seen as essentially separate – can sometimes work from outside to intervene in brain activity, such as by the mind initiating flips of ambiguity. William James discusses this notion, though critically, but Popper and Eccles (who curiously do not refer to James) make the phenomena of visual ambiguity their strongest evidence for a separate mind: mind as a non-material causal agency affecting the brain. This is, indeed, the traditional view of mind in most religions. But if (as the vast majority of brain scientists do) we reject mind–brain duality, holding that mind is generated by brain function, then we may say that *other brain processes* initiate switching between alternatives of ambiguity. This avoids the ghostly pianist play-ing upon the synapses of the brain.

Sir John Eccles has now developed his 'dualist-interaction' view with a more specific account of how mental units (psychons) may affect brain units (dendrons) to account for the mind–brain relation (Eccles 1990). They are supposed to interact by quantum mechanical prin-ciples – avoiding nineteenth-century physics strictures of conserva-tion of energy, for some borrowing and trading of energy is allowable at the quantal level. Here we are not concerned in any detail with the mind–brain relation, beyond realizing there is a deep problem that any black box account must include. The essential issue is whether the box is a *receiver* of consciousness or a *generator* of consciousness.

Here there are both neurophysiological and theological implications. So brain science becomes experimental theology!

Spontaneous brain activity and trying out solutions of visual ambiguities set no special problems; spontaneous shifts and changes are not beyond computers – and so do not require a separate mind. But if the brain is some kind of a computer – what kind is it? In particular, does the brain work *digitally*, or by *analogue* processing? This is an important question which radically determines the design of the black box account (see 'What is the Catch in Neural Nets?' p. 148). Whether the black box works digitally, or with analogues, affects how we interpret phenomena and experiments, of perception, learning and thinking, and may have implications for education. But this is going further – to peep inside the black box, to seek the secret of what we are.

REFERENCES

Allport, D.A. (1993) 'Attention and Control: Have We Been Asking the Wrong Question?' in D.E. Meyer and S. Kornblum (eds) *Attention and Performance XIV: A Silver Jubilee.* (New York: Academic Press).

Eccles, John (1990) 'A Unitary Hypothesis of Mind–Brain Interaction in the Cerebral Cortex', *Proceedings of the Royal Society B*, 240, 433–51.

Gibson, J.J. (1950) *Perception of the Visual World.* (Boston, Mass.: Houghton Mifflin).

Gregory, R.L. (1961) 'The Brain as an Engineering Problem', in: W.H. Thorpe and O.L. Zangwill (eds) *Current Problems in Animal Behaviour* (London: Methuen). Reprinted in: Gregory, R.L. (1974) *Concepts and Mechanisms of Perception.* (London: Duckworth), (pp. 547–65).

Gregory, R.L. (1963) 'Distortion of Visual Space as Inappropriate Constancy Scaling', *Nature*, 199, 678–91. In: Gregory, R.L. (1974) *Concepts and Mechanisms of Perception.* (London: Duckworth), (pp. 342).

Gregory, R.L. (1968) 'Perceptual Illusions and Brain Models', *Proceedings of the Royal Society B*, 171, 179–296.

Gregory, R.L. (1970) *The Intelligent Eye.* (London: Weidenfeld and Nicholson).

Gregory, R.L. (1974) 'Choosing a Paradigm for Perception', in: E.C. Carterette and M .P. Friedman (eds) *Handbook of Perception*, vol. 1. (New York: Academic Press).

Gregory, R.L. (1980) 'Perceptions as Hypotheses', *Philosophical Transactions of the Royal Society B*, 290, 181–97.

Helmholtz, H. von (1856–67) *Handbuch der physiologischen Optic.* (Hamburg: L. Voss). J.P.C. Southall (1924–5) (trans. and ed.). *Helmholtz's Treatise on Physiological Optics*, 3 vols. (New York: Optical Society of America). Reprinted 1963 (New York: Dover).

Helmholtz H. von (1903) 'Concerning the Perceptions in general', in: *Popular Lectures on Scientific Subjects* (2nd Series). E. Atkinson (trans.) (New York: Longmans, Green).

Helmholtz H. von (1903) 'Concerning the Perceptions in General', in: *Popular Lectures on Scientific Subjects* (2nd Series). M. Kline (1962) (ed.). (New York: Dover).

Ittleson, W.H. (1952) *The Ames Demonstrations in Perception*. (Princeton, N.J.: Princeton University Press).

James, H. (1890) *Principles of Psychology*. (New York: Holt).

Popper, Karl and Eccles, John (1977) *The Self and its Brain*. (London: Springer International).

18

WHAT IS THE CATCH IN NEURAL NETS?

Net: Anything reticulated or decussated at equal distances, with interstices between the intersections.
    Samuel Johnson (1755) *Dictionary* 1st edition

Net: Anything made with interstitial vacuities.
    Samuel Johnson (1808) *Dictionary* 8th edition

In the mind–brain sciences we often think of brains as being supremely complicated machines, seen in recent years as super-computers. So, in a sense, brain science is a branch of engineering. I expressed this over thirty years ago in a paper called 'The Brain as an Engineering Problem' (Gregory 1961). A central point was how difficult – impossible – it is to localize brain function, or say where processes are going on, without 'engineering' knowledge of the internal functions. This kind of description overcomes the Phrenologist's Fallacy of supposing that internal functions (in 'bumps') are directly related to external functions of behaviour. We may say without any problem that components in a brain or a machine (nerve cells, or transistors) are spatially localized; but it is impossible to say, for example of an engine, where its power is localized as many component parts contribute to the final result. Brain functions are extended over many interacting neural components, which makes it hard to say where intelligence, or perception, or whatever, lie in the brain. This can make interpreting brain ablation studies very difficult. To quote the example I used in another paper (Gregory 1958):

> If any changes take place upon removal of part of the brain, the changes are either (a) loss of some feature of behaviour, or diminution or worsening of some skills, or (b) introduction of some new behavioural features. Now it is often argued that if some part of behaviour is lost ... the causal mechanism necessary for this behaviour is localized in the affected region. But does this follow? ... We can take an example from radio engineering.

If a main smoothing condenser breaks down (shorting the H.T.
to earth through a low resistance), the set may stop working,
or work in a peculiar manner . . . . Its purpose in the system is
to smooth the ripple for the whole system, but it happens that
this part of the system is more sensitive to reduction in supply
voltage than the rest. Suppose that when the condenser breaks
down, the set emits piercing howls. Do we argue that the
normal function of the condenser is to inhibit howling? Surely
not. The condenser's abnormally low resistance has changed the
system, and the new system exhibits new properties – in this
case howling.

For an engine (which may be more familiar) power is lost if we remove
the spark plugs, or the petrol pump – but this does not mean that
the power is in the plugs or the pump, or the pistons or cylinders:
it is necessary that all work together. This does bring out difficulties
of establishing and localizing functions, even in familiar and well
understood interactive systems. It points, too, to how difficult it is
to explain phenomena of abnormality or malfunction – for here we
are faced with a different, even unique system which may be outside
our experience and beyond any available understanding.

This argument was sometimes taken as a criticism of brain experiments – so it was far from popular with some of my colleagues! Very
often, philosophical warnings of what can't be said or done turn out
to be mistaken and block progress. So they had every right to be
annoyed, though I think this is a rare case of such a 'negative'
argument being useful. For it is true that in an interactive system the
various parts affect each other and so it is exceedingly hard to ascribe
causes and effects to the parts, even though physically they are easily
distinguished by appearance. In practice this situation is helped when
systems are 'modular'. Thus the brain is sufficiently separate from
the heart, or the toes, to be seen uniquely as the organ of mind, even
though it depends on the heart and even sometimes the toes to
function. Fortunately for the understanding of it, the brain itself is
in some degree modular, with the initial stages of perception at the
surface cortex at the back of the brain, memory in the parietal region
to the side, and so on. But these functional regions are not entirely
complete and adequate for perception, memory or whatever (as the
phrenologists believed), but depend on other regions. The modules
are interconnected, so damage or loss at distant regions can produce
bizarre results that may be very hard to explain from knowlege of
normal function. This points to the need for deep understanding, in
very general terms, for seeing what the visible components do and
what happens when there is damage. This requires different kinds

147

or 'levels' of description and explanation. The American philosopher of language Jerry Fodor (Fodor 1983) has recently defended something of the phrenologists' notions of modularity of mind. It is an interesting question how much is separate and how much interconnected. The more modular the brain the easier it is to establish localized functions.

The kinds of description I suggested thirty years ago were illustrated with a simple circuit: a battery, a switch and a lamp (see Fig. 17.1, p. 137). The kinds or levels of description (see 'Mind in a Black Box', p. 136) were given as (Gregory 1961):

- **Blueprints**: showing the *appearance* of components – the anatomy;
- **Circuit diagrams**: showing the *functional properties* of the components – the physiology;
- **Block diagrams**: showing the *flow of power or information* – the software or operating rules.

Localization gets more fuzzy as we move from visible, touchable components to their functional properties; finally to the spatially diffuse and more abstract – though very important for understanding – block diagrams of the operating rules. These kinds of descriptions, with their corresponding kinds of explanations, are very different – justifying anatomy, physiology and so on as different though related sciences. Indeed, science itself may be structured and specialized to match the modularities and levels of nature.

Explanations are very different in each of these kinds of description. The first (anatomical) description is in terms of visible components. If they are missing, damaged, or wrongly connected, bizarre changes and errors may result. The second (physiological) description is of more general functions, involving many components and related complicated biochemical processes, which may be disturbed as by hallucinogenic drugs. The third (cognitive) description is general operating principles and rules, essentially of information. When these are inappropriate, errors may occur even though the anatomy and physiology are in perfect order. For perception, perhaps this is most easily seen in cognitive distortion illusions, where rules of perspective mislead. So these phenomena of illusion should cast light on deep cognitive psychological principles of perception (Gregory 1963, 1968, 1970, 1981). This is discussed here in 'Putting Illusions in their Place'. For these cognitive kinds of phenomena of illusions (including conjuring) there is no useful anatomical or physiological explanation when they are due to operating procedures or perceptual rules being inappropriate to the situation. Cognitive illusions fall neatly into four classes: Ambiguities, Distortions, Paradoxes, Fictions. As perceptions are descriptions (hypotheses) of the external world, surely it is no accident that these are also the errors of language.

Rule-based perceptions are bound to be inappropriate in some situations, for effective rules (including legal laws) must be broad and general, as they must be limited in number, and so cannot exactly apply in every case. Perspective laws are so general that they apply to any conceivable eye–brain or camera–computer system, so they should apply beyond brains to seeing machines. Such rule-based illusions should be much the same for a seeing machine as they are for us, so we can use illusions to test whether the 'mind' of perceiving machines is like ours, and vice versa, though their 'anatomy' and 'physiology' are very different (Gregory 1967). Explanations of these perceptual phenomena lie at deep levels of operating procedures, and how they are applied or misapplied, rather than in the anatomy or physiology of the eye and brain.

It is very important to select the appropriate kinds of description for explaining various kinds of phenomena. Each kind of description allows corresponding kinds of explanations. In my view, these may not lie at different 'levels' (the higher levels 'reducing' to lower level description as more fundamental) but rather, they may be simply different, and all may be important. Thus, the blueprint, the circuit diagram, and the operating rules of the block diagram (Fig. 17.1, p. 137) are all important for describing and understanding any circuit. None can be 'reduced' to the others – all are important. For thinking about nerve cells of the brain, increasing our knowledge of each kind or level enhances understanding of the other kinds or levels of explanation. Each provides insights for what contributes to the system as a whole and how it works. It is not possible to say what an electronic component or a nerve cell is doing without understanding the function of the circuit in general terms. So it is impossible to localise functions without knowing general principles and what are the contributions of the local components.

BRAIN MACHINES

If we are to call the brain a machine we should ask: what is a machine? One might say a machine is a *functional system designed to combine principles of nature to achieve goals*. As machines are designed to perform generally useful functions (for transport, communication, cooking and so on) machines involve purpose. Unlike the universe itself, the purposes are in human terms. For machines, we are our own designing and judging Gods. What can be frightening is that machines may transcend nature to achieve unnatural, even anti-natural goals.

If machines are designed for achieving goals, and so are purposive, does this apply to brains, if brains are machines? Are brains designed?

Yes – we believe that brains are designed, by natural selection, for the survival of their owners against threats of nature and of rival brain-controlled beings. It seems appropriate to say that living organisms are designed by natural selection even though natural selection by 'survival of the fittest' is blind and without initial aim or purpose. Though this is very different from planned invention and design in technology we may call a brain a 'machine', and describe and judge the efficiency of its functions in terms of the perceived purposes for its parts and what they do. This at least is so if we think of understanding the brain in terms of understanding an engineering problem. This is assuming that, in a broad sense, brains are machines. The weakness is that we do not know how to make machines that are comparable to brains.

Wittgenstein in his later writings seems to be opposed to this entire way of explaining brain and mind in terms of machines, saying (in *Philosophical Investigations*, pp. 359–60):

> Could a machine think? – Could it be in pain? – Well, is the human body to be called such a machine? It surely comes as close as possible to being such a machine.
>
> But surely a machine cannot think! Is that an empirical statement? No. We only say of a human being and what is like one that it thinks. We also say it of dolls and no doubt of ghosts too. Look at the word 'think' as a tool.

Wittgenstein suggests that intelligence in machines is more than the solving of problems requiring human intelligence. He considers what criteria should be employed – including social sensitivities (cf. Cook 1969, Neumaier 1987). But for our purposes I shall assume that a machine is intelligent if it can solve, with some originality, what to us are problems, even though its 'thinking' is not as rich or as imbued with social significance as ours. Some philosophers object to any kind of analysis into parts; object to saying that the brain 'thinks', or that it 'perceives' – on the grounds that it is the entire person that thinks or perceives. This would preclude any engineering-type description or explanation. But I see no objection to stressing the importance of the most involved parts of a system, allowing that the brain perceives even though it depends on the heart and much else. Science depends on knowing where and how to look at parts in terms of whole systems. This is assuming that perception and thinking and so on – mind – is given by brain function.

St Thomas Aquinas believed that there were disembodied intelligences, though they were not capable of seeing or hearing (Geach 1967). Adherents of belief in psychic disembodied spirits may hold that seeing can occur without physical eyes or brains. Throughout

150

history most people have believed this; so the neuro-sciences ortho-doxy I am assuming – allowing the brain to be called a machine – is probably a minority view overall though it is held by the great majority of scientists.

For several hundred years, the brain was thought of as a machine though not as a computing machine. The French mathematician, philosopher and scientist, René Descartes (1596–1650) described the bodies and brains of animals, including humans, as machines; but he stopped short of the mind. As is very well known, Descartes thought of the mind as being beyond any machine description, and indeed beyond science. He saw the mind as controlling the machine-nervous system, through the interface of the curious brain structure, the pineal gland, beyond which scientific understanding was powerless to reach. To attempt to push machine notions into mind was dangerous. The French physician Julian Offray de la Mettrie was ostracized by colleagues and friends, and had to leave his work and home in Paris for writing *Man a Machine* (1748), which transcended this limit by suggesting mind is included in machine-man.

If brains are machines, what kind of machines are they? If we decide they are computers, what kind of computers? In particular, do brain processes follow 'software' algorithms at all like the computational procedures of man-made *digital* computers? Or do they work like *analogue* computers? We shall go on to explore the digital-analogue difference in some detail, suggesting that it is ignored to our peril.

Writing just before electronic digital computers were available, the Cambridge psychologist Kenneth Craik (1914–45) thought of the brain in engineering terms as working with physical 'internal models' of reality and imagination. Craik describes this (*The Nature of Explanation*, 1943, p. 51) in these pre-digital computing engineering terms:

> by a model . . . I do not mean some obscure non-physical entity which attends the model, but the fact that it is a physical working model which works in the same way as the process it parallels . . . . Thus the model need not resemble the real object pictorially; Kelvin's tide-predictor, which consists of a number of pulleys on levers, does not resemble a tide in appearance, but it works in the same way in certain essential respects – it combines oscilla-tions of various frequencies so as to produce an oscillation which closely resembles in amplitude at each moment the variation in tide level at any place.

There are certainly no pulleys or levers in the brain. What the brain has are between 10 and 18 billion nerve cells of various identifiable kinds, with as many as 2,000 connections for each cell. In man there are over 500,000,000 cells in the visual cortex (Blinkov and Glezer 1968).

What do they do? Kenneth Craik, writing just before the advent of electronic computers, suggested that perceptions and thoughts are patterns of activity of these billions of interconnected cells, forming working 'models' almost like the pieces of a meccano construction set put together to make a model crane, a flower, a clock, or solar system or anything else.

This is fundamentally different from digital computer accounts, which suggest that neural processes represent much as language represents. Such representing and computing by symbols depends on conventional rules, such as grammar in language and algorithms for computing. Algorithms may be carried out by humans, in the head, or with pencil and paper, as in doing long division. The computer is simply faster and more accurate. In digital computer accounts of mind, the rules – the algorithms – become more important than the physical processes of the machine. So it is a small step to say that if mechanical switches or cogs or transistors can carry out adequate algorithms, then the computer should be intelligent and conscious as we are with our brains. So this notion of rules or algorithms, which might be carried out by a brain or a computer, becomes very important for this discussion.

The notion of brains or minds having operating rules must go back at least to Aristotle's rules for logical thinking, especially his syllogisms, but perhaps the notion of mind following procedural rules was not explicit before George Boole's Laws of Thought (Boole 1847). Most curiously, although Pascal demonstrated quite early in the seventeenth century (1642) that a geared machine could perform the algorithms of arithmetic, only recently has the brain been thought of as a goal-seeking system functioning according to internal operating principles which can be transferred to man-made machines.

That perception operates according to rules was central to the Gestalt psychologists (Kohler 1920, Wertheimer 1923). These rules (or 'laws' as they were sometimes called) were not algorithms for computing but rather were organizing restraints tending towards appropriate perceptions or solutions. The Gestalt laws included preference for simple closed forms (good *Gestalten*) and, as most objects do have rather simple closed forms, this is generally useful. The parts of an object generally move together, such as the leaves of a tree in a wind, hence 'common-fate' as an organizing principle. Another was 'proximity', features close together being likely to be parts of the same object, and 'continuity' of contours. The Gestalt rules or restraints were supposed to be inherited rather than learned. They can be revealed with dots forming patterns (Fig. 18.1).

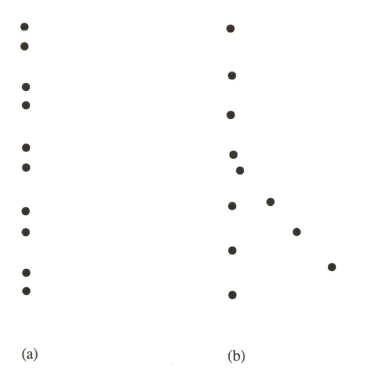

(a)   (b)

Figure 18.1 Gestalt dots. In (a) the dots close together are seen
as 'belonging' – the Proximity Rule. In (b) the dots are seen as two
lines. The first dot of the oblique line 'belongs' to this line although
it is nearer to a dot of the other line. Here, Continuity beats
Proximity.

The Gestalt psychologists' organizing rules have proved useful in
the field of artificial intelligence for creating computers to recognize
objects.

What of meaning? How do brains have meaning? This was a key
question for the Gestalt writers. For Wertheimer (1922) meanings were
supposed to be produced by internal dynamic brain interactions
forming wholes:

> ... we may say in general that a whole is meaningful when con-
> crete mutual dependency obtains among its parts. The mosaic
> or associonistic hypothesis is therefore on principle unable to
> supply any direct approach to the problem of meaning.

The meaning of meaning remains a puzzling problem. We would now give greater weight to learned associations of experiences and concepts and knowledge. But how does the brain learn and associate, to derive or discover meaning? Is this done with digital computing by brain cells? Or can neural patterns of activity serve to represent and give meaning *without computing* – by building 'internal models' or patterns in neural nets?

The notion of brains or machines modifying themselves by building 'internal models' or 'phase sequences' in nets is related to the control systems of cybernetics. The error-correcting feedback concepts of cybernetics (Wiener 1948, Latil 1957) were developed for weapons during the Second World War, especially for anti-aircraft guns and later missiles which would seek out their targets. The trick was to feed errors back to the input, so that the machine would automatically correct errors and seek the goals. There might even be a hierarchy of internal goals (Ashby 1952). This central principle of cybernetics (named by Norbert Weiner from the Greek for steersman) was described by the Greek inventor Hero (or Heron) in the 1st century BC. There were some earlier Greek devices (Hero's *Pneumatics*, Woodcroft 1881); one was used for keeping the flow of water constant for water clocks and another for automatically raising the wicks of oil lamps as they burned away. Windmills steering themselves into the wind is also an early example of a machine seeking and continually finding a shifting goal. But although a few self-regulating devices were known to the Greeks, and have been used ever since, for some reason (Mayr 1970) the concept was not recognized until recently. Once fully recognised, as late as the 1950s, such feedback control and target-seeking was seen as purposeful – conferring lifelike behaviour to machines.

THE BAIT – COMPUTING OR COMMUTING?

There are two very different kinds of computers: analogue and digital. Which kind – if either – is the brain? Digital computers are now so powerful and so familiar it seems natural, even obvious, to assume that the hardware of the brain is some kind of digital computer, and that mind is digital software. But before digital computers were commonplace, very different analogies were drawn for accounts of brain function. I shall suggest that we may be making a major mistake assuming the brain to be a digital computer. Although computer algorithms are very useful for *describing*, it may be deeply misleading to see the brain as *working* by computing with algorithms.

Thirty years ago analogue devices were far more common than digital computers, which were then in their unreliable though very exciting infancy. This was before they demonstrated their immense potential speed and power and flexibility. So then we did not assume the brain was a digital computer. We would ask 'Does the brain work by analogues – or digitally?' No doubt because of the dramatic advantages of digital computing it seems now to be generally assumed that brains are digital. But this assumption could be disastrously wrong. Perhaps we should look more carefully and not ignore the analogue alternative. What, then, are the important differences?

These depend on the chosen level, or kind, of description. It is often said that the primary distinction is between continuous for analogue – and discontinuous for digital. This is a component description. It is true that analogue systems usually work continuously and digital systems always work in steps. But why is this so? We may ask for a reason which gives a deeper distinction. A far more basic point is that digital computers follow the computational steps of algorithms, while analogue systems do not go through computational steps and so can be continuous. By following analogue pro-formas they avoid the need for computing. So analogue 'computers' are *not computers*!

The most familiar example of analogue processing is that of a graph. If, for example, the average heights of children are plotted against age, we can read off the average or expected height for any age with no computing. Analogues like this can be built into a machine in many ways such as using mechanical cams which may have any form; or physical laws may be used, such as those which describe the acceleration of a falling weight or the periodicity of a pendulum. Simple circuits with condensers and resistors (perhaps with amplifiers, which need not be linear) may serve to integrate or differentiate or perform many other dedicated functions – with no steps of computing. This freedom from computing gives even analogue systems with slow components great speed, though they do not give exact answers. As they are not very flexible, they are used mainly for dedicated special purposes. Specialized graphs and analogue devices called nomograms were frequently used in the nineteenth century to solve particular problems, avoiding calculating, or computing.

We may call digital systems computers and analogue systems commuters (following its root meaning of 'changing', as into gold). Computing follows computational steps of algorithms: commuting avoids calculating or computing by following (generally continuous) analogues. This may be less exact but it can be much faster.

What is confusing is that characteristics of analogue systems can be described with algorithms, though they do not work with

algorithms. Alan Turing (1950) showed that any clearly stated function can be described by algorithms – it does not follow that anything can be accomplished with algorithms. For example, the necessary
steps of computing may take too long for their accomplishment in
real time. There is a serious danger of confusing the description
with what is being described. This is a particular hazard for descriptions of brain and mind. Thus algorithms may describe processes of
perception, though perception does not work by the computations
of algorithms.

Let's take this analogue–digital distinction right outside brains
– beyond the earth to the moon. The moon orbiting the earth follows
laws of physics, which may be described by algorithms, and can
be used to compute future positions. But the moon does not itself
carry out computations in order to orbit the earth. It does not compute or use algorithms, though the astronomer may compute using
algorithms to describe and predict its motion. An artificial satel-
lite may, however, have its orbit controlled by a computer or analogue
system for course corrections. A familiar analogue instrument is
a car's speedometer: this does not compute $v = d/t$, though v (velocity)
is defined as distance travelled divided by the time taken. It is
a simple analogue system working without computing or using any
algorithm. No doubt, with our eyes and brains, we see velocities
without computing or using algorithms. The eyes commute rather than
compute.

INTO THE NET

The American neurologist, psychiatrist and philosopher Warren
McCulloch (1899–1969), held that each brain cell is an elaborate computing element, affected by its many inputs (electrical and chemical)
with a subtly regulated threshold for firing. In the early 1940s
McCulloch, with the logician Walter Pitts (McCulloch and Pitts 1943),
saw the brain's nerve cells as working co-operatively in small groups,
forming 'psychons', which were units of thinking which could be
analysed in detail. They drew hypothetical circuits for the psychons,
and these could actually be made with artificial neurons. But of course,
a few artificial psychons could not make a psyche, so the general
appropriateness of their notions was hard to test. The cell's activity
in the nets was not supposed to vary linearly but to fall off gradually,
with use associated with learning, otherwise the net would soon
become saturated. This non-linear feature made mathematical analysis
and predictions for large nets very difficult.

The seminal notion of the brain as a parallel processing neural net
is due to the Canadian psychologist D.O. Hebb. Unlike the Gestalt

writers, Donald Hebb saw learning as centrally important, with innate knowledge as a minor contribution or non-existent. He thought of the brain as initially wired up randomly, gradually forming functional structures (phase sequences) as the cells change their properties through use. The central notion is that the brain develops patterns and operating rules, as the most used cells conduct more freely and so set up patterns of interconnected pathways. (My paper 'The Brain as an Engineering Problem' was written before digital computers were commonplace, when we were thinking in terms of Hebb's interactive neural nets as described in his *Organization of Behaviour* (1949), a book which was much discussed over the next ten years and remains a key contribution.)

Attempts were made early on to construct seeing machines with artificial neural nets. Most famous was Frank Rosenblatt's Perceptron. With excitatory and inhibitory connections (synapses), it could begin to generalize patterns. There were two layers of artificial neurons, generally with every input (retinal receptor) connected to every output. With the cells adapting to frequency of use, this system could give some generalization of patterns.

Marvin Minsky and Seymour Papert (1969) showed, however, that there must be severe limitations in Rosenblatt's perceptrons and, partly due to their valid criticisms, the idea was dropped. Interest declined in this approach, also, because of the evident power and flexibility of the digital computer; though von Neumann, its inventor, did himself realize the potential power of interactive nets for some uses.

There were many exciting papers written at that time, with ideas that should have flowered. For example, there was the conference which produced a book *Neural Networks* (1968) edited by the Italian pioneer E.R. Caianiello; my old friend Gordon Pask lived his life devoted to neural nets and he tried to grow artificial neurons; Albert Uttley very early on built inductive learning machines; and Ross Ashby (1956) and, most fascinating, Grey Walter (1953) with his truly pioneering life-like tortoises, *Machina Speculatrix*, introduced a new way of thinking about thinking.

If interest in perceptrons had not died it might have been realized much sooner that adding more layers between inputs and outputs makes a fundamental difference. These 'hidden units' allow inner patterns to develop which are not driven by the input or closely related to the output. They are hidden and secret, much as mind is hidden and secret. They have remarkable powers to abstract and learn and discover generalizations. They need periods of rest to sort themselves out, apparently to dream!

Donald Hebb's (1949) randomly interconnected nets, which form internal patterns of activity modelling objects and thoughts and memories by each cell becoming more active as it is stimulated more often, is the prototype for all the recent PDP (parallel distributed processing) neural nets. (See Fig. 18.2.)

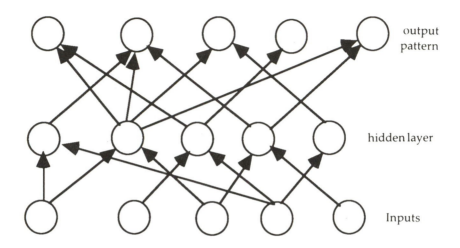

Figure 18.2 A simple neural net. The inputs feed to the 'hidden layer' – which is the ghost in the machine. This is perhaps the nearest a machine can come to mind, as it lies between the world and the behaviour.

The new nets are inspired by the work of John Hopfield (1982), Geoffrey Hinton (1986), and now many others. Michael Arbib, who was a student of Warren McCulloch, has developed interesting ideas (Arbib 1989). Ivor Aleksander worked for years developing the impressive WISARD (Wilkie, Stonham and Aleksander's Recognition Device), which with other recent work is clearly described in *Neural Computing* (Aleksander and Morton 1990). As demonstrated in a recent television programme, Terrence Sejnowski has devised a net that can learn to read English and synthesize its own speech very much as children do, starting with random babbling. His artificial net is faster than babies are at learning from examples, without algorithmic programs, though one does not know how sophisticated they can become.

This is a general query: many nets work well for small problems but rapidly become inadequate with the increasing number of alternative possibilities.

How best to teach artificial neural nets presents unsolved problems. But here may lie some helpful hints and perhaps significant research for human education. The essential point of PDP nets is that analogue interactive systems can learn from successive presentations of, for example, faces, or differently written letters, or sounds of words or whatever, to recognize new objects of the same class. And they may devise the classes. Unlike digital devices they go on working even though a large proportion of their components are destroyed. And, as we can, they can cope with partial or mangled input signals. Is this where the answer lies for how the brain works? Or, are brain processes digital programs of algorithms?

FLOUNDERING COMPUTERS (FISHY DIGITS)

In his influential book *Vision*, David Marr (1982) speaks of algorithms of visual processing. Is he assuming the brain to be a digital computer? Surely he is. As Marr himself emphasized, and did a great deal to discover, in the early stages of vision there are various kinds of filters. But surely it is most implausible to suppose that they work by digital computing. Digital computers are used by us to simulate and investigate properties of analogue filters, but a simulation is not the same as what is being simulated. They are essentially different. It is virtually certain from inspection of the neural components, and for other reasons, that the filters of visual processing are analogue, and so do not work by algorithms – though digital computing is used by visual scientists to simulate and investigate their characteristics for valid research purposes.

David Marr set up his well-known 'levels' of description of visual processing as:

- the *hardware implementation*: the components and how they are wired;
- the *algorithms*: the procedures to be followed for digital processing;
- the *computational theory*: the problem to be solved, in terms of the available algorithms.

For Marr, the most important level is the algorithm. Then comes the computational theory, and last the hardware. This is fine for neural (or silicon or wheeled) computers, working by following steps of algorithms; but surely it is not appropriate for analogue systems as they do not have algorithms or, presumably, 'computational theories'. If we are right that the analogue–digital distinction is not merely verbal but is conceptual, with empirical consequences, this is a matter of real importance.

We may, indeed, want to reconsider much of what Marr says. For example, we might translate (p. 23); 'An *algorithm* by which the transformation may actually be accomplished' (his italics) to something more like: 'A *rule* by which the transformation may actually be accomplished' (my italics). Then the option of analogue or digital with their different implications is left open. To my mind, the neutral term 'rule' is very useful, as it can apply equally to analogue or digital processing.

Let's take this issue right outside eyes and brains. Let's look again at something very different – a steam engine. The parts move with simple, easy-to-state mathematical functions. The piston moves back and forth through the cylinder with a sine wave velocity function; there are circular, linear, and so on mathematical functions. These can be used to describe the motions of the parts, and the pressure changes and so on in the engine. So we could describe the engine with a sequence of algorithms. We might use these algorithms to draw the engine and its internal movements and pressure changes and so on in a digital computer. But it does not at all follow that the engine itself works with these or any other algorithms. The engine works with physical components and forces which, however, can be described and predicted with the computational steps of algorithms. No-one would confuse the engine – the power of its steam and so on with mathematical algorithms. So why should this mistake (if it is a mistake) be made for brains? The reason, clearly, is that an engine delivers power which is not mind-like, while brains deliver answers which are mind-like. Yet analogue devices can produce answers without computing – because working systems can be *described* with algorithms! Thus a steam engine could be made to give, without computing, values of sines from the position of its piston as the wheels turn. Although possible, this would be bizarre. So it may seem equally bizarre that the brain is a physical system giving answers without having to compute. Yet most of us are very bad at using the algorithms of mathematics. Digital computers are far faster and more accurate. It might be said that algorithms turn us into inefficient artificial intelligences.

Let's summarize the differences between analogue and digital systems. Differences appear at each level or kind of description. Do they suggest that brains are analogue processors such as PDP nets, or digital algorithm computers? Let's compare them:

COMMUTER OR COMPUTER?

Analogue	*Digital*
The components can be slow and yet give answers quickly. *Brain components are surprisingly slow given* the speed of perception and behaviour – suggesting analogue.	
Analogue components must be stable and free of drift. *Brain components are neither.*	Digital components can be crude and tolerant to errors as they have a few discrete states, preferably two: 'on' and 'off'. *Brain components do not have discrete states.*
Analogue devices have special components for special purposes. *This is not clearly so for the brain.*	Digital computers have large numbers of identical components for a wide range of uses. *This is so for the brain.*
Analogue systems are fast though not highly accurate – like brains.	Digital computers need very fast components to achieve their high operating speed. *Unlike brains.*
Analogue systems, especially nets, continue though many computing elements fail – like brains.	Digital computers generally fail if even a single computing element is lost.
Analogue systems are not flexible or easily 'programmed'. So they are usually 'dedicated' to special tasks.	Digital computers are extremely flexible and readily programmed for any task.
Analogue systems can work without analytical understanding.	Digital computers generally need precise algorithmic rules to follow.
When analogue systems fail they usually fail 'gracefully'.	When digital algorithms fail they usually collapse suddenly, and often have 'bugs'.

We see that, though with correct inputs and appropriate rules, analogues are seldom if ever exactly correct; digital computers are usually either exactly right or very wrong. When pushed to their limits, or beyond, errors occur very differently for analogue and digital devices. Analogue nets fail gradually and gracefully. What happens with digital computers depends on whether the algorithm collapses suddenly (especially when infinities come in).

161

Errors, such as some visual illusions, might have to be explained differently for analogue and digital systems. Computer scientists choose algorithms, which may not be maximally efficient, in favour of robust algorithms which work over a wide range of conditions without breaking down (Sedgewick, 1989). But the ways algorithms break down, when they do, is typically different from analogue failures. So there should be errors of perception, illusions and so on, which would distingish between, and indicate analogue or digital processing for the functioning of the brain. Adaptations to tilt and curvature may well be a case in point. Such adaptations suggest modifications of analogue physiological processes, rather than breakdown of digital algorithms.

As analogue systems are not flexible and so tend to be used for special purposes, an analogue brain is likely to consist of many modules, each dedicated to special kinds of tasks, and switched in as necessary. Just how they are called upon when needed is an interesting question.

For analogue rules, or for digital algorithms working well within their limits but inappropriate to the situation, similar kinds of errors might be generated – so it may not be clear which is operating. Algorithms of digital systems hold only within the limits of their logic, to break down for logical reasons. But this is not so simple for digital systems may suffer component failure. Thus, drugs might change perception and behaviour in bizarre ways if algorithms can no longer operate.

COMMUTING OR COMPUTING FOR ARTIFICIAL INTELLIGENCE

Recent philosophers of AI have considered digital computers rather than analogue devices. This may be a major mistake.

We have claimed that analogue systems – including neural nets – may be *described* by algorithms though they do not *work* with algorithms. Analogue pro-formas avoid the need to compute. Analogues do not go through the computational steps of computing – so they are not computers. These statements clearly have implications for artificial intelligence. The strong claim is that machines can be built that will display all the intelligence, and have the consciousness, of the higher organisms, including humans.

If the 'strong AI' notion that a machine can have a mind is *true*, a mind-full machine could 'be made of old beer cans'. (See 'Questions of Quanta and Qualia', p. 90.) On a digital algorithm view, this would be so if the beer cans can count. On an analogue view the 'old beer cans' would need to have far more subtle, elaborate characteristics, for the functional units are much larger than the simple switching steps of digital systems, as analogue pro-formas embody wide-ranging functions. An entire range of input–output values might be carried on a single pro-forma.

If we apply these considerations of analogue and digital to AI philosophy, we may want to amend some recent criticisms of AI. A sustained criticism of the AI enterprise was mounted by Hubert Dreyfus with his famous (and for some, infamous!) book *What Computers Can't Do* (1972), which tries with general arguments to set limits to digital processing for intelligence. Other objections have been put forward by the American philosopher John Searle (1984, p. 36):

> The question isn't: 'Can a machine think? or: 'Can an artifact think?' The question is: 'Can a digital computer think?' But again we have to be very careful how we interpret the question. From a mathematical point of view, anything whatever can be described *as if* it were a digital computer. And that's because it can be described as instantiating or implementing a computer program. In an utterly trivial sense, the pen that is on the desk in front of me can be described as a digital computer. It just happens to have a very boring computer program. The program says: 'Stay there.' . . . Of course our brains are digital computers, since they implement any number of computer programs.

Really? Again, any things (following Turing 1950) can be *described* as computer programs, but this does not mean they *are* computer programs. Searle continues:

> And of course our brains can think. So once again, there is a trivial answer to the question. But that wasn't really the question we were trying to ask. The question we wanted to ask is this: 'Can a digital computer, as defined, think?' That is to say 'Is instantiating or implementing the right computer program with the right inputs and outputs sufficient for, or constitutive of, thinking? And to this question, unlike its predecessors, the answer is clearly 'no'. And it is 'no' for the reason that we have spelled out, namely, the computer program is defined purely syntactically. But thinking is more than just a matter of manipulating symbols, it involves meaningful semantic contents. These semantic contents are what we mean by 'meaning'.

John Searle's point is that digital computer programs have syntax (grammar) but not semantics (meaning), and so cannot be genuinely intelligent. Searle holds that computers may be able to *simulate* human behaviour, but 'If we are talking about having mental states, having a mind, all of these simulations are simply irrelevant'. So, he rejects strong AI. Some computer scientists hold, however, that programs can have semantics. After all, computers can tell us which planes have got free seats, and they interact with the world in many civilian and military situations.

We might well ask why Searle thinks that brain programs (he is considering the brain as a digital computer) can have semantics if man-made computers can't. Searle's claim is that:

> Mental states are biological phenomena. Consciousness, intentionality, subjectivity and mental causation are all part of our biological life history, along with growth, reproduction, the secretion of bile, and digestion.

This is a surprisingly Vitalist creed. For over a century the story of biology has been the gradual rejection of special substances for life, since 'organic' chemistry became associated with carbon rather than with special substances for life (following the production of 'organic' urea, by heating 'inorganic' ammomiun cyanate by Friedrich Wohler in 1828). Searle appears to be back-tracking, seeking some special, uniquely biological life-substance in the brain for mind. The snag is, if this is so special and intrinsically associated with living brains, it offers no explanation.

If the brain is not carrying out algorithms but is, rather, an interacting net or some such analogue system without algorithms, does this affect Searle's position? Presumably he would say that we have moved the goalposts of his position – that he is only talking about algorithms. But he might maintain that only biological substance can provide analogue pro-formas, or whatever, for intelligence. How this could be a philosophical rather than an alleged empirical conclusion beats me. The fact is we do not know any limits of this kind. How can we possibly be sure, on any philosophical grounds, that an artificial net or digital computer programs properly carried out, could not embody the full attributes of biological mind? Surely this is a question only experiment can answer.

A more recent and somewhat related attack on AI is made by the highly distinguished mathematician, cosmologist, inventor of Impossible Objects and much else, Roger Penrose in his book *The Emperor's New Mind* (1989). It has very interesting things to say, including fascinating insights on the nature and importance of algorithms. In some ways he follows Searle's objections to AI. Penrose also equates AI accounts of brain function with carrying out algorithms. Does he (as I have suggested for Marr, and rather differently for Searle) conflate the use of algorithms for *doing* (implementing) and *describing* (simulating)? Penrose looks for at present unknown properties of matter to explain mind, especially quantal properties. He speaks of quanta and other physical entities and events as 'computing', and evidently thinks of physical laws as algorithms given by nature. The alternative view is that algorithms are not in nature, but are only in systems that describe – brains and computers. Penrose probably puts algorithms into nature to avoid a mind–brain dualism. But are we worried about this kind of mind–computer dualism? Do our computers become metaphysical if we think of their algorithms as rules not tied to particular matter? Surely not. Even if we think of mathematics as 'Platonic' (existing apart from minds) we do not think of computers as working by resonating with cosmic realities. Mind–brain (or mind- -computer) duality only becames a problem when we consider consciousness.

Like Searle, Penrose equates AI accounts of brain function with carrying out algorithms, though he thinks that mathematical intuitions are different – being non-algorithmic. He gives intuition a special status, seeing it as beyond AI. He bravely discusses consciousness, suggesting that the key may lie in developments of quantum physics. He rejects algorithms as vehicles for intuitive thinking and consciousness – including the mathematician's intuitions, preferring possible quantum properties not yet discovered of matter. But we want to avoid the conclusions that *all* matter (tables, chairs, wood) is intelligent and conscious. So there must be something special about brains. What is it about brains that harnesses such quantum effects? If these supposed properties of matter can be specially used in brains, why not also in man-made, brain-like machines – for their being able to know and perceive and feel much as we do? The following syllogism naughtily suggests itself, (with apologies):

Quantum Mechanics is mysterious
Consciousness is mysterious
  therefore
Consciousness is Quantum Mechanics.

However this may be for consciousness, it has been generally thought, or assumed, over the last two or three decades that intelligent machines must be digital. Recent philosophical objections to AI are aimed at showing that the rules of algorithms are not adequate for intelligence. Of course not: algorithms have to be implemented by hardware components. Thinking of algorithms as sufficient is a non-starter on any brainy account – for this would be to say that mind is not based on any physical processes. Some kind of hardware is essential for any brainy account of mind: the important question is whether the brain works by handling algorithms. We can (though with difficulty) learn to use algorithms of mathematics and (more easily) language; but apart from our (artificial) symbols of mathematics and language, does the brain work with algorithms?

The arch-critic of AI, Hubert Dreyfus, (author of *What Computers Can't Do* 1972) has more recently said (1987)

> I still believe, as I did in 1965, that computers may some day be intelligent. Real computer intelligence will be achieved, however, only after researchers abandon the idea of finding a symbolic representation of the everyday world and rule-governed equivalent of common-sense know-how, and turn to something like a neural-net modelling of the brain instead. If such modelling turns out to be the direction AI should follow, it will be achieved by the massively parallel computing machines on the horizon – not because parallel machines can make millions of inferences per second, but because fast, more parallel architecture can better implement the kind of pattern processing that does not use representations of rules [algorithms] and features at all.

But what of language? Can neural nets give the syntax and semantics of structured language? If the language-like classification of phenomena of perception – ambiguities, distortions, paradoxes, fictions – does, indeed, suggest a close tie-up between the organization of perception and language, we can hardly suppose that nets work for perception but not for language. There is much to suggest that language and perception are closely related, though it may be going too far to suggest that perceptual hypotheses (as I call perceptions) are what logicians call propositions. These are questions on the very edge of understanding.

There is a great deal of work going on which is attempting to make nets (though generally simulated on digital computers) develop concepts with language-like relations (e.g. Hinton 1989). This is promising on the small scale, but whether artificial nets (preferably not simulated digitally) will become comparable to the full richness of human thought and language and perception is an open question.

THE NET RESULT

Allowing – in spite of Wittgenstein's doubt – that we can call machines intelligent that perform tasks for which we credit ourselves with intelligence, we arrive at two potential forms of biological and of artificial intelligence: analogue and digital; biological and artificial. Of course, the brain might be a hybrid of analogue and digital, and so might robots. Let's call Artificial Intelligence AI, and Biological (or Brain) intelligence BI. These might be digital or analogue:

WHAT IS THE CATCH IN NEURAL NETS?

Artificial Digital Intelligence – A D I

Artificial Analogue Intelligence – A A I

Brain (or Biological) Digital Intelligence – B D I

Brain (or Biological) Analogue Intelligence – B A I

The most promising candidate for animal and human learning and perception seems to be B A I, in the form of neural nets. This may well be so also for future robots (A A I) for even with the fastest electronic components, digital computing (A D I) appears to be too slow. Parallel digital computing helps, but probably will never be adequate. We may envisage large numbers of analogue modules – both for nature's B A I's and for robot's A A I's – commuting with distributed nets, rather than computing with algorithms.

THE FINAL CATCH

A practical advantage of nets is that they may be used to provide useful answers without our having to understand the problem. So nets can be used for controlling complex systems and warning of unusual, perhaps dangerous situations, though we have failed to analyse the system to develop algorithms for running it. This, surely, reflects the evolution of brains; for animals survive in extremely complex environments without having any deep understanding of how their world works. It is very hard to believe that analytical brain algorithms developed blindly through evolution, or that our brains are programmed through experience in day-to-day learning. Algorithms need basic understanding – what Marr called 'theories of computation' – which simply are absent for all except a very few well worked out theories in science. They are not available for perception, or for interacting systems such as economics, and are generally only available for 'ideal' linear, somewhat artificial systems. It may be better to run national economies (if indeed, as seems to be so, economists don't know what they are doing) without trying to understand them on self-optimizing nets.

This raises the question: does the *net* understand what it is doing? The answer seems to depend on what level of abstraction it can find. Having found deep levels of abstraction, so far at least nets cannot tell us what they know. For our minds (though this may be an artificial product of science) generalizations are unsatisfactory without explicit theories for our understanding. These seem often to depend on algorithms – so future effective nets may be good practitioners but poor theoreticians.

Digital computer disks contain data and algorithms that can be transferred from one machine to other compatible machines. If mind is digital stored data and operating algorithms, then it should be possible to transfer minds to other brains – or machines – to attain immortality. This should be so if the brain is digital, for algorithms and digital data can easily be transferred or translated into very different physical forms. Suppose, though, the mind works with PDP neural nets: could they be transferred between brains – or transferred to man-made machines? The snag, at least so far, is that the nets cannot be fully analysed or described, that is, copied. Patterns of mind are built into unique nets, which presumably die when they die. So if we are neural nets seeking immortality, we should spur the mathematicians to greater efforts to describe and copy and so preserve our nets, preferably for ever. To do this, we must learn to see clearly what is in the black box of mind. Although physiological and artificial brains wear out, digital minds might never die. They might, indeed, be merged and edited and improved beyond recognition – and have immortality. But if our brains are commuting neural nets, that cannot be fully described or copied, sadly, the net result of human life is *nothing*.

REFERENCES

Aleksander, I. and Morton, H. (1990) *Neural Computing*. (London: Chapman and Hall).

Arbib, M.A. (1989) *The Metaphysical Brain 2: Neural Networks and Beyond*. (New York: John Wiley).

Ashby, W.R. (1952) *Design for a Brain*. (London: Chapman and Hall).

Blinkov, S.M. and Glezer, I. (1968) *The Human Brain in Figures and Tables: A Quantitative Handbook*. (New York: Basic Books).

Boole, George (1847) *The Mathematical Analysis of Logic: Being an Essay Towards A Calculus of Deductive Reasoning*. (Cambridge). (Reprinted 1948 Oxford: Blackwell).

Caianiello, E.R. (1968) *Neural Nets*. (Heidelberg, New York: Springer Verlag).

Cook, J.W. (1969) 'Human Beings', in: Peter Winch (ed.) *Studies in the Philosophy of Wittgenstein*. (London: Routledge & Kegan Paul), pp. 117–51.

Craik, K. (1943) *The Nature of Explanation*. (Cambridge: Cambridge University Press).

Dreyfus, H.D. (1972; revised 1979) *What Computers Can't Do*. (New York: Harper and Row).

Fodor, J.A. (1983) *The Modularity of Mind*. (Cambridge, Mass: Massachusetts Institute of Technology Press).

Geach, Peter (1967) 'Could Sensations Occur Apart from an Organism?', in: H. Morick (ed.) *Wittgenstein and the Problem of Other Minds*. (New York: McGraw Hill), pp. 205–10.

Gregory, R.L. (1958) 'Models and the Localization of Function in the Central Nervous System', *Mechanization of Thought Processes*, Vol. 2. National Physical Laboratory Symposium No 10 (London: Her Majesty's Stationery Office). Reprinted in: Gregory, R.L. (1974) *Concepts and Mechanisms of Perception*. London: Duckworth, pp. 537–42.

Gregory, R.L. (1961) 'The Brain as an Engineering Problem', in W.H. Thorpe and O.L. Zangwill (eds) *Current Problems in Behaviour*. (London: Methuen). Reprinted in; Gregory, R.L. (1974) *Concepts and Mechanisms of Perception*. (London: Duckworth), pp. 547–65.

Gregory, R.L. (1963) 'Distortion of Visual Space as Inappropriate Constancy Scaling', *Nature*, 199, 678–91.

Gregory, R.L. (1967) 'Will Seeing Machines have Illusions?', in N.L. Collins and D. Michie (eds) *Machine Intelligence 1*, (London: Oliver and Boyd).

Gregory, R.L. (1968) 'Perceptual Illusions and Brain Models', *Proceedings of the Royal Society, B*, 171, 179–296.

Gregory, R.L. (1970) *The Intelligent Eye*. (London: Weidenfeld and Nicolson).

Gregory, R.L. (1981) *Mind in Science*.(London: Weidenfeld and Nicolson).

Hebb, D.O. (1949) *The Organization of Behaviour*. (New York: Wiley).

Hinton. G.E. (1989) 'Implementing Semantic Networks in Parallel Hardware', in G.E. Hinton and J.A. Anderson (eds) *Parallel Models of Associative Memory*. (Hillsdale, New Jersey: Lawrence Erlbaum).

Hinton, G.E. and Sejnowski, T.J. (1986) 'Learning and Relearning in Boltzmann Machines', in: David Rumelhart and James McClelland (eds) *Parallel Distributed Processing*, 2 vols (Cambridge, Mass.: Massachusetts Institute of Technology Press), I, pp. 282–317.

Hopfield, J.J. (1982) 'Neural Networks and Physical Systems with Emergent Collective Properties', *Proceedings of the National Academy of Science*, USA, 2554–8.

Kohler, W. (1920) 'Physical Gestalten', in: Ellis, W.D. (1938) (ed.) *A Source Book of Gestalt Psychology*. (London: Routledge & Kegan Paul), pp.17–54.

Latil, P. de (1957) *Thinking by Machine*. (Boston: Houghton Mifflin).,

McClelland, J.L. and Rumelhart D.E. (1988) *Parallel Distributed Processing: Explorations in the Microstructure of Cognition*, 2 vols (Cambridge, Mass.: Massachusetts Institute of Technology Press).

McCulloch, Warren S. and Pitts, Walter (1943) *Bulletin of Mathemaics and Biophysics 5*, 115–33.

Mayr, O. (1970) *The Origins of Feedback Control*. (Cambridge, Mass.: Massachusetts Institute of Technology Press).

Marr, D. (1982) *Vision*. (San Francisco: W.H. Freeman).

Mettrie, Julian Offray de la (1748) *Man A Machine*. G.C. Bussey (1953) (Illinois, La Salle: Open Court).

Minsky, M. and Papert, S.(1969, revised 1988) *Perceptrons: An Introduction to Computational Geometry*.(Cambridge; Mass.: MIT Press).

Neumaier, Otto (1987) 'A Wittgensteinian View of Artificial Intelligence', in: Rainer Born (ed.), *Artificial Intelligence: the Case Against*. (London: Croom Helm). Reprinted 1989. (London: Routledge, pp. 132–73.

Penrose, Roger (1989) *The Emperors's New Mind*. Oxford: Oxford University Press).

Popper, Karl and Eccles, John (1977) *The Self and its Brain*. (London: Springer International).

Rosenblatt, F. (1962) *Principles of Neurodynamics*. (New York: Spartan).

Searle, John (1984) *Mind, Brain and Science*. (London: BBC Publications).

Sedgewick, R. (1988) *Algorithms*. (Reading, Mass.: Addison Wesley).

Turing, A.M. (1950) 'Computing Machinery and Intelligence', *Mind 59*, 433–60.

Walter, W. Grey (1953) *The Living Brain*. (London: Duckworth).

Wertheimer, Max (1922) 'Gestalt Theory', in Ellis, W.D. (1938) (ed.) *A Source Book of Gestalt Psychology*. (London: Routledge & Kegan Paul), pp. 1–11.

Wertheimer, Max (1923) 'Laws of Organization in Perceptual Forms', in: W.D. Ellis (1938) (ed.) *A Source Book of Gestalt Psychology*. (London: Routledge & Kegan Paul), pp. 71–88.

Wiener, Norbert (1948) *Cybernetics: Control and Communication in the Animal and the Machine*. (Cambridge, Mass.: Massachusetts Institute of Technology Press).

Wittgenstein, L. (1953) *Philosophical Investigations* G.E.M. Anscombe, trans. (Oxford: Blackwell).

Woodcroft, B. (1881) *The Pneumatics of Hero of Alexandria*. (London: Taylor, Walton and Maberly. Reprinted 1971 with Introduction by Mary Boas Hall. London: Macdonald).

19

CONNING CORTEX

The ghostly visual phenomena of illusory surfaces were discovered early in this century by Schumann (1904). Most curiously, they were almost entirely ignored for seventy years before Gaetano Kanizsa's beautiful examples, especially the famous Kanizsa Triangle (Fig. 19.1), (Kanizsa 1976; 1979). Why were they ignored for so long? Presumably because they did not fit any prevailing paradigm of vision. Whatever the reason, it is astonishing that they were not investigated – and seldom even seen! – even though Schumann's figure (Fig. 19.2) is given in the most widely-read excellent textbook of psychology of the 1940s and 1950s, Robert Woodworth's *Experimental Psychology* (1938). There it is on page 637. I must have seen this as an undergraduate yet failed to spot its significance. It is to Kanizsa's immense credit that he saw where others were blind. With his evocative examples he made us see also. Perhaps it is no accident that Gaetano Kanizsa was a painter, and in his science, a phenomenalist.

These illusory surfaces can be lighter or darker than the background, with sharp edges which can be straight or curved, convex or concave. Whether or not they are part of normal perception, they present a fascinating challenge for explanation.

Investigators have come up with very different suggestions which generally reflect their theoretical positions or philosophies of perception. Some look for explanations simply in the appearance of these phenomena (Phenomenalists). Others turn to physiological processes, ranging from interactions between cells believed to give edge-sharpening (lateral inhibition), to effects of spatial filtering (Fourier components), to stimulation of edge-detector cells (following the discovery of Hubel and Wiesel in 1962 that there are cells in the visual cortex that respond to lines of specific orientations). Others suggest, very differently, that these are cognitive phenomena, induced by information rather than by stimuli. Whatever the explanation they are certainly ghostly, and very likely to be the basis of many reported apparitions.

171

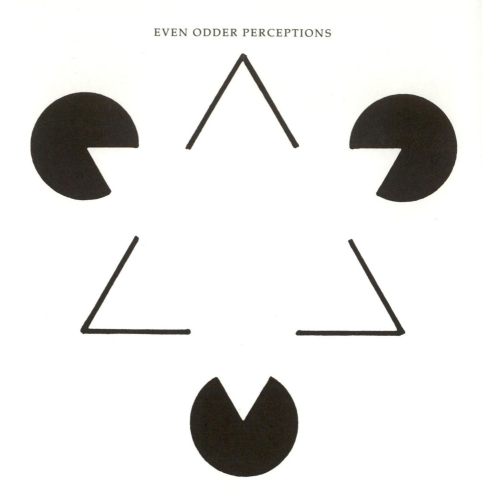

Figure 19.1 The Kanizsa triangle. The illusory white triangle seems to lie in front of the 'cakes'. It is a perceptual postulate to explain the missing slices.

With my cognitive bias, I suggested just over twenty years ago that they are postulated by the visual system, to explain surprising gaps as due to nearer or eclipsing objects. I called them 'cognitive contours' (Gregory 1972; 1987), but this was not a good name, as it begged the question: it assumed that they are cognitive phenomena. A name should not presuppose an answer!

The point as we saw it is that as, very often, distant objects are partly hidden by nearer objects and yet we recognise partly hidden things as complete though parts are missing to the eyes, we can create what is hidden. In a figure with actual gaps this process may create nearer objects or surfaces that 'ought' to be there. As predicted from this notion we found that illusory surfaces must be nearer – in front

Figure 19.2 Schumann's figure (1904). A vertical white stripe appears, bounded by straight lines at the right and left sides, and separated from the semi-circular shapes. This is the first recognized example of illusory contours and surfaces, though once noticed the effect is commonly observed.

of – the gaps (Gregory and Harris 1974). So we claimed that the visual system creates these surfaces as useful fictions to explain unlikely gaps.

It is a very interesting question just what can, and what can't, the visual system create? Faces with missing noses are common on Roman statues in museums, and what we see is a face with a missing nose. So here our eyes and brains do not create, or fill-in, what is to be expected from our knowledge of faces. However, a hollow mask is seen as a normal, nose-sticking-out face (p. 259). Why it is that a hollow face is seen – wrongly – as a normal nose-sticking-out face, though a nose-missing face is seen – correctly – as a face minus a nose, may not be at all easy to answer. If probabilities affect what we see, why should perception of the hollow face be affected by likelihood, but not in the case of the missing-nose face? One might say that creating a nose requires more of vision than switching depth. But Kanizsa's figures show that creation of surfaces (whether for fiction or fact) is within the powers of vision. This also appears from the completion of blind spots, or scotomas (Ramachandran and Gregory, 1981; see 'Virtually Real', p. 81). So, if vision can create these illusory surfaces – why not also noses?

The notion that illusory surfaces and illusory contours, as we may call them, are postulated from the surprising absence of parts of objects, such as the missing slices of the three 'cakes' in Kanizsa's Triangle,

Fig. 19.1, implies that cognitive processes are operating, requiring quite high-level brain processes. Certainly we would not expect to find such processes in the retinas of the eyes. They must be higher up, in the brain, but how high? It seems that what is created here is normally given by quite simple rule-following, without drawing upon knowledge of specific objects. This is 'side-ways' rather than 'top-down', as described in 'Putting Illusions in Their Place' (p. 259. But when we consider hallucinogenic drugs, the situation is different. Drugs such as LSD do evoke objects – scenes – weird universes – generated in the disturbed brain.

Discovering the physiological location of visual, as for other functions, can yield important insights which may have practical importance. This is, however, surprisingly difficult in systems with a lot of interaction. It is easier where there are parallel channels, or where there are clear hierarchies of command. The fact that presenting one curved illusory contour to one eye, and a different curve to the other eye, can give stereoscopic depth, suggests that this processing is within each eye system, and so quite low in the brain's hierarchy.

The most direct way to find out where these phenomena originate was to record from single cells of a (cat's) brain; but as I am not a physiologist with the necessary skills, and my laboratory was not at all equipped for this kind of study, my colleague Priscilla Heard and I collaborated with the distinguished electrophysiologist Adam Sillito, who was then at the University of Birmingham. This question was far removed from his own interests and superb work so this project, to which he contributed time and skills entirely beyond ours, must have been quite disrupting, especially as his laboratory was about to move. The scheme was to present for us illusory contours, to the receptive fields of brain cells that had been identified as responding to true, low-contrast contours. The question was whether the illusory contours would 'stimulate' these cells. We looked at the primary projection area 17(V1), predicting that this would be too early in the visual system for cognitive activity, and so on this kind of theory there should be no activity at this first stage of visual brain processing corresponding to illusory contours. We did, however, expect to find activity related to the illusory contours higher up in later stages of processing. To show no activity at the first stage would rule out a retinal origin, which would be strong evidence against many possibilities but would make a cognitive explanation such as creating eclipsing surfaces that 'ought' to be there appropriate.

The choice of experimental controls was tricky as we wanted the stimulus to be as nearly as possible the same for the true contours and the illusory contours; but obviously they could not be entirely identical. This is a general problem for any experimental control situations, for comparisons never can be entirely identical to what one is interested in, or they would be no more than repetitions. One must make sure the differences are as small as possible and appropriate to the question the experiment is addressing. There is an art to selecting what needs to be the same, and what can be allowed to be different for experimental purposes.

In 'Good as Gold' (p. 200) it is suggested that virtually all experiments were impossible when it seemed necessary to consider the positions of the planets – when they were supposed to have causal astrological influences. This must have made experimental science impossible, for any failure to confirm an observation could be attributed to a change in the pattern of the sky. As we did not believe in astrology, at least we didn't have this problem! We didn't even consider the planets or anything else that didn't seem directly relevant to what we wanted to find out. Rightly or wrongly, we worked within the unspoken assumptions of a paradigm that allowed feasible experiments. This assumes that nerve cells and their connections are very important, and that information proceeds upwards from the eyes to physiological systems carrying out cognitive processes. For any science the assumptions are horrendous; but one cannot do experiments without assumptions, and it would be tedious beyond belief to make all the assumptions explicit. This is where some knowledge of the history of one's science is so useful, for history reminds us that there are assumptions that may always be wrong and deeply misleading. It is only a few generations ago that the eminent psychologist William MacDougall (MacDougall, 1926) believed that the brain works by telepathic communication between its cells, or what he called 'monads', rather than by the electrical signals that for us are essentially necessary. This is an astonishing change of paradigm which affects the interpretation of just about every experiment and observation of the brain sciences.

To return to our – as it turned out failed because it was incomplete – experiment: following hours in the darkroom, Priscilla Heard produced three very nice sets of stimulus slides. One set had low-contrast rectangles. Another had four 90° sector disks – like cakes with a right-angular piece cut out of each – which produced for us an illusory rectangle, with the centres of the disks forming the corners. The third of Priscilla's sets of slides had the same four sector disks but each was rotated through 90°, so they did not produce illusory contours. We first searched around for cells responding to true, low-contrast contours. Then, trying the various stimulus patterns, we found that the selected cells did not respond to the rotated sectors which gave us no illusory contours. Much more interesting – they did not respond to the sector-disk patterns that *did* give us illusory contours.

We might conclude that the Area 17 (V1) cells do not respond, or are not involved in producing, illusory contours. This in turn might be accepted as evidence that the phenomenon must have its origin higher up, where it could be cognitive. All this could well be true. We did, however, have some doubts. We were not sure that we had tested enough cells to generalize adequately. More profound, there was a nagging doubt whether in this kind of case it is ever possible to get a convincing *negative* result. We were bothered by the non-drama of pictures showing *no* activity. They could indeed be genuine pictures of nothing happening – which indeed we believed to be the case – but would pictures of nothing happening be convincing to anyone else looking them? They might be too like pictures of a black cat in a dark room! Though this would hardly win the Cat-of-the Year competition it could be an accurate picture of no cat. But there might be a nagging doubt that there is a cat but it is hiding. It was disconcerting to have to publish a picture of no cat – or of no electrophysiological signals – because one is so used to pictures showing the presence of something.

As someone who works on phenomena of vision, rather than on physiological recording, something struck me which may be worth consideration. In order to stimulate these cortical cells it was necessary to sweep the stimulus display across the selected receptive fields. But to study the phenomena of illusory contours in us, about the last thing one would do is to sweep the display across the line of sight. One looks at the figures with more or less fixed eyes. So the situation is artificial and not comparable to how we look at the figures. I tried looking at these figures while moving the display across my line of sight, as though I was the cat. If there was no phenomenon in this situation, there would be no interesting reason for not finding physiological activity. This kind of control is, surely, very important for relating physiology to visual phenomena.

I think I do see illusory contours when the figures are swept across the eyes, though not as strongly as with a normal stationary display. This control of moving the stimulus as required for the electrophysiology is quite easily done, though conceivably there are differences here between cat and human vision. There is a more subtle problem. The cat's eye is stationary during the experiment, but ours can move freely. When we move our eyes the world remains stable. But do we know what happens, at the early stages of the brain's representation, when the eyes move though the perception remains fixed? What has been reported is that when the human eye is willed to move, but for some reason cannot do so, the visual world appears to move in the direction the eyes should have moved. Now does this thwarted compensation (as most authorities if not all would describe it) change the position of the cortical representation? How do we know that the cat is not 'willing' its eyes to move, so changing the cortical representation?

For various reasons, we never did complete these experiments though we did present a brief paper at the summer meeting of the Physiological Society at St Andrews in 1982. This was abstracted in the *Journal of Experimental Psychology*. Our paper had a title that was so good (as we saw it) that the rest of the paper came as an anti-climax. It was called: 'Can Cognitive Contours Con Cat Cortex?'

Having got our title, which was so good it made any further text look dull by comparison, and realizing that the pictures supporting our conclusion would be showing *nothing* – perhaps it is hardly surprising that the paper remains unfinished to this day, though there were other more serious reasons for our failure. A major problem was the move of the laboratory from Birmingham to Cardiff. Another was that the building started falling apart!

The answer, however, was found by the excellent work of Baumgartner, Peterhans and van der Heydt, working in Zurich (von der Heydt et al 1984; Peterhans et al 1984). In short, they found that activity associated with illusory contours is not present in the first stages of brain processing (Area 17) but is found at the next stage (Area 19), where it could be cognitive. They concluded (Peterhans et al 1984): 'Mechanisms such as lateral inhibition, spatial-frequency filtering, or interpolation by elongated fields [are ruled out] as explanations of illusory contours'. This is assuming that brain processing works upwards from the eyes without massive downward 'loops' in the early stages. No doubt, as for all experiments, there are many other assumptions but this was an unusually important finding.

Did Baumgartner, Peterhans and van der Heydt consider problems of eye movements that might conceivably upset such cortical recording? Yes they did. They thought of the problem and they investigated it, with highly ingenious experiments. They asked the right questions and did the right experiments and so they achieved fully deserved success.

Oh well – one can't win them all.

REFERENCES

Gregory, R.L. (1972) 'Cognitive Contours', *Nature* 238 51–2.

Gregory, R.L. (1987) 'Illusory Contours and Occluding Surfaces', in: Petry, Susan and Meyer, Glenn E. (1987) *The Perception of Illusory Contours*. (New York: Springer-Verlag), pp. 81–9.

Gregory, R.L. and Harris, J.P. (1974) 'Illusory Contours and Stereo-depth', *Perception and Psychophysics*, 15, 3, 411–16.

Hubel, D.H. and Wiesel T.N. (1962) 'Receptive Fields, Binocular Interaction and Functional Architecture of the Cat's Visual Cortex', *Journal of Physiology*, 160, 106.

Kanizsa, Geatano (1976) 'Subjective Contours', *Scientific American*, 234, 48–52.

Kanizsa, Geatano (1979) *Organization of Vision: Essays on Gestalt Perception*. (New York: Praeger).

MacDougall, William (1926) *Abnormal Psychology*. (London: Methuen).

Peterhans, D. von der Heydt, R. and Baumgartner, G. (1984) 'Illusory Contour Stimuli Reveal Stages in Visual Cortical Processing', *Perception*, 13(1), A16.

Ramachandran, V.S. and Gregory, R.L. (1991) 'Perceptual filling in of Artificially Induced Scotomas in Human Vision', *Nature* 350, 6320, 699–702.

Schumann, F. (1987) 'Contributions to the Analysis of Visual Perception. First Paper: Some Observations on the Combination of Visual Impressions into Units', in: Petry, S. and Meyer, G.E. (eds), *The Perception of Illusory Contours*. (New York: Springer Verlag), pp. 21–34.

Sillito, Adam, Gregory, R.L. and Heard, Priscilla (1982) 'Can Cognitive Contours Con Cat Cortex?' Talk presented to the Experimental Psychology Society Meeting at St Andrews, Scotland.

Von der Heydt, R., Peterhans, E. and Baumgartner, G. (1984) 'Illusory Contours and Cortical Neuron Responses', *Science*, 224, 1260–1.

20

PERCEPTIONS OF WILLIAM JAMES IN *THE PRINCIPLES OF PSYCHOLOGY*

As *The Principles of Psychology* appeared a little over one hundred years ago, in 1890, this seems an appropriate time to review what is probably the best-known book in the literature of psychology.

William James was born in New York in 1842. His brother, the novelist Henry, was born in the same city fourteen months later. Their parents were second-generation Americans, their father Henry being a wealthy amateur philosopher who espoused the views of Swedenborg. His father, who came from Ireland, had three wives and thirteen children and amassed a fortune, giving his grandsons leisure and confidence to make good use of their exceptional literary gifts and psychological insights. It has been said that Henry wrote like a psychologist and William like a novelist. However this may be, William James was the first important American psychologist; with the beauty and verve of his writing over a brave range of enquiry, he graced the subject indelibly and remains significant today.

Although James set up a laboratory at Harvard he did virtually no experimental work himself, yet he espoused the cause of physiologically based psychology by discussing behavioural experiments on learning, emotion, attention, thinking, perception and much else. His caste of mind was philosophic (certainly not mathematical) yet he was critical of contemporary philosophy, as we see from his *Pragmatism* (1907). This held that meaning is use, and was a forerunner of Logical Positivism. James did not object to psychology at Harvard being within the Department of Philosophy, his main concern being to interpret experiments and experience with philosophically phrased arguments.

Pehaps James's best-known theory in psychology is his account of emotion as being sensations of visceral responses to situations of danger and so on. This idea, which was conceived independently by the Swedish physiologist C.G. Lange (1834–1900), reflects James's interest in physiology. It stimulated a number of experiments but it has now been largely abandoned, except as being a rather small contribution to the understanding of emotions which are now seen to be brain-based. In spite of his leanings towards physiology James was not shy of writing about consciousness.

What makes him so interesting to read is his willingness to consider questions right across the board of experience and behaviour, from many points of view and with the tools of the philosopher and the scientist. Here I shall look mainly at sections on perception in *The Principles of Psychology*. These are in Volume II starting with Chapter XVII, 'Sensation'. This begins: 'After inner perception, outer perception!' Admitting but a loose distinction, James starts by saying that in adults sensation always involves perception. For him sensation is simple and is 'mere *acquaintance* with a fact'. Perception's function is 'knowledge *about* a fact; and this knowledge admits of numberless degrees of complication'. Both (unlike thinking) give immediate outward reality. But James does not take a direct view of perception. His General Law of Perception (*The Principles*, Vol II, p. 108) is

> whilst part of what we perceive comes through our senses from the object before us, another (and it may be the larger part) always comes (in Lazarus's phrase) out of our own head.

Here he offers a physiological account of consciousness, suggesting that previous experiences are laid down physiologically and when called upon slow down electrical activity; the slower the more conscious. He criticises the Scottish philosopher Thomas Reid (1710–96) and Helmholtz for saying that 'true sensations can never be changed by the suggestions of experience'. Did Helmholtz say that? However this may be, James makes an interesting distinction between the individual's necessarily ever-changing concepts for perception and the changeless concepts of logic with the aim of science to produce changeless concepts of objects.

James asks 'Is perception unconscious inference?' He considers a kind of syllogism (where 'this' is perception of an object):

'this' is M;
but M is A;
therefore 'this' is A.

Although he rejects this as unnecessary 'wheelwork in the mind' he uses it to explain illusions as logical errors (footnote, Vol. II, p. 112):

> When not all M, but only some M, is A, when, in other words, M is 'undistributed' the conclusion is liable to error. Illusions would thus be logical fallacies, if true perceptions were valid syllogisms. They would draw false conclusions from undistributed middle terms.

But, who would suppose that any perceptions are logically certain? – Certainly not Helmholtz.

There follows an extended discussion of perception of space. This starts with the importance of local signs (different feelings for different parts of the body) and the problem of how the many sensed features come together to form integrated perceptions. On what we would call the scaling of Size Constancy, James merely says, as he looks along his dinner table (Vol. II, p. 180):

I overlook the fact that the farther plates and glasses *feel* so much smaller than my own, for I *know* that they are all equal in size; and the feeling of them, which is a present sensation, is eclipsed in the glare of the knowledge, which is a merely imagined one.

But constancy works for unknown sizes of objects, so we have to say that this is no advance on René Descartes writing two and a half centuries earlier (*Dioptrics*, 1637):

[Size of objects] is judged according to our knowledge or opinion as to their distance, in conjunction with the images they impress on the back of the eye. [And for shape] Again, our judgements of shape comes from our knowledge, or opinion, as to the position of the various parts of the objects, and not in accordance with the pictures in the eye; for these pictures normally contain ovals and diamonds when they cause us to see circles and squares.

But it is easy to show, and is obvious from daily experience, constancy does not depend on knowledge of size or distance or shape. James stresses the problem of how the disparate and often conflicting sensations from the different senses are somehow combined into coherent perceptions, and here he is looking at a genuine problem still too often ignored.

Throughout all this confusion we conceive of a world spread out in a perfectly fixed and orderly fashion, and we believe in its existence. The question is: How do this conception and belief arise? How is the chaos smoothed and straightened out?

How indeed. James considers effects of muscular action to be important. This leads James to consider the world of the blind, and cases of recovery from early blindness. He picks up the important point (often forgotten) that negative results may be due to

general mental confusion at the new experience, and to the excessively unfavourable conditions for perception which an eye with its lens just extirpated affords.

So although failures may be attributed to irrelevant factors sucesses are significant:

> as in the young man operated on by Dr. Franz who named circular, triangular, and quandrangular figures at first sight.

James gives more weight to consciousness, to *feeling*, than we do now. He speaks of the feeling of depth as of primary importance and objects to Helmholtz's statement 'only qualities are sensational, whilst almost all spatial attributes are results of habits and experience.' James is concerned to show that visual perceptions of size or depth (including by stereopsis) are not at all simply related to patterns, sizes or positions of retinal stimulation. This leads him to phenomena of distortion and other illusions, and here he does have much of interest to say. He does, however, conceive what is accepted as 'physical reality' to be given by choice, such that (p. 237, his italics):

> we have native and fixed optical space sensations; *but experience leads us to select certain ones from among them to be the exclusive bearers of reality; the rest become mere signs and suggesters of these.*

James complains that Helmholtz and Wundt are vague; but is he clearer when suggesting that

> The factor of selection, on which we have already laid so much stress, here as elsewhere is the strong word of the enigma . . . .
> If they had gone on definitely to ask and definitely to answer the question, What are the size and distance in their proper selves? they would not only have escaped the present deplorable vagueness of their space-theories, but they would have seen that the objective spatial attributes 'signified' are simply and solely certain other optical sensations now absent, but which the present sensations suggest.

Is this clear? I for one prefer Helmholtz; but surely we are still not at all clear why, for example, a Necker Cube only has two spatial configurations, or why the moon looks the same size, high in the sky, when there are no 'signs' or 'cues', or 'clues' to its distance. These may be 'default' values – but is this clear?

James discusses ambiguous figures in *The Principles* (Vol. II, p. 254 and beyond). Here, surely, he misses their most interesting phenomena. It is the change of brightness of the shadow of Mach's folded card (see Fig. 15.1, p. 111) that is interesting (for it shows sensation modified 'downwards' by whether it is seen as a mark or a shadow) though this is not mentioned. The movement in the direction of motion of reversed cubes and the hollow mask are incredibly striking, yet again not mentioned. Here surely James is too much the passive philosopher and too little the active observer. Of the hollow mask James says (Vol. II, p. 254):

> Habit or probability seems also to govern the illusion of the intaglio profile, and the hollow mask. We have never seen a human face except in relief – hence the case with which the present sensation is overpowered. Hence, too, the obstinacy with which human faces and forms, and other extremely familiar convex objects, refuse to appear hollow when viewed through Wheatstone's pseudoscope. Our perception seems wedded to certain total ways of seeing certain objects.

No perception in laboratory or practical class is complete without a hollow mask! But isn't it odd that James leaves out its apparent rotation, following the observer wherever he moves at twice the speed he moves? This, indeed, shows the importance of having actual three-dimensional objects and models and not only pictures for appreciating perception.

James would agree. He points out that line diagrams indicate rather than produce perception of form. Returning to appearance-reality, he points out that ambiguous objects such as Mach's card appear fully real when depth-reversed:

> In these changes the actual retinal image receives different complements from the mind. But the remarkable thing is that the complement and the image combine so completely that the twain are one flesh, as it were, and cannot be discriminated in the result.

Yet James limits the creative contribution of the mind, (Vol. II, p. 269): In completely educated space-perception, the present sensation is usually just what Helmholtz (*Physiological Optics*, p. 797) calls it: 'a sign, the interpretation of whose meaning is left to the understanding'. But the understanding is exclusively reproductive and never productive in the process; and its function is limited to the recall of previous space-sensations with which the present has been associated and which may be judged more real than it. Did James ever say that to the newborn babe the world is 'a blooming, buzzing confusion?' Though often quoted, I have not come across it. Discussing the difficulty of seeing creatively he asks (Vol. II, p. 343), 'Why does it take a Newton to notice the law of squares, a Darwin to notice the survival of the fittest?' Suggesting that the child sees vaguely, without discrimination, as is the case for new experiences for the adult:

A library, a museum, a machine shop, are mere confused wholes to the uninstructed, but the machinist, the antiquary, and the bookworm perhaps hardly notice the whole at all, so eager are they to pounce upon the details. Familiarity has in them bred discrimination.

He thinks these are selected according to practical and aesthetic interests. How far selection is modified by the prevailing interest or needs of a task – perhaps with basic differences of information processing – seems still to be scarcely investigated. He says (Vol. II, p. 442): 'The image in the mind *is* the attention; the *preperception* ... is half the perception of the looked for thing.'

James was of course writing before Behaviourism. For him consciousness is primary, even though he finds consciousness and will impossible to reconcile with the physical sciences without ambiguity and paradox. He likes to think of mind as affecting the matter of the brain but, by his own confession, he has no evidence or reason beyond considerations of ethics to see mind or consciousness as causal over brain. He returns many times to whether freedom of the will is more than sensation of volition. In avoiding repetitive reflex arcs, James (Vol. II, Chapter XXVI) introduces ideas remarkably close to the later phase sequences of D.O. Hebb's *Organization of Behaviour* (1949) and recent notions of neural nets, with explicit physiological speculations of how new-formed sensory irradiations keep draining things forward, so 'breaking up the "motor circle" which would other-wise accrue'. There is here a fascinating to-ing and fro-ing between physiological and 'psychic' explanations of associative learning and the ability to break free from neural patterns, which puzzle us now with our computer models as they inspired James's creative thinking on these imponderables of matter and mind a century ago.

William James sums up his view of mind more poetically early on in *Principles*, Vol. I (pp. 288–9):

The mind, in short, works on the data it receives very much as a sculptor works on his block of stone. In a sense the statue stood there from eternity. But there were a thousand different ones beside it, and the sculptor alone is to thank for having extricated this one from the rest. Just so the world of each of us, howsoever different our several views of it may be, all lay embedded in the primordial chaos of sensations, which gave the mere matter of the thought of all of us indifferently. We may, if we like, by our reasonings unwind things back to that black and jointless con-tinuity of space and moving clouds of swarming atoms which science calls the only real world. But all the while the world *we* feel and live in will be that which our ancestors and we, by slowly cumulative strokes of choice, have extricated out of this, like sculptors, by simply rejecting certain portions of the given stuff. Other sculptors, other statues from the same stone! Other minds, other worlds from the same monotonous and inexpressive chaos! My world is but one in a million alike embedded, alike real to those who may abstract them. How different must be the worlds in the consciousness of ant, cuttle-fish, or crab!

William James was writing a century ago. Now we know far more of the details. Will we be able to see the grand pattern of the mind in a hundred years hence? Will its questions remain unanswered? It is a safe bet that *The Principles of Psychology* will still be worth reading a century from now.

REFERENCES

Descartes, René (1637) *Dioptrics.*(1965) Paul Olscamp (trans.) (Indianapolis: Bobbs-Merril).
James, William (1890) *The Principles of Psychology*. (London: Macmillan).
James, William (1907) *Pragmatism; A New Name for some Old Ways of Thinking*. (New York: Longmans, Green).
Hebb, Donald O. (1949) *The Organization of Behaviour*. (New York: Wiley).

21

FORGOTTEN GENIUS OF BRISTOL: WILLIAM GEORGE HORNER

The city of Bristol is founded on five sins: piracy, slaves, booze, tobacco and weapons of war. Here I have lived for more than twenty years.

This merchant city, a hundred miles southwest of London, has Roman origins. Although not on the sea it became a port in the tenth century, being readily defended from the sea as it is approached by a narrow gorge with high cliffs from which rocks could be dropped to sink attacking ships. Reaching its peak in the eighteenth century, Bristol still has fine houses and merchant palaces dating from when it was the second port and the second city of the realm. Now it is the same size as Edinburgh, with its population of somewhat over half a million citizens.

It has a stirring, adventurous history. Giovanni Cabot (1425–*c*. 1500), born in Genoa, moved from Naples to Bristol in about 1490, and set sail in 1497 under letters-patent from King Henry VII – to discover the mainland of America. Sailing from Bristol with his three sons, in two ships, he sighted Cape Breton and Nova Scotia on 24 June. The letters-patent from the British King ensured that America virtually belonged to Britain. On his second voyage, Cabot mysteriously disappeared. An almost equally famous if less significant sailor was Alexander Selkirk, who sailed from Bristol in 1708 in a crew of merchants and privateers. Quarrelling with his captain, he was left to rot on the island of Juan Fernandez where he was marooned for over four years, inspiring Defoe's *Robinson Crusoe*.

Bristol architecture reflects and preserves the spirit of this merchant adventuring, and at least three of its five founding 'sins' survive. It has always been noted for generous benefactors, with names such as William Canynges (a medieval shipbuilder) and Edward Colston (the source of his wealth is left vague in the history books) in street names, almshouses and societies of learning and the arts. The university was founded by the Colston Society. The Wills tobacco family have endowed the university with great generosity from its founding just over a century ago.

186

Bristol has traditions that have passed into common currency. The Plimsoll line painted on all ships is the invention of 'the Sailor's friend' Samuel Plimsoll, an effective Member of Parliament, in 1824. The expression 'paying on the nail' is from the bronze 'nails' on which the merchants struck their bargains. 'Shipshape-and-Bristol-fashion' comes from the Natural Selection through Survival of the Fittest of vessels, in the hazardous passage through the six-mile tidal gorge from the docks to the sea with the danger of landing on their bottoms in the mud of the narrow winding gorge. The Bristol Channel has the second highest tide in the world, next only to the Bay of Fundy in Canada. The largest ship built in Bristol broke her back on her maiden voyage in 1831 when she stuck fore and aft on the most extreme bend on the tidal gorge, in which she met her end at the moment of birth. This was the end of shipbuilding in Bristol. It signalled the migration of large ships, and heavy industry, to the huge harbours of Manchester and Liverpool. So Bristol was stranded in time; stuck fast (or slowly) in the eighteenth and early nineteenth centuries though later it became a pioneer in the building of aircraft and aero engines.

Throughout its history there have been flashes of originality and invention, especially from the great engineer, Isambard Kingdom Brunel, who came to Bristol to recover from nearly drowning in the Thames Tunnel and then left his mark as an inspiration of what an original, single-minded person can achieve (see Fig. 25.1, p. 230). Brunel's *Great Western*, launched in 1837, was the first steamship to cross the Atlantic commercially, sailing from Bristol on 8 April 1838 with seven brave passengers, arriving in New York fifteen days later. His second ship, the *Great Britain* was built in Bristol and launched in 1843 (Fig. 21.1). After a long and honourable service she returned to the very same graving dock in which she was built. She was towed 7,000 miles from the Falkland Islands, where she had lain abandoned for sixty years (Goold-Adams 1976). So now we can travel back in time, visiting the world's first screw-driven double-hull iron ship, as she lies inert yet beautiful in her stone womb.

The Clifton Suspension Bridge, spanning the gorge, designed in 1830 when Brunel was a young man, is a major triumph of Victorian engineering, though it was not completed until after his death (Fig. 21.2). The world's first mainline railway station with its then enormous 74 foot roof span, built by Brunel about 1841, is still impressive. His drawing office and the train shed where the broad-gauge engines were serviced houses our Exploratory, a hands-on Science Centre, open every day for the public to explore, discover and perceive principles of science. (See

187

Figure 21.1 Isambard Kingdom Brunel's *S.S. Great Britain*, now preserved at Bristol

the essay, 'Switching Brains on by Exploring Hands-on'.) Brunel visits us in spirit.

There were other engineers and inventors who are remembered. The Scottish, road-making John McAdam settled in Bristol, and was

188

Figure 21.2 A contemporary picture of Isambard Kingdom Brunel's design for Clifton Suspension Bridge, Bristol. The bridge was completed in 1864

made a freeman of the city in 1805. He lived at 23 Berkeley Square. The idea of making lead shot by dropping molten lead from a great height into water came in a dream to a Bristol plumber, William Watts. He made a fortune from his shot tower, invested in lavish local building projects and ended famous but bankrupt. Anaesthetics were almost discovered in Bristol, when Humphry Davy (1778–1829) as a young man joined Dr Thomas Beddoes in his Pneumatic Institute for curing diseases by the inhaling of gases, in a house (No. 6) still standing in Dowry Square. Here he discovered the effects of laughing gas, trying it out on Coleridge and Southey among other notables of the day.

The university has been the home of many celebrated scholars, including the quantum physicist Paul Dirac who was born and did most of his important work in Bristol and received the Nobel Prize in 1933. Cecil Powell was Wills Professor of Physics, winning the Nobel Prize in 1950 for photographing cosmic rays and discovering in 1947 the first fundamental particle to be predicted from theory – the Pion.

More recently, Tony Epstein (now Sir Anthony Epstein), working in the university Medical School, discovered the first cancer-producing virus. Although Bristol did not produce its university until the end of the nineteenth century, it has proved itself as a major centre of discovery.

The city of Bristol has not always been praised or liked. When a young man, David Hume spent a year here training to be a merchant; he had a nervous breakdown and went back to Edinburgh to immerse himself in philosophy. This city of merchants did not always get a good press, even in her heyday in the eighteenth century. Thus the minor poet Richard Savage, friend of Samuel Johnson, wrote of Bristol:

Upstarts and mushrooms, proud, relentless hearts,
Though blank of sciences, though dearth of arts.
Such foes as learning once was doomed to see,
Huns, Goth and Vandals, were the types of thee.

The famous local tragic young genius Thomas Chatterton, who tried to sell poems as being the work of the Bard, wrote on the day before his suicide:

Bristolia's dingy piles of brick
Lovers of mammon, worshippers of trick
and its 'guzzling aldermanic fools'.

Bristol has something of this reputation today. Has it made full use of its geological grandure? Does its more recent architecture raise the spirit? Bristol has the oldest theatre in the country (the Theatre Royal), and through the efforts of many dedicated individuals, the largest art centre outside London (the Arnolfini), and the first hands-on Science Centre in the country and the largest (the Exploratory). With almost no support from the city they serve, they are all struggling against the odds for survival. Is Bristol sufficiently imaginative, or generous in supporting its arts and sciences? Like all of us, the in-many-ways delightful city of Bristol has sins of commission and even more grave sins of omission.

One minor sin of omission I shall now try to repair: Bristol's forgetting of its inventive son Wiliam G. Horner.

As other cities, Bristol has its special spirit – its own genius. (The word comes from 'genial', the spirit of family celebrations.) As we have seen, Bristol has produced its share of outstanding individuals: merchants, builders, writers, inventors, philanthropists. In addition must be added Wiliam Horner (1789–1837), who invented the first effective device for showing moving pictures. He invented the simple yet stunningly effective zoetrope. This was a vital first step in the history of the cinema. I can find no reference to Horner in local histories

190

(such as Hutton 1907, Foot 1979, Shory 1989). In his native city, this important inventor and mathematician, as well as something of a poet, William George Horner, is forgotten. As a mathematician, he discovered a way of solving numerical equations of any degree. This is regarded as of the highest importance (Boyer 1968), and his method is known to mathematicians by his name (though apparently it was in part anticipated by Chinese mathematicians many centuries earlier who used a similar method for deriving accurate values of Pi).

Although forgotten by Bristol historians, some background of Horner's life *is* given in the Dictionary of National Biography (the DNB). Here we learn that his father was a Wesleyan Minister in Bristol, the Rev. William Horner. The son, William George, was educated in Bristol at Kingswood School, which no longer exists. At 16 he was an assistant master of the school and four years later he became its Head. In 1809 he founded his own school at Grosvenor Place in near-by Bath, where he remained for the rest of his life.

His invention of the zoetrope is not mentioned in the DNB. Horner's zoetrope (it changed its name several times) is, however, mentioned by C.W. Ceram (1965) in his *Archaeology of the Cinema*.

Following the dissolving magic lantern projections which go back to the end of the seventeenth century, Ceram attributes the first truly moving picture to Dr John Ayrton's (of Paris) thaumatrope: a spinning disk with different pictures on the front and back. But this illustrated persistence of vision rather than apparent movement which, though this is not always realized, is very different. The two pictures of the thaumatrope blended into a single stationary composite but they did not move. Following the discovery of the stroboscope for stopping motion, by Faraday and Brunel (see 'Michael Faraday's perception', p. 231–2), the physicist J.F. Plateau (1801–83) of Brussels simultaneously invented the spinning disk with equally spaced slots, with the same number of slightly different drawings placed in a ring round the disk, which produced the first moving pictures. This cunning arrangement was viewed from the front, through the slots, to a mirror placed behind the spinning disk so that the pictures on its back were seen in the mirror. The intermittent vision given by the slots allowed the pictures to be seen in sequence, one at a time, producing illusory motion.

The drawings chosen were usually of rotating gear wheels, which appeared to rotate around their centres when the disk was spun. Plateau's slotted wheel and Wiliam Horner's zoetrope cylinder with its slots for interrupting vision between each picture, for the first time allowed successions of slightly different still pictures to be seen as moving.

One might say that this results from what later became known as 'phi movement'. This was the term used by the Gestalt psychologists who made a big thing of it, supposing that dynamic brain fields are necessary to explain it. One might say, more simply, that the movement-system of the eye is tolerant of small interruptions for signalling real movement. And of course there is real movement: from each still picture to the next, slightly different picture – giving what we call – if not quite accurately – the *illusion* of movement of the cinema. The eye's tolerance allows just a few pictures per second to give smooth realistic movement, which makes the cinema and television commercially feasible. We may now see the Gestalt brain fields as a conceptual illusion derived from a visual illusion!

The zoetrope was followed by the praxinoscope, invented by Emile Reynaud and patented in Paris in 1877. By replacing the zoetrope's slots the paxinoscope, with its inner ring of mirrors placed half-way along the radius, gave a brighter picture. This principle is used in modern film-editing machines.

The snag these first moving devices shared was the limited length of the sequence – a dozen or so pictures – so only short, repeating sequences could be used. The goal of indefinitely long, moving pictures was almost achieved by Louis le Prince (1842–90). Through 1886–8 he was developing such a camera, with a separate projector with a maltese-cross mechanism, and celluloid perforated film. But in September 1890, on a train journey from Paris to Dijon to visit his brother, he disappeared. This is a complete mystery. Neither his body, nor his baggage which might have held the secret of the cinema, were ever found.

William Friese-Green (1855–1921) was also an inventive genius, though he died in poverty. He was the first – in 1890 – to demonstrate cinematograph projection of moving pictures. Where was *he* born? In Bristol!

REFERENCES

Boyer, C.B. (1968) *A History of Mathematics*. (New York: Wiley).

Ceram, C.W. (1965) *Archaeology of the Cinema*. (London: Thames).

Foot, David (1979) *Famous Bristolians*. (Bristol: Redcliffe Press).

Goold-Adams, Richard (1976) *The Return of the Great Britain*. (London: Weidenfeld and Nicholson).

Hutton, S. (1907) *Bristol and its Famous Associations*. (Bristol: Arrowsmith).

Shorey, J. (1989) *Tales from old Bristol, Bath and Avon*. (Newbury: Countryside Books).

22

GOOD AS GOLD
Newton's alchemy of matter and mind

We may see alchemy as a scientific and philosophical failure. Yet the greatest of all scientists laboured for over thirty years on alchemical experiments and theories. Isn't it bizarre that Sir Isaac Newton, for thirty years an alchemist, as Master of the Royal Mint became the keeper of the nation's gold! Yet Newton was not alone among great seventeenth-century scientists in believing it possible to transmute base metals into noble gold. (See Fig. 22.1.) The idea was accepted by such distinguished men as Robert Boyle (1627–91) and Gottfried Leibnitz (1646–1716). It is likely that, as did many others, Newton suffered mercury poisoning through alchemical experiments (Lenihan 1988). This may have killed the royal alchemist, founder of the Royal Society, King Charles II.

Why did transmutation of metals seem plausible at that time? This was long before the atomic theory of matter was accepted, and so the word 'element' had a different meaning. All substances were supposed to be made of various proportions of the four Aristotelian 'Elements' – Air, Earth, Fire, Water (see Fig. 11.1, p. 69). But Aristotle meant principles, or properties, rather than elements in the modern chemical sense. Proportions of (tenuous) airy, earthy, hot and humid characteristics were seen as imposed on a central *prima materia*. It was a familiar observation that substances changed into other substances, such as earth becoming fruit. But as it was incorruptible, gold had a special status making it uniquely hard to transmute. It was known well before the seventeenth century that gold could be dissolved by ordinary – not magical or 'philosophic' – *aqua regia*, a mixture of nitric and hydrochloric acids. It was thought, however, that this did not change the essential nature of the gold, but dissolved it essentially unchanged into small particles. Great efforts went into dissolving gold for transmutation. Robert Boyle would quote the alchemical saying: 'It is harder to destroy gold than make it.'

The father of chemistry (and uncle to the Earl of Cork) Robert Boyle destroyed alchemy's conceptual basis, by denying Aristotle's four

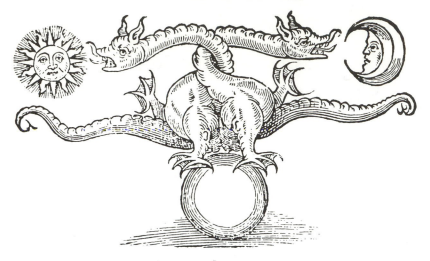

Figure 22.1 An alchemical symbol of the transmutation of base metal (the earth, at bottom) into gold (the sun) and silver (the moon), through the agency of the dragon (mercury, or volatility)). This illustration appeared in *Theatrum Chemicum Britannicum* by Elias Ashmole. Newton is known to have had a copy in his library.

elements. Boyle defined 'elements' as substances which, by all chemical means, cannot be changed to other substances. Alchemy lost its power and influence at this time, yet there were some attempted later demonstrations. As late as 1782 an English chemist, James Price (who had been elected a fellow of the Royal Society in 1781), demonstrated in public turning sulphur, with the use of some mysterious powders, into fifty or sixty times as much silver or gold, which passed assay tests. Concerned with the honour of the Royal Society its President, Sir Joseph Banks, requested Price to repeat the experiment before the Fellows. This time it failed to work. Price took poison on the spot – dying at the demonstration.

Paradoxically, the discovery at the start of the twentieth century that elements *can* transmute, by radioactivity, finally destroyed alchemy. This seems a rare case of a successful prediction serving to destroy the hypothesis supporting it. Strictly speaking, the transmutation of atoms by radioactivity makes a nonsense of the chemical meaning of 'atom' and 'element'. Their definitions should have been changed, to allow transmutation as a logical possibility, though after the event. The problem was avoided by denying that these effects of radioactivity are 'chemical'. The old alchemists had no such semantic or logical problem with their Aristotelian sense of elements as these were seen as being mixtures, not unsplittable particles or 'atoms'.

Newton built furnaces with his own hands, for his alchemical laboratory in Trinity College, Cambridge. He wrote an estimated one million words on alchemy and he assembled the largest private collection of books and papers, copying many in his own hand. Searching for meanings hidden in these obscure texts he became, it is now realized, the most deeply read of all the alchemists. Yet Newton did not publish one word on alchemy. Why should this be? One interpretation is that he doubted that his experiments really worked. Another, and it would seem the more likely interpretation, is very different – that he regarded the potential powers of alchemy as too dangerous for public knowledge. This is the view taken of Newton's silence by B.J.T. Dobbs (1975), which I shall follow. Golinski (1988) points out that secrecy was a characteristic of alchemists who, like those in the priest crafts, disliked sharing noble knowledge with the base public. This was also the attitude held by the Guilds.

There is striking evidence of Newton's concern about the dangers of alchemy in what we may see as a dramatic seventeenth-century parallel to the recent cold fusion debacle, in which it was claimed that nuclear fusion can take place in a test-tube at room temperature to generate heat beyond that which could occur by chemical means. Over three hundred years ago Robert Boyle claimed that philosophical sulphur could heat gold by alchemical power. This was in 1675, which was the year Newton first met Boyle. Newton was so disturbed by Boyle's claim that he wrote privately (on 26 April 1676) to the Secretary of the Royal Society, Henry Oldenburg, urging that it should:

> not to be communicated without immense damage to the world if there should be any verity in the Hermetic writers, therefore I question not but the great wisdom of the noble Author [the Hon. Robert Boyle] will sway him to high silence till he shall be resolved of what consequence the thing may be. [Newton ends this letter] I have been so free as to shoot my bolt but pray keep this letter private to yourself.

What exactly was this claim or discovery of Boyle's that Newton was so worried about? It was an alchemical experiment carried out by Boyle which he reported in a paper 'Of the Incalescence of Quicksilver with Gold', published in *Philosophical Transactions of the Royal Society* of 1675 (Vol. 10, Contrib. 155, p. 515). It was introduced by Henry Oldenburg who translated it from the Latin. It starts:

In this long paper Mr. B.R. (Robert Boyle) enters into an inquiry whether or not the commixtion, or amalgamation, of gold with mercury, is accompanied with a sensible production of heat; which he decides in the negative, in respect to common mercury, and in the affirmative with regard to purified, or (as he terms it) ennobled mercury. I took, says he, to one part of the mercury, sometimes half and sometimes an equal weight of refined gold reduced to a calx or subtle powder. This I put in the palm of my left hand, and putting the mercury upon it, stirred it and pressed it a little with the finger of my right hand, by which the two ingredients are easily mingled, and grew not only sensibly but considerably hot, and that so quickly, that the incalescence sometimes arrived at its height in a minute.

With his usual excellent scientific method, Boyle guards against the possibility of a sensory illusion of heat through irritation of the skin:

I had the curiosity to keep the mixture in a paper, and found not its interposition to hinder me from feeling the incalescence, though it abated the degree of my sense of it.

He tried it out with successful confirmation on Oldenburg and on the President of the Royal Society, Viscount Brouncker.

Boyle makes it clear that this is not ordinary mercury. But he gives no details of it. Indeed, curiously, he makes too many excuses: that he lost 'a considerable quantity of it', and there was 'the almost sudden death of the only operator I trusted in the making of it', and that he was 'diverted by business, sickness, and more pleasing studies'. It would seem that Boyle shared Newton's fear of this alchemical reaction, supposedly producing heated gold, not with normal but only with specially prepared 'philosophical' mercury.

Should we account, now, for this seventeenth-century cold fusion-like heat, as being due to some impurity? I am no chemist, but presumably modern chemists would prefer an assumption of impurity to magic or to alchemical effects. What has changed is assumptions of possibility. Such assumptions are sometimes changed by experiments. Cold fusion looked so interesting because it looked like relaxing the assumptions of impossibility, in the world of new possibilities that opened so dramatically with the splitting of the atom by radioactivity. But, like Boyle's alchemical claim of three centuries ago, it seems these experiments were not sufficiently powerful to shift the current assumptions – some other though unknown cause is more likely than cold fusion, or alchemy.

Following many years of dedicated, dangerous work, Newton claimed to have remarkable success developing a 'philosophical mercury' for producing gold, and later an effective 'philosophical sulphur'. We find a clue to why he saw these as possible from his attraction to the *star regulus* of antimony. Antimony is a semi-metal, occurring naturally as antimony sulphide, now called stibnite. The crystals are long and thin and form themselves into patterns like ferns. But under special conditions, which the alchemists discovered, they form patterns radiating from a centre, like stars. It was called by alchemists the *regulus* ('little king'), probably referring to the star Regulus in the constellation of Leo. In any case, Newton saw a relation between the 'regulus of antimony' and the star Regulus. The alchemist Basilius spoke of the star of antimony as having 'a spirit which is its strength, which also invades it invisibly, as the magnetic property pervades the magnet'. It seems that this greatly appealed to Newton, leading him to think that by analogy with celestial gravity it would draw the 'philosophical mercury' out of other metals.

Traditionally, alchemy is closely tied to astrology, as to each planet is ascribed a metal: mercury for Mercury, lead for Saturn, tin for Jupiter, copper for Venus, iron for Mars, silver for the moon, gold for the sun. Newton looked for alchemical relations between substances and certain stars, especially Regulus. Wouldn't Newton have loved the spectroscope! He would have seen all the alchemical elements in the stars – even gold!

Although Newton did not publish explicitly on alchemy there are strong hints of alchemical ideas in his printed papers. It seems that he looked to alchemy for principles underlying mathematical accounts of mechanisms. Evidently he found the mechanistic account of nature, in terms of forces and motions of bodies which he did so much to develop, unsatisfactory as a complete account of nature. It has even been suggested that his interest in alchemy was a revolt against mechanistic philosophy, though this may be too strong. Newton wrote two unpublished papers on underlying principles, with rich hints of alchemy, in 1699. The first contains:

> The vital agent diffused through everything in the earth is one and the same.
>
> And it is supremely volatile, which is dispersed through every place.
>
> The general method of operation of this agent is the same in all things; that is, it is excited to action by a gentle heat, but driven away by a great one, and when it is introduced into a mass of substances its first action is to putrefy and confound into chaos; then it proceeds to generation. . . . In a metallic form it is found most abundantly in Magnesia [Antimony].

The second paper has no name, but is usually called 'The Vegetation of Metals'. The distinguished Newton scholar Richard Westfall summarizes it (Westfall 1980, his italics):

His focus in 'Vegetation' was the earth and its mineral products. He described how the metallic spirit ascends from the bowels of the earth, is fixed with salts and minerals, when it meets water, and is thereby alienated from its metallic nature. The alienation arises because concretion is not a process of vegetation but only *'a gross mechanical transposition of its parts.'* If the spirits can be freed from their fixed compositions, they can again *receive metallic life & by degrees recover their pristine metallic forms.* ... 'The Vegetation of Metals' *proclaimed Newton's conviction that mechanical science had to be completed by a more profound natural philosophy which probed the active principles behind particles in motion.*

Newton never abandoned his view (1675) that: 'The whole frame of nature [might] be nothing but aether condensed by a fermental principle'. Newton's final account, published in the *Queries* of the *Opticks*, reads:

Are not gross Bodies convertible into one another, and may not Bodies receive much of their Activity from the Particles of Light which enter their Composition? For all fix'd Bodies being sufficiently heated emit Light so long as they are sufficiently hot ...

The changing of Bodies into Light, and Light into Bodies, is very conformable to the Course of Nature, which seems delighted with Transmutations.

Newton was deeply interested not only in matter and forces operating in the material world but also in mind: how we can sense things, and appreciate principles by which the universe works. His interest in mind is bound up with his concepts of space, the aether and absolute motion. Although he did not simply assume absolute motion, but questioned it and sought experimental evidence, absolute motion, in a fixed space or in aether, was important for him on theological grounds – for he saw space as God's mind. He thought of the laws of the physical world as God's ideas, which He might change at any time, or have other ideas, giving different laws for different parts of the universe. Considering how with his mathematics he could discover the laws of the universe, Newton thought he had a kind of telepathic communication with God's mind, which somehow existed in the space between the stars. For Newton, the laws of motion of the heavenly bodies must lie not in the bodies but in space; because any heavenly body, of any composition of the same mass, would behave the same. The mystery was how the symbols of mathematics could reveal astronomical forces and laws. The hope was that symbols might reveal powers and laws of mind. For Newton, living organisms, very differently, determine their own behaviour from within themselves – as different organisms behave differently and may show free will.

Here it is surely right to think of the immense power that symbols have for us in everyday life. We are just as affected by symbols as by physical forces: by patterns of pictures, words, music, logical (and illogical) arguments. We live (and with modern advertising we may drown) in a sea of symbols. It does seem odd that Newton thought of the pattern of crystals of antimony as drawing in power and attracting principles of metals, perhaps making gold. But alchemy made no sharp distinction between living and non-living, so it is hardly surprising that symbols were seen to have powerful influences in the inorganic world.

The mechanical philosophy was set up in the generation before Newton. René Descartes (1596–1650) had suggested that mind is essentially separate from matter – seeing the body as a machine controlled by a separate mind, through a quixotically identified link, the pineal gland of the brain. Newton greatly disliked this Cartesian dualism of mind and matter. He looked for matter–mind links in the symbols of the experimental theology of alchemy.

It is interesting that Newton's teacher, Isaac Barrow – who set Newton's interest in optics, the possibility of the calculus, and other of his great achievements – held similar views on Descartes' dualism. Barrow gave up his Chair at Cambridge for Newton. He became a noted preacher in London, his sermons at St Pauls going on so long that the congregation would bribe the organist to play to make him stop! Barrow said, of the mechanism of the universe:

> He thinks unworthily of the Supreme Maker of things who supposes that he created just one homogeneous Matter, and extended it, blockish and inanimate, through the countless acres of immense space, and moreover, by the sole means of Motion directs those solemn games and the whole mundane comedy, like some carpenter or mechanic repeating and displaying *ad nauseam* his one marionettish feat . . .

Wouldn't it be interesting to know how Newton would accept current ideas of a different kind of dualism – of machines handling symbols as the hardware of computers control and are controlled by their software – as an analogy for the brain–mind relation.

The Greeks realized the power of symbols and that symbolic processes can be handled by mechanisms: counting on the fingers (digital), and moving pebbles (calculate) as is done for the abacus. Yet this ancient notion of matter-mechanisms carrying out symbolic processes did not become a paradigm for physiological psychology until as late as the middle of the twentieth century. Charles Babbage showed in the 1830s that a machine could make its own decisions during calculations, and mechanical calculators were well known right through the nineteenth century; yet they never seem to have been even mentioned by psychologists concerned with how the brain works for thinking, learning and seeing. In spite of the obvious powers of modern electronic computers for handling symbols and learning and even seeing, explanations in terms of cognitive concepts are still taboo for many distinguished physiologists. Perhaps they are frightened of being branded alchemists! The really interesting general question is why experimental science took so long – thousands of years – to get going effectively, and took so long to challenge and defeat the paradigm of alchemy. An answer may lie in the sister 'science' of astrology. It seems very likely that all progress in experimental science using inductive method and critical experiments was held up by astrology. For controlled experiments must have been virtually impossible when it was supposed to be necessary to have to wait for the planets, the moon and the stars, to return to the same positions in the sky for each comparison trial of an experiment. So Francis Bacon's experimental method, of the *Novum Organum* (1620) which we follow today, could not be carried out before the general demise of astrology within the community of scientists.

But if this is so, as I suggest, how could the ancient queen of sciences – astronomy – have been successful? A reasonable answer is that observational astronomy escapes the problem – because it does not use controlled experiments. Events happen and patterns form and change in cycles which, though beyond human control, can be described and used for prediction. It is these that Ptolomy explained mechanistically with his epicycles and Kepler and Newton made sense of with their mathematical models. On this view, astronomy is a special case, making it the first, but atypical science, to be successful in spite of astrology. For just because the heavens could not be controlled but could be observed, alchemy's marriage partner astrology did not inhibit conceptual models for describing the dance of the stars.

Newton saw symbols, with the operations of arithmetic and mathematics, as extremely powerful and dangerous in physics and mind. He did not refer to the first manmade engine to do mental arithmetic with a mechanism of metal gears. This was Pascal's calculating machine, invented in 1642, the year Newton first opened his eyes to the light.

REFERENCES

Dobbs, B.J.T. (1975) *The Foundations of Newton's Alchemy: or; The Hunting of the Greene Lyon.* (Cambridge: Cambridge University Press).

Fabricius, J. (1976) *Alchemy: The Medieval Alchemists and their Royal Art*, (Northampton: The Antiquarian Press/Thorsons).

Golinski, J. (1988) 'The Secret Life of an Alchemist', in: Fauvel, J., Flood, R., Shortland, M. and Wilson, R. (1988) *Let Newton Be!* (Oxford: Oxford University Press), pp. 147-67.

Gregory, R.L. (1983) *Mind in Science.* (London: Weidenfeld and Nicolson. Reprinted 1986, London: Penguin).

Holmyard, E.J. (1957) *Alchemy.* (London: Penguin).

Kuhn, T.S. (1962) *The Structure of Scientific Revolutions.* (Chicago: University of Chicago Press. 2nd edn, enlarged, 1970).

Lenihan, J. (1988) *The Crumbs of Creation: Trace Elements in History, Medicine, Industry, Crime and Folklore* (Bristol and Philadelphia: Adam Hilger).

Sherwood Taylor, F. (1952) *The Alchemists.* (London: Heinemann).

Turnbull, W.H. (1959) *The Correspondence of Isaac Newton.* (Cambridge: Cambridge University Press).

Westfall, R.S. (1980) *Never at Rest: A Biography of Newton.* (Cambridge: Cambridge University Press).

23

COUNTING ON EYES

We all know that you can't count on eyes. Eyes go wrong, unaccountably. Yet in Egypt over five thousand years ago there was an eye you could count with: the eye of Horus. The god Horus, represented as a man with the head of a falcon, was the earliest of the Egyptian gods, worshipped predynastically as the face of the sky, his eyes being the sun and the moon. When neither sun nor moon was visible the sky was called 'Horus dwelling without eyes'.

Horus was the son of Isis, and the posthumous son of Osiris, who was murdered by his uncle the evil god Set. The young Horus was brought up among tall papyrus leaves to hide him until the time when he could avenge the death of his father. This led to a series of good-against-evil, light-against-dark, violent fights between Horus and Set. In one encounter Set destroyed Horus's right eye, breaking the eye into six pieces which were scattered over the country. This explained the recurring cosmic drama of the eating of the sun, at solar eclipses.

Horus's left eye, the moon, was owned by Atum, the creator of many gods, who had but a single eye. Atum sent his single eye, the moon, to look for Shu and Tefnut in the dark waters of Nun. When they returned with the eye, Atum wept for joy and from his tears grew men.

The many Egyptian gods, with animal and human forms, represented all aspects of nature with charm and a wit that is irresistible. For us now, this is the attraction of their art and, in some ways, their religion (or so it seems to me from amateur reading), which may have contributed to the stability over thousands of years of the Egyptian civilisation. In these earliest records of conflicts, victories and disasters, wealth and poverty, loving and hating, we find not only the eternal human fears and hopes and dramas, but also hints of pre-historic sciences (or proto-sciences) and of how the first inventions of ancient technology were accepted and applied. Detailed drawings sometimes show surprisingly sophisticated mechanisms and how they were made and used from very early times.

My favourite Egyptian god is the ibis-headed Thoth. The god of wisdom, of writing and of mathematics, unlike the other gods he was self-created, without parents. At the creation of the universe it was Thoth who determined the patterns of the stars. Isn't it suggestive that in ancient Egypt the soul of the dead person was weighed against the feathers of truth, with an elaborate, beautifully constructed balance, whose calibration was in the hands of the god Thoth. Neither god nor man made the judgement: the eternal fate of souls was decided by the same mechanism that was trusted for the weighing of gold.

In the earliest accounts of the conflict between Horus and Set, in the *Book of the Dead* before 4000 BC (Budge 1960), they fight unarmed. Later Horus is shown fighting with iron weapons, accompanied by beings called *mesniu* (or *mesnitui*) who were workers in metal. It is thought (Budge 1904) that this represents an otherwise unknown historical event, at an early dynastic time, of people invading parts of Egypt with iron weapons and tools. History and myth are inextricably mixed; but surely this is true also for modern history, and even today's news!

Thoth collected the pieces of Horus's broken right eye 'with his fingers' (counting on his fingers?). He mended the eye, returning it whole to its owner. The now healthy eye of Horus – the *Hekat* – became a widely used symbol of vision and of fecundity.

Horus's eye was represented as the eye of a human and of a bird. It was shown with a human iris, with an eyebrow. Beneath were the two long curved lines below the eye of a peregrine falcon.

The six parts of the broken eye of Horus became symbols for counting. The eye was divided into six pieces representing the six fractions ½, ¼, ⅛, 1/16, 1/32, 1/64 (Fig. 23.1). These were used especially for

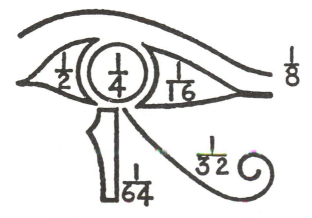

Figure 23.1 The division into six parts of Horus's eye

grain and other products of agriculture, with the unit of measurement of a *hekat*, which was a volume of about 4.8 litres in our measure (Gillings 1972, pp 202-6).

There is no doubt that number systems and units for measurement were extremely important, both for commerce and for stimulating general and abstract ideas. The invention of counting with its appropriate systems of symbols released the human mind from a basic limitation: we cannot, at a glance, assess numbers of objects beyond about seven. (Hence the delightful title of the American psychologist George Miller's (Miller 1956) celebrated paper, 'The Magic Number Seven, plus or minus Two'.) It is the strongest evidence of the powers of symbols that without them we are numerically feeble beyond words; yet with language and numbers, human thinking and calculating have taken us far beyond the ancient dreams of achieving power over nature and seeing behind appearances.

It has turned out over the millennia that some symbol-systems work much better than others. The Egyptian number system had a decimal notation with special signs for units, tens, hundreds and so on, but there was no sign for zero. Multiplication was carried out by successive additions. Although digital computers carry out multiplications in this way, it is cumbersome for us, and it did not serve the Egyptians well.

The powers and limitations of Egyptian mathematics are revealed in the Rhind papyrus (Robins and Shute, 1987) so named after its American discoverer and first owner. This unique document of ancient methods of calculating originates at least from the 19th century BC, the existing papyrus having being copied by a scholar named Ahmose in the 16th century BC from a still earlier version. Just why some symbols and number systems work well, though others such as the Egyptian and Roman systems are clumsy, suggests something of how the mind works – dramatically helpful aids are generally very different from what already exists.

Thus, screwdrivers are different from fingers. There would be no point in finger-like screwdrivers as we already have fingers. Similarly, we may suppose, both the pre-historic abacus and modern pocket calculators are so useful for us because the unaided brain does not work like them. This at once tells us something important about the brain: that the brain, or mind, is not like an abacus or an electronic calculator. This suggests a curious paradox for considering mechanisms of mind. This is: we should expect useful mechanical mental aids to be unlike human thinking – and so be unlike minds or brains they seem to model by analogy.

Perhaps it is even odder that the pre-historic aid to counting – the abacus – has come alive, to work by itself with powers beyond conceptions of magic.

From the enchanting Egyptian story of mending and lending eyes has come our medical ability to hand on parts of eyes to bring new sight from death. So we owe much to the ancient dreams expressed by Horus and to the eye-mending skill of the ibis-headed god of learning Thoth who, thousands of years before the existence of classical Greece, respected writing, measurement and counting, which were the magical beginnings of science.

It is recorded (Ifrah 1987) that an Egyptian apprentice scribe pointed out to his master that the fractions of the Horus eye did not add up to 1; but are equal to only $63/64$. The master replied that Thoth would always supply the missing $1/64$ to the reckoner who placed himself under his protection. The missing $1/64$ is still the 64,000 dollar question – just how do eyes and brains confer sight? We only know a fraction of the answer.

REFERENCES

Budge, Wallace E.A. (1904) *The Gods of the Egyptians*. (Chicago, Ill: Open Court; reprinted, 1969, New York: Dover).

Budge, Wallace E.A. (1960) *The Book of the Dead: The Hieroglyphic Transcript of the Papyrus of ANI*. (New York: University Books).

Gillings, R.J. (1972) *Mathematics in the Time of the Pharaohs*. (Cambridge, MASS: Massachusetts Institute of Technology Press; reprinted, 1982, New York: Dover).

Ifrah, G. (1985) *From One to Zero: A Universal History of Numbers*. L. Blair (trans.) (Harmondsworth: Penguin), p. 212.

Miller, G.A. (1956) 'The Magic Number Seven plus or minus Two: Some Limits on our Capacity for Processing Information', *Psychological Review* 63, 81–97.

Robins, G. and Shute, C. (1987) *The Rhind Mathematical Papyrus: An Ancient Egyptian Text*. (London: British Museum).

24

SWITCHING BRAINS ON BY EXPLORING HANDS-ON

> We shall not cease from exploration
> And the end of our exploring
> Will be to arrive where we started
> And know the place for the first time
>
> T.S. Eliot 'Little Gidding' *Four Quartets*

Hands-on science centres are designed to introduce the world of science and technology to children and to adults, literally at first hand, with simple interactive demonstrations and experiments. The interaction is not just making passive push-button movements. It is active experimenting, with choice and initiative, sometimes with surprising results. If such hands-on experience of phenomena and methods of science turns on curiosity, it succeeds. If it turns curiosity into understanding, it achieves more than can be said of most schools.

This is not a criticism of schools, who have well-intentioned and often devoted teachers doing a very difficult job against all manner of odds. The strange fact is that in spite of several thousands of years of experience of education – from the Babylonians, the Egyptians, the Greeks, on to state education for all – we still have such a feeble understanding of how to present facts and ideas effectively; it is not at all clear how we should introduce science and technology now. Perhaps our lack of knowledge of how to instil knowledge is because methods of science are hard to apply to research for improving school education, as groups of children can hardly be sacrificed as experimental 'controls' when they would be denied what is believed to be important for their learning. Education goes through fashions, presumably because empirical data on effects of various methods are hard to come by; aims are not clear, and may conflict; the education system has to cope with a wide range of abilities and interests; it is set by traditions which may become inappropriate, and yet may rightly be treasured and protected. There are uneasy conflicts between perceptions of the past, the present and possible futures, central to education. As science centres are outside the structures and strictures of schools they can experiment in presenting ideas and questions and answers in all manner of new ways – occasionally to illuminate understanding by chance lights as a new idea flashes into existence.

Most things are opaque, many intimidating, without our having some understanding of science and inventions of technology. The universe looks like a vast conjuring trick, understood if at all by the closed magic circle of scientists who speak in a secret language and produce not only wonders but also some frightening tricks. The aim of science centres is to open this magic circle to all who wish to step inside to appreciate the hidden wonders of reality, as made visible and useful by the questions and explorations of science. Visitors – the Explorers – may learn and question science and its discoveries by experiencing often beautiful phenomena and playing games against nature with ancient and modern experiments.

Presenting hands-on science and technology for the public is not a new idea. It is clearly expressed by Francis Bacon in his unfinished book *New Atlantis* (1627), which described how the technology and knowledge of his day could be made available to the population in the imaginary House of Salomon, where all could share the drama of seeking truth through experiment and share the harvesting of its benefits. Bacon described his House of Salomon as having:

> Perspective Houses, where we make demonstrations of all lights and radiations; and of all colours; and of things uncoloured and transparent, we can represent unto you all several colours; not in rain-bows, as it were in gems and prisms, but of themselves single. We represent all multiplications of light, which we carry to great distance, and make so sharp as to discern small points and lines; also all colourations of light . . . . We procure means for seeing objects afar off, and things afar off as near; making feigned distances . . .
>
> We have also engine houses . . . . We imitate also flights of birds; we have some degree of flying in the air; we have ships and boats for going under water, and brooking of seas; also swimming girdles and supporters. We have diverse curious clocks, and other like motions of return, and some perpetual motions. We imitate also motions of living creatures, by images of men, beast, birds, fishes and serpents . . .
>
> We have also a mathematical house, where are represented all instruments, as well as geometry and astronomy, exquisitely made.

Francis Bacon saw that science could and should be a social activity, to which all kinds of contributions could be made according to individual abilities and personal interests. He emphasized methods of enquiry and discovery, which enhance individual abilities and allow individuals to co-operate in the great venture of discovery and invention. He stressed the importance of useful inventions, which derive from questioning and research, to improve men's lives. It could well be claimed that he invented planned organized experiments and the use of discoveries for practical ends. Bacon's *Novum Organum* of 1620 set up rules for scientific method. It inspired the foundation of the Royal Society in 1660; but nothing came of his *New Atlantis* dream though then, as now, the future depends on children coming to appreciate how science works and what it does and fails to do.

The principal modern pioneer of hands-on is Frank Oppenheimer, (1912–85) (Fig. 24.1) who founded the Exploratorium in San Francisco in 1969. He was inspired by visiting the essentially hands-on Children's Gallery of the London Science Museum dating from the 1930s. Oppenheimer wrote (1976):

I suspect that everybody – not just you and I – genuinely wants to share and feel at home with the cumulative and increasingly coherent awareness of nature that is the traditional harvest of scientists and artists.

Figure 24.1 Frank Oppenheimer, founder of the San Francisco Exploratorium
(Photo: P. Clements 1970)

He said of his exhibits in the Exploratorium (Murphy 1985):

> We do not want people to leave with the implied feeling: 'Isn't somebody else clever.' Our exhibits are honest and simple so that no one feels he or she must be on guard against being fooled or misled.

Yet he loved visual and other illusions. He saw them as a way to introduce the observer – us – into science's account of the universe. Three and a half centuries earlier, Francis Bacon had included in his House of Salomon – in which there were to be Houses of Mathematics, Engines, Instruments for measuring and all the science and technology of the time:

> We have also Houses of Deceits of the Senses; where we represent all manner of juggling, false apparitions, impostures, and illusions; and their fallacies. And surely you will easily believe that we have so many things truly natural which induce imagination, could in a world of particulars deceive the senses, if we could disguise those things and labour to make them seem more miraculous.

Present-day hands-on, interactive science centres are delightful: full of the fun of surprises, of discovering new phenomena, and seeing how things work. This kind of experience is stimulating for adults and may switch on children's creativity. Surely this is all to the good for the individual and society. Traditionally, education has perhaps been more geared to training for needed skills and providing secure employment than preparing for unpredictable dangers of creative novelty. This policy used to be safe and probably necessary but now, because of the explosive growth of science and technology, the world and its possibilities and dangers are changing so fast that basic and updateable understanding is needed for planning of all kinds, and for individuals to cope with their unpredictable futures.

The recent popularity of exploratory science centres shows that a significant proportion of the public of all ages find direct experience of science entertaining and interesting (Pizzey 1987). Examples include: the pioneering major Exploratorium in San Francisco, the well-endowed Toronto Science Centre, the almost over-the-top Parc La Villette in Paris. Britain is on a smaller scale: the first independent centre is the Exploratory in Bristol. The first specially designed museum gallery is Launch Pad, in the London Science Museum, which had its prescient though largely unrecognized Children's Gallery in the 1930s. Now there is Techniquest in Cardiff and a dozen other Centres and Galleries in cities throughout Britain including Birmingham, Manchester and Liverpool. But, it has to be said, lack of funding is a very serious problem from which they all suffer. There are more-or-less hands-on centres generously endowed by their governments in most European countries. Science centres are to be found in various forms around the world: in America, Australia, India, Singapore and many more countries, though not yet in Russia. So it is a widespread, rapidly growing movement, co-ordinated in America by ASTC (Association of Science and Technology Centres) and more recently in Europe by ECSITE (Consortium of Science, Industry and Technology Exhibitions) which co-ordinates European countries and should help to share ideas and resources.

The scientific establishment of all countries, it must be admitted, has been slow in promoting public understanding of science. But American science is now taking it seriously and, in the mid-1980s in Britain, the Royal Society with the Royal Institution and the British Association for the Advancement of Science formed a committee, COPUS, chaired by Sir George Porter (now Lord Porter OM) for promoting public understanding of science in many ways including encouraging the setting up of hands-on science centres.

But do such science centres really convey science? Bluntly, are they with their necessarily quick and easy demonstrations much more than funfairs? Certainly there are similarities. But even when there is similar apparatus – such as almost zero-friction pucks (i.e. like those used in ice hockey) on an air table for a funfair game and exactly the same in a science centre to demonstrate Newton's First Law of Motion – they are handled very differently and apparently are seen very differently. Context and atmosphere evidently are important for how things are seen and appreciated. It is possible though, as suggested by Michael Shortland (1987), that we have been too free with phrases such as 'Science is fun', for much of science is tedious, difficult – sometimes dangerous! This charge of triviality is important. It needs to be met with evidence of what people do get from hands-on experiments, to learn how to make them more effective.

These are challenges to understand and try to overcome. From its beginning, an essential feature of Frank Oppenheimer's Exploratorium has been and is its team of friendly Explainers, who initially were imaginatively trained by Sheila Grinell. An atmosphere of social interaction was a key element for its success which later centres do well to follow, as we have done in the Bristol Exploratory with its vitally important team of Pilots. But by avoiding the 'stuffiness' of many traditional institutions of learning, we risk a danger of hands-on science failing to convey the essential spirit of enquiry and scholarship, and so be misleading as 'science' centres. The situation is very different for schools and universities which have far more time available for reading and writing and discussion, with students working for qualifications. There are also financial considerations which can and do distort the aims of science centres. Many lack government support and depend on sponsors who have to look for commercial possibilities. How can the financial risk be taken of introducing depth and difficulty to a paying public? However, it may well be that these would not necessarily be a turn-off: on the contrary, they could increase science centres' appeal and help to make them financially viable. But we must learn how to present questions and ideas, puzzles and knowledge, without assuming a formal background of science, without being intimidating or boring to those not committed to science.

It is hard to believe that serious learning can't be fun. One has only to watch kittens learning skills of survival by playing to see fun-learning in action, and there are experiments conducted with children which show that games aid their learning (Hodgkin 1985). There is strong evidence that babies learn to see by their active hands-on – and of course mouth-on – experience. (This has come especially from the germinal work of Jean Piaget, such as Piaget 1929, 1952, 1955.) The power of hands-on experience as the basis of visual perception is perhaps most dramatically borne out by some investigations into rare cases of adults born blind at birth, or from infancy, who received successful eye operations when adult (Gregory and Wallace 1963; Valvo 1971). For Gregory and Wallace's patient, S.B., upon first being shown an object which for years he had wished he could see and use – a lathe – he was at first frustrated, for although it was there in front of him he could not see it – it was meaningless. Then he shut his eyes, ran his hands over it, stood back and said 'Now I've felt it, I can see'. Then he described the lathe as he saw it for the first time. It turned out that his ability to see depended on his earlier knowledge from touch experience. Touch could switch on his sight. (See 'At first sight', p. 53.)

We can see the importance of hands-on experience for discovery and learning throughout the history of science. There is evidence that crafts and technology, and the making of toys and models, have always been important for suggesting questions and providing means for answering problems of science and philosophy. Recently it has become clear that there was an infrastructure of surprisingly sophisticated technology behind Greek science and philosophy. This is shown dramatically with the find, in 1900 AD, in an ancient ship sunk off the small Greek island of Kythera, a lump of bronze dated c. 85 BC with unusual inscriptions, and a spoked wheel evident on one face. The distinguished historian of science, the late Derek de Solla Price, arranged for the bronze lumps to be X-rayed, which revealed inside an elaborate geared mechanism (Price 1975). He showed that it was designed to represent and predict with great accuracy astronomical cycles, especially those of the sun and moon. There are several classical references to such Greek mechanisms of several hundred years earlier being on public display in temples and probably in the still-existing 4th century BC Tower of the Winds in Athens. For their design and construction there must have been a sophisticated technology and applied mathematics with high mechanical skills, at the time of Plato and Aristotle. This means that, for example, Ptolomy's system of epicycles for explaining planetary movements could have been and almost certainly was built with working models being used as thinking tools for explaining the science of the day. That these Greek references are so little known does no credit to classicists – who presumably failed to see their significance through lack of understanding of technology! As shown by the work of Joseph Needham, a scientist with an appreciation of technology, essentially the same is true of the very different history of China (Needham 1970). It seems that the development of organized science has always required interactive experience with working devices and tools and models in order to appreciate phenomena and discover and invent conceptual principles. We see this also in the work of many of the greatest individual scientists: Galileo, Newton, Faraday, Herschel, Watson and Crick, and in that of many more who also made models and toys for playing creatively with their deepest thoughts.

Exploratory playing seems to be a basic need for the development of perception and intelligence. There are many studies on animals showing the importance of active exploration for learning to see, such as the ingenious experiment of Richard Held and Alan Hein (1963) with a pair of kittens. They were put in baskets which were free to move but were linked together so that one of the kittens was free to move as he wished, but the other could only follow in his linked basket and so had similar visual inputs but lacked voluntary control of where he moved. It was found that the 'active' kitten learned normally, but the linked, 'passive' kitten did not learn to see. Though his eyes were open, he remained effectively blind.

Young children are extremely active, picking things up and breaking them and generally trying things out, including of course trying their parents' patience. It seems that young children do not start with a blank sheet, but rather they have from very early on their own explanations, which are remarkably Aristotelian, and may be very hard to shift (Driver, Guesne and Tiberghien 1985; Matthews 1980). Presumably, children's 'naive theories of science', as they are sometimes called, derive from everyday, hands-on experience from infancy. The conclusion is inescapable that although hands-on experience is in many ways effective – essential indeed for learning to see, and in some ways to understand – it cannot be sufficient for

212

arriving at scientific understanding. Clearly, more is needed, for infants and young children are intensely active, hands-on. More is needed, if only because perceptions are ambiguous, and must be interpreted with knowledge or assumptions for them to have clear meaning. Our 'naive' assumptions may mislead, even to the extent of producing errors of primary perception. Hopefully, some of these are corrected by encountering at first-hand surprises in hands-on Exploratories. But it would be naive of us to think that explanations are not important.

There are some moral doubts to consider if indeed we can change children's initial naive theories and increase their creative powers. Is it possible that children *need* to live for several years with an Aristotelian view of things? Is there some kind of innate structuring and inborn development that we may upset, with risk of harm? Is it perhaps best to let children learn facts isolated from interpretation, so they can build up their own cognitive structures, in their own ways, appropriate to their generation? There is certainly a danger of teachers imposing unhelpful ways of seeing and thinking. The alternative is to promote originality in children and expect them to develop in unpredictable ways. But if we are able to stimulate originality, how do we know that children will be better off than when given at least a basis of accepted knowledge and beliefs? If we stimulate originality with the aim of improving the future, do we have a reasonable right to set up goals for the future?

If we cannot predict effects of science centres on children and adults, how can aims be claimed? Surely we should try to assess the effects of hands-on experience through controlled experiments, comparing this kind of experience with other ways of presenting phenomena and ideas. But for such educational research on how understanding may be gained informally, how can we *measure understanding*? The traditional kinds of examinations may be inadequate for such informal though possibly extremely useful learning. We will come to this later, for it turns out that how to assess such understanding is intimately bound up with the hands-on situation. How can we present difficult concepts in what must, to attract the public and be financially viable, be an entertaining toyland of science? It is a toyland, for the typical experiments of 'real' science are long and tedious and so are switch-offs for the public. We have to be selective, and this creates the danger of distortion. The greatest danger is discouraging visitors – potential Explorers of all ages – by appearing intimidating; the habits of mind needed for entering the magic circle of science are not those held by most people – perhaps because interactive science centres have not been previously available to them! It is well known that mathematical formulations are generally daunting, because incomprehensible. Indeed, for someone to look for logical structures in ordinary discussions can be seen as rudely challenging; evidently the problem goes far beyond mathematics and is very general.

Research is needed on how to introduce science-thinking into Science Centres. In fact, it is remarkable how little science there is in traditional science museums! In most it is impossible to find demonstrations of the essential principles of science or of science thinking, such as the distinction (which amazingly appears not to be taught in our schools, though these omissions may be made good in the new National Curriculum) between *deduction* and *induction*; or of probability, or of testing hypotheses. Where in museums does one find concepts of force, energy, relativity, quantum physics, or computing? There are specialist motor museums that do not show how a petrol engine works; computer museums with not a clue as to how mechanisms can represent and handle numbers; natural history museums with little or no physiology, anatomy, biochemistry, genetics or evolution. Stuffed animals without explanations of how they live, or lived, have little more than visual appeal. There are a few notable exceptions, even though they are improving, this is still the general rule for most museums. This conceptual vacuum may be a hangover from museums' concern with collections, which indeed are extremely valuable, when they can be understood. This collections preoccupation should not apply to science centres based on specially built demonstrations and experiments. Conventional museums should also gain greatly from hands-on experience, for without it visitors are blind to the often superb collections: fossils revealing origins of species; instruments revealing how technology serves and inspires basic discoveries; historical developments showing dramas of individual and socially important inventions; follies of wasted effort; static and working models representing philosophical ideas.

What kinds of phenomena and experiments should be chosen to introduce hands-on science is clearly important, though at present the selection is largely intuitive. As both Bacon and Oppenheimer saw, it is first of all important to appreciate *ourselves* as intelligent observers – so phenomena of odd and even odder perceptions are peculiarly appropriate. Frank Oppenheimer (1983) said:

> The Exploratorium introduces people to science by examining how they see, hear and feel. Perception is the basis for what each of us finds out about the world and how we interpret it – whether we do so with our eyes, or develop tools, such as microscopes or accelerators, art, poetry or literature to help us.

Yet the human observer is almost ignored in the natural sciences. We are sacrificed for 'objectivity', though without us there would be no science! How we perceive and learn and discover is hardly considered in science, or in schools. No doubt this is because for the last three or four hundred years, following the immense success of mathematical physics and the use of instruments, the role of the observer's judgement has been reduced in importance. This has made individuals almost interchangeable, so making science objective and impersonal, with the additional unfortunate side-effect of making it also appear cold and intimidating.

We find that among the most immediately accessible and intriguing phenomena are those of perception. Paradoxically perhaps, the most effective way to see our own roles and limitations as observers and understanders is through illusions of vision and the other senses, and errors of prediction and thought. However curious this may be, illusions reveal essential links of perception by which we appreciate ourselves and our relation to the world. Apart from their own intriguing interest they serve to warn us that we must check our perceptions and question even what seems most clearly true. As Frank Oppenheimer found (and I helped him in this at the start of the Exploratorium) these 'subjective' though often explainable phenomena help the visitor to be aware of what it is to observe and understand, through failing to observe or understand correctly. Then pendulums, levers, locks and keys, spinning water, clocks, frictionless pucks floating on air, elliptical billiard tables, pointer readings – almost *anything* can take on significance. But to see these as meaningful phenomena of science, considerable help may be needed. It takes the genius of a Faraday to read new phenomena unaided.

Even without knowledge of the ways things work, it is wonderful to experience the surprising forces of gyroscopes, magnets, Bernouli air-flow, or patterns of spectral lines in glowing gases, to discover the same patterns in light from the stars – universal fingerprints of chemistry linking the universe. But to go on, to appreciate the red shift and how this tells us the universe is expanding, and that from these displaced patterns of light we can see billions of years back in time, it is essential to understand some abstract principles such as the Doppler shift. This effect also applies to sound and is commonly experienced though seldom understood. So, evidently, familiar experiences such as approaching sounds rising in pitch and falling as they recede are very often not sufficient in themselves for conveying understanding. In other words, we do not normally understand much of what we experience, so why should hands-on experience help? There is something about the context of a hands-on science centre that is important for seeing beneath the surface. But explanations are also needed. These may be provided by the helpful Explainers, or Pilots, but of course their own knowledge may be quite limited. Indeed, Pilots with a physics background may not have a feel for biology, and vice versa, and rather few scientists are good at providing short, clear explanations on demand and matched to the listener's interests and needs in the time he or she will spare. Also, Explaining, or Piloting, is very tiring. So additional sources of information are needed, though it is not clear how these should be provided or what kinds of explanations are appropriate. Can we journey into explanations and abstract concepts *hands-on*?

HANDLING EXPLANATIONS

Explanations are needed so that we may draw analogies from appearances for relating what is experienced to what it may mean, in terms of more or less general principles. Observed correlations can suggest that events are causally related – but not which way round the cause works. Thus, does increasing interest produce more learning, or does improved learning increase interest in what is being taught? Only a theory can indicate directions or arrows of causation. 'Does day cause night – or night cause day?' With understanding of the solar system, we can see that this question is inappropriately put as neither is true, for both day and night come from the earth spinning in space beside the sun. This explanatory model provides the answer, and shows that observed phenomena and correlations are not adequate for understanding. We need explanations to be creatively intelligent. And we need to be creatively intelligent to discover explanations. Hands-on experience can help but cannot be sufficient. Evidently, explanations from teachers and books (and now perhaps from computers) are very important.

What kinds of explanations are most interesting and useful? Following initial *hands-on* experience, there are surely two very different kinds of explanations and understanding. There are intuitively held 'mental models' of how things work, and there are explicitly formulated accounts which may be mathematical. Intuitive mental models, we may call *hand-waving* explanations. Explicitly formulated, especially mathematical accounts I shall call (if again somewhat rudely) *handle-turning*. This refers to solving problems by following rules of mathematics, which can be surprisingly easily mechanised (dating from Pascal's wheeled calculator of 1642) and expressed for all to see as equations and algorithms. On this view, mathematicians need hand-waving intuitions to select algorithms; but once selected the handle-turning is automatic and is often better carried out by quite a simple machine.

So, we arrive at a handy terminology:

HANDS-ON	*Exploration*
HAND-WAVING	*Explanation*
HANDLE-TURNING	*Computation*

For perceptual experience to be meaningful it has to be interpreted, generally by hand-waving intuitive accounts. Equations in mathematics also have to be interpreted to have meaning, again, generally from hand-waving intuitions. These intuitive accounts or theories very often become drastically modified with advances of science. But they may then disappear from common view, as they depart from common sense. This is one reason, surely, why science teaching is so difficult. Traditional science teaching concentrates on what I am calling handle-turning. Hands-on practical classes are also traditionally important for many sciences including medicine; but the middle category – hand-waving, intuitive explanations – are traditionally disparaged in the teaching and science communities. I suggest this is a major mistake.

For many 'hard' scientists all that matters are handle-turning mathematical formulations but at least for the rest of us, equations get their meaning (when they have meaning for us) from actual situations or from our hand-waving intuitions. How far this is true for mathematicians is an interesting question; but at least for some mathematicians (Penrose 1989) intuitive understanding is vital. It may be changed and hopefully corrected by experience and experiment – or by logic and mathematics. But what we live with, and what we use for almost all decisions and judgements, are intuitively held, very possibly naive theories that may be hard to express to ourselves or convey to anyone else. We discover them by trying them out. We discover they are incorrect when they lead to false predictions. They are our 'inner life' – which is challenged by science.

So hands-on science centres are challenging. They must challenge and change beliefs to be interesting or effective.

We might say that hand-waving intuitions, when made explicit, are essentially philosophy. We can, however, express a great deal of science in this kind of way, without using handle-turning mathematics. For an example, let's consider the gyroscope's curious tendency to 'precess' at right angles, to a tilt or turn of the spinning wheel. This is a favourite in hands-on science centres – but is seldom if ever explained or understood! It may be described by equations, but do they give us understanding of what is going on? Playing hands-on with a gyroscope (such as a bicycle wheel, held by its axle) one discovers a curious law. When the spinning wheel is (like going round a corner on a bicycle) *turned* – it *tilts*. And when it is *tilted* – it *turns*. Which way it turns or tilts depends on which way round the wheel is spinning. Why? Consider the following hand-waving account –

directly from Newton's First Law of Motion: Moving bodies resist imposed changes of direction or velocity.

Imagine – or actually hold by its axle – a spinning bicycle wheel vertically in front of you, with the top rim moving away. Imagine the wheel (especially its rim) as made up of small point-masses. (These may be atoms or much larger.) Now, consider the *changes of direction* of these horizontally moving point-masses, at the top of the wheel as it is *turned*, say, to the right. The point-masses are forced to change direction, to the right. This change they *resist*, by Newton's First Law (inertia). So the point-masses at the top of the wheel produce an effective force to the left (because they resist being forced to turn right) which pushes the top of the wheel left; so the wheel precesses to tilt to the left.

The bottom point-masses are also forced to change direction. They exert a force at the bottom of the wheel to the right. Why? Because they are moving in the opposite direction, towards you.

What of the vertically moving point-masses at the front and back of the wheel? They are shifted sideways as the wheel is turned – but they *do not change direction*. So they hardly resist the turn of the wheel to the right. So the action is in the top and bottom point-masses. The front and back point-masses are merely shifted sideways, as though the wheel were not spinning. Their direction of motion is not changed, so they do not contribute to the precession making the wheel tilt when it is turned.

But if you tilt the wheel, then the top and bottom point-masses are merely shifted – without their direction being changed – so the action is now in the vertically moving front and back point-masses – making the wheel precess by *turning* to the left.

If the wheel is set to spin the other way round (top towards you) the forces are reversed, so now a turn produces the opposite tilt, and a tilt produces the opposite turn.

This is much easier to understand by trying it out with an actual wheel. Once one 'sees' the point one understands the essential principle of gyroscopes. Then one can predict from one's mental model which way it will precess, for any turn or tilt, with either direction of spin – with no mathematics. Having seen it in this 'hand-waving' way, the mathematics comes to take on meaning.

It may have been hard to follow these words. Hand-waving understanding is really pre-verbal. This may be conveyed better with pictures – better still with actual objects and working models. This is why we need hands-on science centres!

SIGNS OF UNDERSTANDING

There are well-established ways of assessing knowledge in schools – especially by answering questions, as in exams. There are also open-ended essays. The former are more easily marked, the latter are more revealing but require more time-consuming assessment, which is expensive.

If we are interested in hand-waving, rather different methods may be needed to measure this understanding. It is best seen in a hands-on environment, with signs of understanding such as these:

Making predictions A powerful technique is to set up situations for *predicting* – where correct prediction requires, and so demonstrates, understanding of what is going on. False predictions can be clear evidence of inappropriate mental models of the situation. A classical example is Aristotle's rejection of the theory that the stars appear to move across the sky because the earth spins round. He jumped up – and landed in the same place – so how could the earth have been spinning under him?! What Aristotle lacked was the concept of inertia. He could not 'see' that he continued moving with the earth when he left it. This example shows how important concepts are – and how soon we depart from common sense in science.

It may be noted that although prediction-surprises are exciting for the curious, and are powerful signals and spurs to questioning for deeper understanding, for some people they are unsettling – as appears right through the history of science. This presents problems for planning science centres, for what appeals to scientists as being intellectually stimulating (somewhat like the more physically frightening rides at Alton Towers) may be seen as threatening the common sense which is accepted, and protected as safe, by sponsors. There is a general fear and rejection of conceptual surprise – yet surprise is what exploration and explanation are all about.

A favourite hands-on example of surprise is what happens when air is blown between a pair of freely suspended beach balls. Practically everyone expects them to fly apart – but they are drawn together, by the flow of air between them. This failed prediction tells the Explorer (as well as the investigator of hands-on learning) their appreciation of the situation. The failed prediction is a powerful and useful internal signal that they *do not understand*. They may accept this as a signal to explore further. So from failed predictions they may learn to appreciate their assumptions (which are seldom conscious: a useful product of philosophy is to make us aware of assumptions) so they may correct their 'mental model' of the situation. As such surprises show limits and failures of understanding, they are pointers to discovery, both for individuals and for science itself. For scientists, failed predictions may suggest the next step for advancing human knowledge. For the child, or the aware but not especially knowledgeable adult, failed predictions can signal the need for further experiment to see the phenomenon in a fresh way. But questioning and restructuring require effort, which is not to everyone's taste. If parents and schools taught science effectively from the very beginning of children's development, perhaps they would not need to back-track and restructure later on; but this is hardly realistic. It is, however, an intriguing thought that just possibly young children would take to the paradoxes of relativity theory and quantum mechanics as ducks to water, if they were presented early and as a matter of course. But at present we do not know how to get over these concepts hands-on – which may be why they are so difficult for all of us. And would there be some danger in cutting short the usual Aristotelian phase of development in children – though few adults ever succeed in escaping from it?

Seeing analogies An important test of understanding, at a more-or-less deep level, is the ability to see analogies. If one understands, for example, *resonance* then similarities and deep identities are seen between on-the-surface different-appearing things and phenomena such as: musical instruments, the divisions of Saturn's rings, tuned radio circuits, the positions of spectrum lines given by resonances within atoms. It is clearly important to have many examples of different-appearing things and phenomena to practise and test for seeing analogies. We may look for an increased ability to see deep analogies to assess effects of hands-on experience; or indeed to assess any science teaching.

Inventing and filling gaps We may look for ability to fill in gaps, and invent novel solutions – where gap filling or inventing requires more-or-less deep understanding. An example would be filling in or inventing hidden parts of mechanisms. One can only see into Black Boxes by understanding them!

Seeing conceptual jokes With an increasing spread of understanding of science and technology we may look for more widely shared humour – which will surely enliven literature and life. Ability to see and to make jokes is clear evidence of relevant understanding. This is the basis of 'in-group' jokes. At present science is too in-group and exclusive. Science centres should share science – and its jokes; they should be run with a sense of humour.

Seeing small effects Appreciating the significance of small effects or phenomena shows they are appreciated as *conceptually* important though they are not *perceptually* dramatic. (Thus the photoelectric effect heralded quantum mechanics, and the precession of the perihelion of the planet Mercury was a key to relativity. Though conceptually dynamite these effects are physically almost insignificantly tiny. There are many such examples.)

Seeing nothing Perhaps the most dramatic evidence of understanding is seeing significance in *nothing*. This is the point of experimental controls. We should widen the notion of experiencing phenomena – for in science a great deal comes from significant small effects and especially from nothing happening. But nothing can only be seen when the situation is understood.

Nothing happening can be extremely important in any experimental science. Most experiments are controls to establish where the action is, or isn't, by finding nothing. The Michelson-Morley experiment, challenging the existence of the ether, is the most celebrated non-effect. But any nulling test where the unknown cancels the known (such as weighing something with a balance) depends on nothing happening.

Unlike King Lear's admonition to Cordelia, much may come from nothing in science – but nothing does not make a 'Gee-whiz' science centre demonstration. Science centres will have grown up when their Explorers stare, in entranced wonder, at nothing.

BEYOND HANDS-ON EXPLORATORIES – TO EXPLANATORIES?

We have admitted there is a danger of interactive science centres trivializing science. Should we, indeed, speak of a *science* centre which lacks the rigour of science? Should we move beyond Exploratory, hands-on activity to more thoughtful explanation – to develop what we might call Explanatories?

Here we may return to conventional science museums. Looking at the traditional museums of science we find remarkably little science. There are very few explanations or clear examples of methods. It is hard to find Kepler's or Newton's Laws; how spectral lines may be related to atomic structure; concepts of quantum physics or relativity. This general lack extends to technology. It is quite hard to find clear explanations of how motors, radios, freezers or computers work – yet the principles of technology are in many ways exciting, with their conceptual and human interest. For a technical example: it is most imaginative to use a microscope *backwards* – to shrink design drawings into thousands of tiny integrated circuits (with components as small

221

as nerve cells of the brain), even to make molecular motors and geared mechanisms. And we can actually see electron charges moving through the logic gates of microchips (with a beam-switched scanning electron microscope strobing repeated signals to slow things down to match speeds that we can see). This technology takes us right inside Alice's wonderland, while CCDs (charge coupled devices) are so sensitive they take us to the edge of the universe. The eyes and hands of technology and its computer-brains extend us way beyond our biological origins – provided we can take off from common sense to live conceptually with our new senses.

Can museums help? Do so few museums attempt explanations merely because explaining is not their traditional aim? Or have they found it impossible to present ideas in a museum context? Are the concepts and principles underlying appearances just too hard to present, without the kind of background knowledge instilled over years in science courses in schools and universities? This is an important question.

Only experiment can establish whether hands-on science centres can become conceptual, and whether conventional science museums can present abstract concepts – for helping us to see the wonders they display to, at present, blind eyes.

Possibly existing schools and universities *are* the Explanatories we need. But in schools and universities explanations are built up gradually, on a carefully planned, slowly growing basis of knowledge. Can we speed this up? Can we introduce the often difficult concepts of physics, chemistry, life, time, symbols, intelligence, chaos or whatever in minutes rather than years? This is the challenge. Possibly but few people will wish to step from the familiar assumptions of everyday life into non-intuitive, sometimes bizarre concepts of the sciences. But many people, of all ages, do find the world of science incredibly exciting, even to finding it gives new meaning to their lives.

So, how can we explore abstract concepts hands-on? Some can be experienced quite directly, by removing contaminating effects. Indeed, this is how many experiments have led to discoveries in laboratories. A good example for a science centre (or museum) is the use of air tracks and air tables to remove contaminating friction; for revealing Newton's Laws of Motion as they apply in frictionless space. Such very direct demonstrations form excellent bridges between Exploratories and potential Explanatories and should be in both. Less direct, but vital for moving from particular instances to principles, is the provision of a wide variety of examples. Technology plays many games with a few pieces – the same principles coming up time and again in different forms in which they are hidden. It is the seeing of the common features underlying many on-the-surface different phenomena which vitalises invention and creates understanding.

Unfamiliar ways of thinking are the barrier, for they can be intimidating. Here perhaps familiar technology can help to introduce unfamiliar and strange ideas of science. It is remarkable how little the common devices of everyday technology are noticed or observed. It is a small step to ask how radios, freezers, microwave ovens, water taps, locks, TV, thermostats, CD discs, soap, sponges, calculators – actually work. Yet such devices of technology, and many more, are wonderfully successful experiments and demonstrations of principles often on the edge of scientific understanding. For example, the solid-state devices found in the electronic machines of any western home rely on principles of quantum physics, that have only been dreamed of by physicists for the last few years, and are still largely mysterious even to them. By taking such familiar examples and presenting them as the amazing experiments they are, we can see principles of science captured by human intelligence, combined in unique ways to serve our needs. Rather than being inhuman, technology has plucked solutions to our problems from nature and presented us with dreams (with occasionally nightmares) come true. It is nice to know that we now own wonders far beyond the ancient claimed powers of magic. But for most of us, the wonders are held secret in opaque Black Boxes that we may own yet not be able to see inside. It would be an interesting experiment to reveal these hidden principles of technology – and so of science – in an Explanatory.

New computer technologies of data search could be very useful. The coming interactive, multi-media, computer-video disk technology could provide explanations and provide journeys with individual adventures through facts and ideas. But, apart from the expense, there are problems to be solved. It is important to be able to approach the same facts or ideas from different starting points, when they then appear in a different light. In a museum each artefact may be seen in various ways, and returned to many times as new questions are asked. Similarly, the same pictures and descriptions will no doubt appear for many computer-based 'journeys'. But how are they selected? Random access precludes helpful structure, and pre-set structures precludes free choice. Some kind of compromise is needed, but difficult to attain for a wide range of questions and Explorers.

In any such search simulation there is the problem that the pictures and text with the information they give have already been selected by their creators. For the linear presentation of a book, selection according to context is an essential part of the art of the author's presentation and message; but here the context should change depending on the chosen 'journey'. This may be a new problem for artists and writers. It is, however, typical of what happens for all of us when we are selecting from our memories and thoughts. For our memories were made years ago, in quite different contexts from the present situations in which we use them to illuminate and resolve. So the problems of providing data and ideas for many individuals to search and explore are extensions from our uses of our own memories. Learning how to switch minds on with Explanatory technologies should illuminate how minds work.

TURNING THE HANDLE OF MATHEMATICS

Finally, should interactive science centres introduce what is for most people difficult, handle-turning mathematics? Perhaps so many people find the simplest mathematics intimidating because they have not linked equations with phenomena. It may be that physical interpretations have to be abandoned by pure mathematicians, to allow them to float away from our shores, to adventures on their own sea of symbols way beyond most of our horizons. Either possibility has implications for a philosophy of hands-on learning. Here again computers can come to the rescue. They remove so much of the sweat and tears of handle-turning, and their graphics reveal to the eye abstract principles and functions with great beauty. This is especially so of the new computer science-art of fractals (Mandelbrot 1982; Peitgen and Richter 1986). (See Figs. 16.1 and 16.2, p. 132.)

Computers can be linked to actual experiments, to show mathematical functions and underlying principles operating beneath appearances in real time. Very promising is the interactive power of computers. This is the basis of Seymour Papert's work (Papert 1980) on Logo, in which the computer controls a mechanical tortoise which interfaces the object world with the symbolic world of mathematics. It has even been suggested, by Philip Davis and Reuben Hersh in *The Mathematical Experience* (1980), that computer interaction allows dimensions to be visualized beyond the three of space and one of time that we normally experience. A computer-generated rotatable hypercube looks meaningless but upon taking up the controls:

> I tried turning the hypercube around, moving it away, bringing it close, turning it around another way. Suddenly I could *feel* it! The hypercube had leapt into palpable reality, as I learned how to manipulate it, feeling in my fingertips the power to change what I saw and change it back again. The active control at the computer

console created a union of kinesthetic and visual thinking which brought the hypercube up to the level of intuitive understanding.

This truly is turning minds on, hands-on.

CONCLUSION

For some people, making decisions by methods of science is alien and even dehumanizing. Perhaps they see scientific method, which objectifies judgements, as conferring a kind of artificial intelligence on human beings, even to turning us into machines. Although it may be admitted that science and technology transcend political and racial boundaries and confer many undoubted benefits, evidently this is not how very many people want to see the world. Is this because science has been inadequately presented? Or is it perhaps because science is simply unable to answer questions that people see as over-ridingly important? Is scientific method too slow to provide answers in real-time for planning decisions? This may all be true; but most people lack the understanding for a comfortable, intuitive feel for science and everyday technology. It may be that formal mathematics over-dominates much science education, intimidating many people and putting them off science. But this might be solved with better ways of presenting mathematics and making fuller use of computers for the handle-turning.

Although hand-waving explanations have low standing in the academic and teaching communities, they are surely important for giving context to facts, for remembering and structuring knowledge for thinking. Although vital for much of science, some great scientists, including Michael Faraday and Charles Darwin, never used handle-turning mathematics but succeeded wonderfully with intuitive, hand-waving explanations, suggested and tested with hands-on evidence. Einstein had an extraordinarily rich intuitive imagination. He would express in mathematics frankly hand-waving intuitive mental models (Miller 1984), tested later with astronomical observations and laboratory experiments.

Discovering how to help children and adults explore phenomena and principles will keep Exploratories and, we may hope, Explanatories re-inventing themselves as viable mutations in futures that they help to create: to introduce science by shaking hands with the universe.

REFERENCES

Bacon, Francis (1620) *Novum Organum*. F.H. Anderson (1960) (ed.). (New York: Macmillan/Library of Liberal Arts).

Bacon, Francis (1627) *New Atlantis* Oxford: Oxford University Press (1915).

Churchland, Paul M. (1989) *A Neurocomputational Perspective: The Nature of Mind and the Structure of Science.* (Boston, Mass: Massachusetts Institute of Technology Press).

Davis, Philip J. and Hersh, Reuben (1980) *The Mathematical Experience.* (Boston, Mass: Houghton Mifflin).

Driver, Rosalind, Guesne, Edith and Tiberghien, André (1985) *Children's Ideas in Science.* (Oxford: Oxford University Press).

Gregory, Richard L. (1970) *The Intelligent Eye.* (London: Weidenfeld).

Gregory, Richard L. (1983) 'The Bristol Exploratory – A Feeling for Science', *New Scientist*, 17 November, 484-9.

Gregory, Richard L. (1986) (with contributions by James Dalgety and Francis Evans) *Hands-On Science: An Introduction to the Bristol Exploratory.* (London: Duckworth).

Gregory, Richard L. (1988) 'First-Hand Science: The Exploratory in Bristol', *Sci. publ. Affairs*, 3, 13-24. (London: The Royal Society).

Gregory, Richard L. and Wallace, Jean (1963) *Recovery from Early Blindness: A Case Study.* (Cambridge: Heffer). Reprinted in: Gregory, R.L. (1974) *Concepts and Mechanisms of Perception.* (London: Duckworth), pp. 65-129.

Held, Richard and Hein, Alan (1963) 'Movement-produced Stimulation in the Development of Visually Guided Behaviour', *J. Comp. and Phys. Psychol.*, 56.

Hodgkin, Robin A. (1985) *Playing and Exploring.* (New York: Methuen).

Mandelbrot, B.B. (1982) *The Fractal Geometry of Nature.* (San Francisco: W.H. Freeman).

Matthews, G.B. (1980) *Philosophy and the Young Child.* (Cambridge, Mass.: HUP).

Miller, Arthur J. (1986) *Imagery in Scientific Thought.* (Cambridge, Mass.: MIT Press).

Murphy, Pat (ed.) (1985) *The Exploratorium:* Special Issue. (San Francisco: The Exploratorium).

Needham, Joseph (1970) *Clerks and Craftsmen in China and the West: Lectures and Addresses on the History of Science and Technology* (Cambridge: Cambridge University Press).

Oppenheimer, Frank (1979) 'Everyone is You ... Or Me'. Reprinted in Murphy, P. (ed.) (1985) op. cit.

Papert, Seymour (1980) *Mindstorms: Children, Computers, and Powerful Ideas.* (New York: Basic Books).

Peitgen, H-O. and Richter, P.H. (1986) *The Beauty of Fractals: Images of Complex Dynamical Systems.* (Berlin: Springer-Verlag).

Penrose, Roger (1989) *The Emperor's New Mind.* (Oxford: Oxford University Press).

Piaget, Jean (1929) *The Child's Conception of the World.* (J. and A. Tomlinson trans.). (London: Basic Books).

Piaget, Jean (1952) *The Origins of Intelligence in Children.* (New York: Basic Books).

Piaget, Jean (1955) *The Child's Construction of Reality.* (Margaret Cook trans.) (London: Basic Books).

Pizzey, Stephen (1987) *Interactive Science and Technology Centres.* (London: Science Projects Publishing, 67 Eccles Road, London SW11).

Price, Derek de Solla (1975) *Gears From the Greeks: The Antikythera Mechanism.* (New York).

Rumelhart, D.E. and McClelland, J.L. (1986) (eds) *Parallel Distributed Processing: Explorations in the Microstructure of Cognition*. (Boston, Mass.: Massachusetts Institute of Technology Press).

Shortland, Michael (1987) 'No business like show business', *Nature*, 328, 213.

Valvo, Alberto (1971) *Sight Restoration Rehabilitation*. (New York: American Foundation for the Blind, 15 West St., New York).

25

MICHAEL FARADAY'S
PERCEPTION

Michael Farday was the greatest experimental scientist of the nine-teenth century. He was born just over two hundred years ago (22 September 1791), the son of a blacksmith. As a boy, with a fascination for science, Faraday learned to see and question by reading customers' books while he was apprenticed to a kind and generous bookbinder, Mr Riebau, in London. He also became interested in art and learned perspective drawing, later contributing to the new art-science of photography.

He attended Sir Humphry Davy's lectures on chemistry at the Royal Institution. His neat notes so impressed Davy that he took the unknown apprentice on as his assistant. He later became Davy's successor, as Professor of Chemistry and Director of the Royal Institution, where Faraday spent his incredibly creative working life. His laboratory with much of its original apparatus is still to be seen at the Royal Institution in Albermarle Street, London.

Faraday's achievements cover an astonishing range and number of electrical and chemical discoveries, including: magnetic rotation and the first electric current motor (1821), production of electricity by moving a magnet in a coil, and electric induction (1831); the relation of electricity to magnetism, and that all forms of electricity are essentially the same (1833); electrochemical decomposition (1834); Faraday's Cage, for isolating electricity (1837); rotating the plane of polarization of light by magnetism, and also by diagmagnetism (1846). There were many more, including field concepts that led away from aether theories towards Einstein's conception of space. His experimental work is meticulously recorded in his *Diary* (Martin 1932) which is a uniquely detailed account of the methods of discovery of an experimental genius. These are most interestingly discussed in *Faraday Rediscovered* (Gooding and James 1985).

Much less well known is Faraday's interest in perception and illusion. In the same year that he discovered electricity could be produced by moving a magnet in a coil of wire, he wrote (1831):

The pre-eminent importance of the eye as an organ of perception confers an interest upon the various modes in which it performs its office, the circumstances of which modify its indications, and the deceptions to which it is liable, far beyond what they otherwise would possess.

Farday goes on to describe an illusion of motion, which is a *physical* effect in that it is explained quite apart from the particular optics of the eye or neurology of the brain. This would now be called a stroboscope, used for making moving machinery apparently appear to be stationary. It is the basis of cinema and television and is further described below. Faraday wrote:

Mr Brunel, jun. described to me two small similar wheels at the Thames Tunnel: an endless rope, which passed over and was carried by one of them, immediately returned and passed over in the opposite direction over the other, and consequently moved the two wheels in opposite directions with great but equal velocities. When looked at from a particular position, they presented the appearance of a wheel with immovable radii.

A word on the scene of discovery may be in order. The Thames Tunnel (Clements 1970; Rolt 1970) was a triumph of Victorian engineering. Following an earlier brave attempt (which was abandoned) to cross the Thames beneath the water, the challenge was accepted by Sir Mark Brunel (1769–1849) and his son Isambard Kingdom Brunel (1806–59). The first successful underwater tunnel in the world, it took two remarkable men, father and son, nearly twenty years to complete. (See Fig. 25.1.) It was accomplished with a boring machine invented by Mark Brunel, based on a biological model – the tunnelling shipworm *Teredo navalis* – which, by boring through oak, sank more ships than gunfire could achieve! Sir Mark got the idea for his successful tunnelling shield, which is still used today, by watching this beetle boring its tunnels through oak. There were numerous serious mishaps before the Tunnel opened in 1843. It nearly killed Isambard Brunel when he was trapped and the foul water of the Thames poured in. His magnificent ship the *Great Eastern*, just one of his achievements, was the only ship in the world big enough to carry the entire transatlantic telegraph cable, weighing 21,000 tons, which she laid successfully in 1866. The Thames Tunnel is still in use, unrecognized by thousands using it daily, as it is incorporated in the London Underground.

It is strange that the greatest scientist and the greatest engineer of their day – Michael Faraday and Isambard Brunel –shared this curious observation of stilling seen motion, in the dramatic setting of the

Figure 25.1 The entrance to the Thames Tunnel built by Mark Brunel and Isambard Kingdom Brunel. It was begun in 1825, completed in 1842 and not used for transportation until 1865

workings of the world's first underwater tunnel, under the muddy waters of the Thames. The engineer Brunel saw it in his machinery, and Michael Faraday took it further, as a phenomenon worthy of experimental investigation. He had an apparatus built for seeing how illusory stationery, forwards or backwards motion could be produced, and why strange and beautiful phenomena (moving moiré patterns) occurred with rotating spokes placed in front of parallel lines or bars, that reminded him of his observations of magnetic fields with iron filings.

Faraday wrote (1831):

If the wheels revolve in opposite directions, then the spectral lines, originating at each axis as a pole, have another disposition, and instead of running the one set in to the other, are disposed generally like filings about similar magnetic poles, as if a repulsion existed; not that the curves or the causes are the same, but the appearances are similar.

It could be argued that the lined-up filings *produce* the lines in a continuous magnetic field, as they line up in chains. If so, these lines are misleading fictions, suggesting non-existing lines of force. Was Faraday misled here by appearances? Was his notion of magnetic lines of force based on an artefact? However this may be, the notion was useful as a thinking tool and for describing extremely puzzling phenomena.

He used the stroboscopic principle to observe structures of electric discharge sparks. At first, he waved his hand with open fingers; then, using a rotating mirror system developed by Charles Wheatstone to measure the speed of electricity, Faraday and Wheatstone used this illusion to make entirely new observations. Faraday saw that though stroboscopic effects are essentially physical, there is also a physiological component – persistence of vision. He observes its effects by creating illusory transparent surfaces, produced by waving a white rod in front of a dark background, or a dark rod upon a light background. Pairs of moving rods at different distances gave 'Two or more distinct impressions, or sets of impressions, being made upon the eye, but appearing to the perception as one.'

Most ingeniously, he looked through a spinning spoked wheel at a mirror – when the wheel appeared perfectly stationary for any speed of rotation:

> A very striking deception may be obtained in this way, by revolving a single cog-wheel between the fingers before the glass, when from twelve to fifteen feet from it. It is easy to revolve the wheel before the face so that the eyes may see the glass through or between the cogs, and then the reflected image appears as if it were the image of a cog-wheel having the same number of cogs, but perfectly still, ·and every cog distinct . . .

This is the basis of the first device giving illusory continuous motion from a sequence of pictures – and so the first cinema. The phenakistoscope (as it came to be called) was described a year later (1832) by J.A.F. Plateau of Brussels, and independently by S. Stampfer of Vienna and P.M. Roget (inventor of the *Thesaurus*.) This addition to Michael Faraday's experiments with the cogs and spokes gave a new dimension – perception of movement from stationary pictures. By stopping motion with an illusion, Faraday made a major contribution to the invention of the moving cinema.

Have illusions of stroboscopic appearances misled scientific observation? Yes – Faraday himself gives an example. An *animalcule* was described by several early microscopists as having two rotating wheels, one on each side of the head, having some fourteen teeth or spokes. These are never seen as wheels except when in motion. Faraday says:

So striking are the appearances of these animalcula, that men of much practice in microscopical observation are at this day convinced that they do possess wheels which actually revolve continuously in one direction.

He quotes the well-known microscopist Henry Baker (1698–1774) (*Baker on the Microscope*, Vol. II, p. 266, the first edition of which appeared in 1742):

As I call these parts wheels, I also term the motion of them rotation, because it has exactly the appearance of such. But some gentlemen imagined there may be a deception in the case, and that they do not really turn round, though indeed they seem to do so. The doubt of these gentleman arises from the difficulty they find in conceiving how or in what manner a wheel or any other form, as part of a living animal, can possibly turn upon an axis supposed to be another part of the same living animal, since the wheel must be a part absolutely distinct and separate from the axis whereon it turns; and then they say, 'How can this living wheel be nourished, as there cannot be any vessels of communication between that and the part it goes round upon, and which it must be separate and distinct from?' To this I can only answer, that place the object in whatever light of manner you please, when the wheels are fully protruded they never fail to show all the visible marks imaginable of a regular turning round . . . . Nay, in some positions you may, with your eye, follow the same cogs or teeth, whilst they seem to make a complete revolution; for the other parts of the insect [!] being very transparent, they are easily distinguished through it . . . as a man can move his arms or legs circularly as long and as often as he pleases by the articulation of the ball and socket, may there not possibly be some sort of articulation in this creature whereby its wheels or funnels are enabled to turn themselves around.

It is certain all appearances are so much on the side of the question, that I never met with any who did not, on seeing it, call it a *rotation*; though, from a difficulty concerning how it can be effected, some have imagined they might be deceived.

Drawings of wheel-animalculae, including Baker's Branchionus, are given by Jabez Hogg in his *The Microscope* (1854) on page 143. These are reproduced in Fig. 25.2 (with a magnification of ×200) with the original caption. Jabez Hogg writes, (p. 142):

THE ROTIFERA, ROTATING OR WHEEL-ANIMALCULAE

This higher grade of the Infusoria derives its name from the appearance presented by the motion of its circles of cilia on the

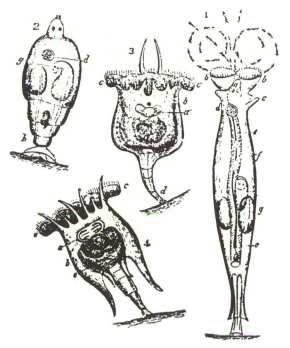

1. The common Wheel-Animalcule, with its cilia or rotators pointed. 2. The same in a contracted state and at rest; at *g* is seen the development of the eyes in the young. 3. The Pitcher-shaped Branchionus: *a* the jaws; *b* the shell; *c* the cilia, or rotators; *d* the tail. 4. Baker's Branchionus: *a* the jaws and teeth; *b* the shell; *c* the rotators; *e* the stomach.

Figure 25.2 The drawings of the wheel-animalculae at a magnification of ×200, reproduced here with the original caption from Jabez Hogg's *The Microscope* (1854)

superior part of its body, which resembles the turning round of a wheel, as they rapidly vibrate. Many have been the speculations as to the mechanism of this beautiful movement: some have considered it as a magnetic or electrical force; and as one passes out of sight and while the next appears, adding to the optical illusion, a philosopher of considerable note was led to look upon the whole as a deception of the sight, and affirmed they had no existence.

Jabez Hogg also accepts that these are rotating wheels.

Unlike these distinguished naturalists and microscopists, Michael Faraday understood the principle and was familiar with the appearances of stroboscopic illusions, so he could reject the observation. He was sure the animalculae do not have rotating wheels.

He was of course also sure that the appearances he described of rotating spokes over parallel lines are not really like iron filings in magnetic fields. Throughout his work, Faraday used active exploratory experiments to separate illusions of perception from phenomena of nature – then presented the phenomena in such a way that anyone could see the truth of the matter. This he did in his main lectures at the Royal Institution; thus his private thoughts and discoveries became public knowledge (Gooding and James 1985). The stroboscope experiments are unusual because these are phenomena of perception itself that he investigated, with, as it turned out, practical uses for physical discovery and the later invention of the cinema.

Faraday also described a different kind of illusion (Faraday 1826): 'a curious aerial phenomenon'. This he observed on 19 August 1826 on the Isle of Wight just above Puckaster Cove:

> The sky was clear, the sun had just set, when several enormous rays of light and shade were remarked towards the E., N.E, and S.E., all radiating in straight lines from a spot rather south of east, and just upon the horizon. . . . The phenomenon seemed inexplicable, but after a little consideration was referred (and as it appeared from after observations correctly) to an effect of aerial perspective. The rays which seemed to originate from a common centre on the east, were really only the intervals between long shadows caused by the occurrence of clouds far to the west, and were in fact passing to the place from which they *seemed* to originate. . . . All these phenomena, with their variations, were easily referable to their causes, and may be observed at almost any sun-set in fine weather . . . . It is with a view to guarding persons who may observe the same effect, against any mistake as to its origin, that the appearance, with its nature, has been thus particularly described.

So far we have not considered intentional delusion or delusions of the supernatural. Faraday considers both in experiments he conducted on table-turning (Faraday 1853). His methods were 'precisely of the same nature as those I should adopt in any other physical investigation'. He stressed that table-turners he investigated were honourable and truly believed

> the table draws their hands; that it moves first, and they have to follow it, that sometimes it even moves from under their hands.

He made plates of a great variety of materials, having very different physical and electrical properties and, placing them under the table-turner's hands, found that the table still moved. He then tried low-friction plates, and marked their position on the table, he found that the plates moved though the table did not. He found no evidence of

> any peculiar natural force ... nor anything which could be referred to any other than the mere mechanical pressure exerted inadvertently by the turner.

So he investigated these pressures from the hands and found that it is exceedingly difficult to press purely downward for any length of time without some sideways pressure. This may not be known to the turners, especially as their fingers become numb with the constant pressure. So he arranged for indicators of side-ways movement to be visible to the turners; then the movements no longer occurred. With a mechanical lever arrangement to see whether the table or the hand moved first, he found that hand movements always preceded table movements. He suggested that

> the apparatus I have described may be useful to many who really wish to know the truth of nature, and would prefer that truth to a mistaken conclusion; desired, perhaps only because it seems to be new or strange.

Although relatively simple, these studies of illusion illustrate how, with his subtle use of experimental methods and his extraordinarily powerful imagination, Michael Faraday could see beneath appearances to very different hidden realities, to understanding we now share.

REFERENCES

Beer, G de (1966) *Humphry Davy*. (London: Nelson).

Clements, P. (1970) *Mark Isambard Brunel*. (London: Longman Green).

Faraday, M. (1826) 'On a Peculiar Perspective Appearance of Aerial Light and Shade' *Quarterly Journal of Science*, 22, 81. Reprinted in: Thomas, J.M. (1991) *Experimental Researches in Chemistry and Physics: Michael Faraday*. (London: Taylor and Francis), pp. 215–17.

Faraday, M. (1831) 'On a Peculiar Class of Optical Deceptions', *Quarterly Journal of Science*, Vol. 2, 205. Reprinted in: Thomas, J.M. (1991) *Experimental Researches in Chemistry and Physics: Michael Faraday*. (London: Taylor and Francis), pp. 291–311).

Faraday, M. (1853) 'Experimental Investigation of Table-moving', *Athenaeum*, July 2. Reprinted in: Thomas, J.M. (1991) *Experimental Researches in Chemistry and Physics: Michael Faraday*. (London: Taylor and Francis), pp. 385–91.

Gooding, D. and James, F.A. (1985) *Faraday Rediscovered: Essays on the Life and Work of Michael Faraday, 1791–1867*. (London: Macmillan).

Hogg, J. (1854) *The Microscope: History, Construction, and Applications* (London: The Illustrated London Library and W. S. Orr and Co.).

Martin, T. (1932) (ed.) *Faraday's Diary (1820–1862)*, Vols I–VI. (London: G. Bell and Sons).

Rolt, L.T.C. (1970) *Isambard Kingdom Brunel* London: Longmans Green; London: Pelican).

Tyndall, J. (1869) 'On Faraday as a Discoverer', in: *The Royal Institution Library of Science*. Vol. 2. Lawrence Bragg and George Porter (eds). (London: Applied Science Publishers).

Williams, L.P. (1965) *Michael Faraday* (London: Chapman and Hall).

Williams, L.P. (1971) *The Selected Letters of Michael Faraday*. (Cambridge: Cambridge University Press).

26

ADELBERT AMES

Interactions with Hermann Helmholtz, Albert Einstein and the Universe

Adelbert Ames is celebrated for evoking surprising perceptions that illuminate the nature of normal perception. The Ames Demonstrations are indeed unforgettable lessons from illusions.

Ames came from a distinguished American family. Confusingly, his father's name was also Adelbert Ames, who also worked on vision – on the optics of the eye, measuring its chromatic aberration and changes of focus with different colours. I shall now refer only to his son, Adelbert Ames Jnr. He started out as a lawyer but not being successful he turned from man-made laws to seeking laws of vision – first in painting with carefully graded colours, then in perceptual experiments with weird-shaped objects and distorted rooms. Like his father he became expert in optics, designing camera lenses from structures of the human eye. He designed lenses giving different magnifications horizontally or vertically, which he came to use in his perceptual research. (These are aniseikonic lenses, like astigmatism: Ames 1945, 1946.)

His formal scientific papers were few but indications of how he worked and something of the development of his ideas are to be found in the occasional jottings that he called his *Morning Notes*. These are disjointed, somewhat repetitive memoranda, starting in August 1941 and ending in May 1955. Not intended for publication they were, however, published in 1960, together with a correspondence with John Dewey, late in his life, entitled *The Morning Notes of Adelbert Ames Jr.*, edited by Ames's friend and colleague, Hadley Cantril (Cantril 1960). They are mainly on perception seen as *transactions* between the observer and the world. A principal question is: What are the day-to-day transactions we make with reality, to survive? As with any transactions, time is important.

The predictive power of perception is central to the musings of the *Morning Notes*. They touch also on purpose, free will, and on the nature of God. Ames saw perceptions as interactions with an essentially unknowable universe. The physical world is left as mysterious 'forms', serving as catalysts to evoke perceptions from 'assumptive common sense' derived from past experience. This assumptive, never certain, common sense is the seeming-reality of perceptions.

Although for Ames perception is individual adventure, there is also this shared 'assumptive common sense', such as acceptance of converging lines and size-graded objects as representing depth by the power of perspective. As these assumptions are shared, we have general perceptual agreement; but there are also individual assumptions so, in spite of general agreement, observers differ to some degree in what they see.

The musings of *Morning Notes* were the basis of the Ames Demonstrations which are – or should be – central for art students and for anyone, including philosophers, interested in visual perception. Once experienced they remain in the mind, to be mulled over as significant phenomena raising disturbing questions such as how we appreciate the universe.

The Demonstrations began to appear at Hanover in 1938. They were later set up and investigated by Ames with several colleagues at the University of Princeton. As they cannot be experienced in pictures or described in words, it is essential to have access to actual models: the Distorted Room, the Trapezoid Window, the Chair that looks like a chair only from a certain viewpoint, as its parts are spread out on radiating 'perspective' strings. These are reproduced in many Departments of Psychology, and are to be found in science centres world wide. The Leaf Room, however (which is discussed below), has seldom if ever been duplicated. The Ames Window is especially striking. It is a window in perspective, as viewed from an oblique angle, so that one side is shorter than the other. And it has shadows painted on it. As it slowly rotates it appears to change size – expand and contract as it rotates or sometimes appears to oscillate from side to side – and when a rod is placed through it the window and rod may appear, impossibly, to rotate in opposite directions. The point is that, unlike a rotating rectangle, the inbuilt perspective trapezoid shape of the Ames Window does not change significantly to the eye and, unlike a normal object, its painted shadows move with it. The dramatic upset of perception demonstrates the ever-present power of perspective, and visual 'clues' such as shadows, to reveal shape and depth – and also to generate bizarre illusions. Questions of how and when this happens bridge the science of seeing with the visual arts.

The visual phenomena elicited by these demonstrations are so surprising and compelling they impressed many distinguished scientists, especially physicists, including Albert Einstein. Although visiting physicists loved the Ames Demonstrations, there was resistance among psychologists. To put this more frankly, the Demonstrations were largely ignored and even resented by psychologists. Why was this? Were demonstrations – rather than formal experiments – not seen as respectably scientific? Were the implications too upsetting for current views of perception? They did indeed challenge the safe notion of stimulus–response links from events to perceptions.

For the most part there were few controls and hardly any statistics in Ames's experiments. There were, however, some systematic studies, such as comparing various trapezoid shapes of the Rotating Window with normal rectangular windows (Ames 1951). These variations and controls for teasing out what is important in these complex effects add greatly to the interest of the Demonstrations yet they are seldom if ever shown, which is unfortunate. Generally, the effects were hard to measure or evaluate objectively. But this did not prevent these dramatic sights giving insights, for visitors and students, with profound effects on how to see perception.

Some of the phenomena are strong evidence that perceptions can take off from the physical world and so are not slaves to stimuli. This makes perception even odder than physical science. No doubt this taking off from physical reality was not popular with psychologists anxious to look respectable in the traditions of physics. Ames's friend Hadley Cantril (1960, p. vii) was very well aware of this. Showing the Ames Window to Einstein one day, Cantril complained of psychologists' recalcitrance, saying: '"Stimulus bound" psychologists opposed the view [we] were trying to develop of perception.' Einstein smiled broadly, saying, 'I learned many years ago never to waste time trying to convince my colleagues'.

Of course, Ames had predecessors, especially the founder of modern studies of perception, Hermann von Helmholtz. Although he does not refer to Helmholtz in *Morning Notes*, there are marked similarities in their views. Helmholtz also saw that perception is not 'stimulus bound' and readily takes off on its own. Perhaps, as he was a distinguished physicist, he was not bothered by surface scientific respectability! A century earlier Helmholtz had appreciated the significance of perspective for depth perception, realizing that it can be more powerful than stereoscopic disparity for seeing distances and three-dimensional shapes. In fact, Helmholtz described the basis of the Distorted Room ninety years before Ames. He realized that an infinite range of shapes and sizes of objects can give the same image to the eye and that a suitably 'distorted' room, designed to give the same retinal image as a rectangular room, must look like a normal, rectangular room. Helmholtz's description follows a discussion of how and why a normal, familiar room appears rectangular in dim light, with no abrupt transition to full vision in brighter light. Thus Helmholtz wrote, in 'Concerning the Perceptions in General' (1866):

But even when we look around a room of this sort flooded with sunshine, a little reflection shows us that under these conditions too large a part of our perceptual-image [perception] may be due to factors of memory and experience. The fact that we are accustomed to the perspective distortions of pictures of parallelepipeds and to the form of the shadows they cast has much to do with the estimation of the shape and dimensions of the room, as will be seen hereafter. Looking at the room with one eye shut, we think we see it just as distinctly and definitely as with both eyes.

Helmholtz then says:

And yet we should get exactly the same view in case every point in the room were shifted arbitrarily to a different distance from the eye, provided they all remained on the same lines of sight.

This is a precise description of the Ames Room, written almost a century earlier; but it seems that Helmholtz did not get round actually to making a distorted room and trying it out in practice. So, in Ames's terms, he did not enter into transactions with it and so did not discover its full potentialities. This is what Ames, to his great credit, did. By placing objects in the Room he discovered new effects and raised new questions that we are still trying to answer.

The relations between the ideas of Helmholtz and Ames, on perception and illusion, seem not to have been at all fully explored. The passage from Helmholtz just quoted gives his emphasis on the importance of experience from the past for making up deficiencies in current sensed data. What Helmholtz says here relates closely to his general account of illusion given in his lecture, 'The Recent Progress of the Theory of Vision' (1867, his italics):

We always believe that we see such objects as would, under conditions of normal vision, produce the retinal image of which we are actually conscious.

So Helmholtz would expect that any odd-shaped object, giving the same retinal image as a familiar object, would appear the same as the familiar object. On almost any theory of monocular vision the Distorted Room must look like a normal room – provided it is built according to the perspective rule that each point lies on a line radiating from the eye, so that every feature doubles in size with each doubling of distance – because this gives the same image to the eye as a normal, rectangular room. This is indeed why a perspective flat *picture* of a room looks much like a room though the texture of its paper, or canvas, produces a paradox of perception: perspective pictures looking flat and in depth at the same time. The Ames Room does not have these paradoxes so it is really simpler than a picture.

I have said that *almost* any theory of perception would predict that the Ames Room will appear as a normal room. An exception is Euclid's theory of the 3rd century BC, that light rays shoot out of the eyes to touch objects (see 'What Are Perceptions Made of?', p. 109). The probing touch-rays would give distances directly, giving the game away. For very different reasons J.J. Gibson's 'Ecological Optics' (Gibson 1961) account would also have a lot of trouble with the Ames room – as it has also with pictures. This is no accident as the Distorted Room has the same logic as a flat picture except that one can get inside the Room! The difficulty for Gibson's account is that, as it does not suppose that perceptions are constructed by following rules (such as perspective) and assumptions (such as right angles and parallel lines), it lacks the concept of being misled, in atypical situations, by normally useful rules and assumptions. As this account has no other explanation, instead of being suggestive tools for understanding perception more deeply, these queer shapes and perspective pictures are embarrassing.

Any theory based on perspective projection at the eye must predict what Helmholtz expected, and what Ames found with the Distorted Room. Ames went further by discovering that the Room really takes off as an experimental situation when objects, including people, are placed in it. People placed at the further sloping wall appear the same distance, and impossibly different sizes, when in fact they are the same size but different distances. This is entirely different from the Muller-Lyer illusion (Fig. 27.5, p. 256), in which perception from the retinal image is distorted. Looked at in depth this is a subtle issue.

What Ames discovered, by trying it, is that the Room sets up a betting situation for the observer: Is the room an odd shape – or are the objects or people in it odd sizes? Usually the room is assumed to be rectangular though it is not, so the room 'wins' – remaining a typical room though objects in it have absurdly different sizes. But the bet does not always go this way. There is a story that newly married wives resist their husbands shrinking as they walk away in the Room. This is a bet between the wife's faith in the constancy of her husband and acceptance of the normality of reality. At first the husband is the preferred truth: isn't it sad if this applies only to newly-weds?

Which way the bet goes should depend on familiarity with rectangular rooms; this suggests cross-cultural experiments with people who live in odd-shaped or round houses.

It is rather surprising that familiar laws of physics may be violated by the eyes. Thus, in the Ames Room, a ball rolling down a trough, which actually slopes down, can appear to roll up the slope. This makes one question the power of cultural or any experience on perception.

But it is very important to be able to see unusual and even downright impossible things. It would be dangerous to be blind to the unlikely for surprises can be life-threatening. Fortunately, it is possible to see unlikely, non-illusory occurrences, such as objects lifted by magnets or (as in science centres) balls riding on jets of water or invisibly on air. By its surprises science provides even odder perceptions. Without them it would be impossible to make discoveries.

Discoveries and inventions also lead to even odder perceptions. With the invention of bicycles in the last century several 'magnetic hills' were discovered – one's bicycle seeming to go uphill without need of pedalling. Investigating the best example in Britain, actually in Scotland, I found it both compelling and puzzling. A small stream seemed quite clearly to be going uphill! The visible horizon was a long, slightly sloping line of hills; but when I looked away from this not quite horizontal horizon, the water still seemed to flow uphill! Thinking about it since, I wonder whether *memory* of reference contexts affects perception? This seems very reasonable, as they can only be sampled visually from time to time. This is a dramatic, real-life example of perception depending on assumptions. The perceptual assumptions are important for driving and flying and so on but are not easy to investigate experimentally.

Recently I had the opportunity of examining one of Ames's original Distorted Rooms, also his Leaf Room. The opportunity occurred while visiting the Exploratorium hands-on science centre in San Francisco. The Exploratorium had just been presented with an original Distorted Room and the Leaf Room by Ames's son, so they are now in safe keeping. I had seen them some thirty years before at Princeton so this was a déjà-vu experience, combining perspectives of space and time. The Distorted Room was still convincing – especially the ball rolling apparently uphill. The Leaf Room also worked well. But I came to doubt Ames's explanation of why this looks distorted when viewed with an aniseikonic lens over one eye – though a normal room looks much as usual.

The Leaf Room is a rectangular enclosure, the inside entirely covered in randomly arranged leaves. The aniseikonic lens changes the scale of the retinal image on one meridian, just like astigmatism. When horizontal this magnification in one eye upsets the usual stereoscopic disparity. The effect is that walls of the Leaf Room look weirdly tilted. A normal room, however, is very little if at all affected. Ames and his colleagues took this to mean that the vague shape of the Leaf Room succumbed to distorted stereo-vision – which normal rooms resist as the distortion is too unlikely. This is a reasonable interpretation, on Helmholtz's or Ames's accounts. But the recent finding that stereoscopic 'disparity', as it is called, from the two eyes is surprisingly poor at signalling the slant of surfaces should give pause for thought. (Important experiments on this include: Gillam (1968), Mitchison and Westheimer (1984), Mitchison and MacKee (1990), Gillam (1992).

From informal observations with just a few observers, it seemed to me that the aniseikonic lens produced distortion whenever there was marked texture, but little or no distortion occurred with smooth surfaces whether or not they formed right angles, as in normal rooms, which are virtually unaffected. The rough stonework of the outside of the Exploratorium building was markedly affected, though distortion of this heavy masonry was highly improbable.

No doubt for evolutionary reasons associated with our ancestors the arboreal primates, random patterns of leaves have optimal texture for stereoscopic depth. It is indeed quite remarkable how effective leaves are for stereoscopic demonstrations. So we may question Ames's interpretation that it is uncertainty of its shape that renders the Leaf Room so liable to distortion though normal rooms are almost unaffected. If it is the exceptionally strong stereoscopic signals given by leaves that make the Leaf Room so vulnerable to stereoscopic distortion, a prediction is that an Ames Room covered in leaves – a Distorted Leaf Room – should look its true, non-rectangular shape when viewed by both eyes without aniseikonic lenses. Is this so? It seems worth trying.

ANALOGUE AMES

How were the queer shapes of the Distorted Rooms designed? They were based on intricate calculations from the essentially simple geometry of the situation (Kilpatrick 1952; more available is Ittelson 1952). It is, however, possible to use a simple analogue technique which avoids tedious calculations.

The trick is to use a small, bright light to cast shadows of windows or whatever on to sloping surfaces. This will produce correct perspective projections for any slope or any curved surface from the viewing position of the shadow-casting light. So if any object (or wire model) is projected onto a screen by a point-source, the shadow remains as a perfect perspective projection – however the surface is tilted – when viewed from the position of the point-source (Anstis et al. 1964). This is a useful trick for experiments on perspective and for producing exact perspective pictures on any surface.

The Ames Window can be made from the shadow of a normal (or rectangular model) window projected on a sloping card cut to this shape. The Ames Room can be made similarly by shadow-projecting a cutout of rectangular windows and so on, on to the sloping wall. The perspective is correct for the Room – whatever its shape – from the viewing position of the shadow-casting light – so it is bound to work.

Let's call this 'Analogue Ames'. It allows any Ames Room or Ames trapezoid Window to be set out easily, and the underlying perspective principle is clearly seen. Alternatively, a model window may be photographed from an oblique angle to give the trapezoid shape, with realistic shadows. A pair of photographic prints of the window thus photographed may be glued back-to-back on a transparent sheet of perspex ('plexiglass' in America) and cut to the trapezoid shape of the prints. The photographed shadows are correct according to lighting of the model window; they confuse the eye, as being frozen photographs, because they do not change when the trapezoid Window rotates.

It is thanks to the imaginative genius of Adelbert Ames, playing about with queer-shaped models, that we have such simple, powerful demonstrations to delight experimental philosophers willing to give up their visual grip on the world, to see how we see. Whether Ames was quite right to describe perceptions as 'Transactions' is not so clear: it has a metaphysical ring. Transactions with earthly objects, if not with the universe, are more hands-on than eyes-on.

REFERENCES

Ames, A. (1945) 'The Space Eikonometer Test for Aniseikonia', *American Journal of Ophthalmology*, 28, 248–62.

Ames, A. (1946) 'Binocular Vision as Affected by Relations Between Uniocular Stimulus-patterns in Commonplace Environments', *American Journal of Ophthalmology*, 28, 248–62.

Ames, A. (1951) 'Visual Perception and the Rotating Trapezoid Window', *Psychological Monographs*, 7 (65), 1–32 (Washington D.C.: American Psychological Association).

Anstis, S., Shopland, C.D. and Gregory, R.L. (1964) 'Measuring Visual Constancy for Stationary or Moving Objects', *Nature*, 191, 416–17.

Cantril, H. (ed.) (1960) *The Morning Notes of Adelbert Ames Jr.* (New Brunswick, NJ: Rutgers University Press).

Gibson, J.J. (1946) *The Senses Considered as Perceptual Systems*. (Boston, Mass.: Houghton Mifflin).

Gibson, J.J. (1961) 'Ecological Optics', *Vision Research*, 1, 253–62.

Gibson, J.J. (1979) *The Ecological Approach to Visual Perception*. (Boston, Mass.: Houghton Mifflin).

Gillam, Barbara (1968) 'Perception of Slant when Perspective and Stereopsis Conflict: Experiments with Aniseikonic Lenses', *Journal of Experimental Psychology*, 78, 299–305.

Gillam, Barbara (1992) 'Perspective, Orientation Disparity, and Anistropy in Stereoscopic Slant Perception', *Perception*, 21, 427–39.

Helmholtz, H. von (1866) 'Concerning the Perceptions in General', *Treatise on Physiological Optics*, Vol. III, 3rd edn, J.P.C. Southall (trans.), *Optical Society of America*, New York, 1925, Section 26. (This classic is reprinted by Dover, New York, 1962.)

Helmholtz, H. von (1867) 'The Recent Progress of the Theory of Vision', *Popular Scientific Lectures*. (New York: Appleton). (This is a course of lectures delivered in Frankfurt and Heidelberg in 1867, translated by P.H. Pye-Smith.)

Ittelson, W.H. (1952) *The Ames Demonstrations in Perception*. (Princeton: Princeton University Press).

Kilpatrick, F.P. (1952) (ed.) *Human Behavior from the Transactional Point of View*. (Washington DC: Office of Naval Research, Neuropsychiatric Branch, Bureau of Medicine and Surgery, Department of the Navy).

Mitchison, G.J. and Westheimer, G. (1984) 'The Perception of Depth in Simple Figures', *Vision Research*, 24, 1063–74.

Mitchison, G.J. and MacKee, S.P. (1990) 'Mechanisms Underlying the Anisotropy of Tilt Perception', *Vision Research*, 30, 1781–91.

27

PUTTING ILLUSIONS IN THEIR PLACE

Although at first sight illusions of the senses seem trivial, they challenge some of our deepest beliefs. They were the basis of the rejection by Plato of perception as being a valid source of knowledge. He even discarded the world of objects we seem to perceive in favour of timeless mathematics and perfect Forms existing in a world beyond the senses. Much later, British Empiricism based all knowledge on perception – playing down and even ignoring the wonderful, philosophically disturbing phenomena of illusions.

The historical watershed in the history of illusions is the writings of the Arab mathematician Abu Ali Al-Hasan Ibn Al-Hasan Abn Al-Haytham (*c.* 965–1038), born in Basra. He is better known to us simply as Alhazan. Alhazan was the first to give an account of atmospheric refraction and of reflection from curved surfaces. He feigned madness to escape from a boast that he could prevent the flooding of the Nile; but, much more important, he was the first to write at length on sources of vision illusions. Until recently his work has only been available in fragments (Ronchi 1970), but now we have the entire text of his *Optics* translated into English (Sabra 1989). What do we find? Writing in our Dark Age of the 11th century, Alhazan described perception as depending upon knowledge and inference, most illusions being, he thought, false unconscious inferences. This idea did not surface for almost another thousand years, with the ideas of the nineteenth-century German polymath Hermann von Helmholtz (1821–94), who founded modern studies of vision and hearing. Alhazan was, by a thousand years, a pre-Helmholtzian! He also saw perception as depending on knowledge and (syllogistic) inference.

Alhazan gave eight causes of illusions, some having multiple causes. His explanations of illusion and their classification reflect his understandings and misunderstandings of perception. No doubt the very different categories of illusions that I shall suggest here reflect our thinking, a millenium later, and no doubt in time these will come to seem quaintly inadequate. Islamic rugs and books contain *deliberate* errors to avoid any pretence of challenging the gods by creating perfection. I have no such excuse for mistakes or confusions in this attempt to put illusions in their place. Illusions may be described as deviations of perception from the world which is described by the Natural Sciences. So we may call their study Unnatural Science. Although illusions appear trivial they are genuine phenomena, deserving explanations just as much as did the quirky phenomena of rubbed amber that puzzled the Greeks, and the floating lodestones that mysteriously pointed North–South and were used by the Chinese to aid navigation. Understanding of these led to further, deeper understanding of matter with the unprecedented, present-day technologies of control and energy, including the atomic bomb.

The natural sciences describe, they explain, and they classify. There is no clear sequence for these activities of describing, explaining and classifying, for each affects the others and is in turn affected by the others. Thus, whales may be described initially from their appearance as vast fishes; but with further examination and understanding they become mammals. Lightning may start as thunderbolts from the gods but becomes a manifestation of electricity. The heart starts as the seat of the soul but becomes a pump. For the ancients the brain was unimportant; for Aristotle it cooled the blood, so he would describe and classify the brain and its works quite differently from us. At various times, and with each change of notions of magic or technology, the brain has been seen in many ways. As technology changes, so we explain the brain and processes of perception differently: receiver of truth from some outside source (magic); tweaking puppet strings (from the Greek fascination with puppet automata); reservoir of Vital Spirits (from seventeenth-century pumps and fountains); complex switches (from telephone exchanges); now, creator of our thoughts and sensations as some kind of computer. As explanations modify descriptions they force changes in classifications of phenomena. Classifications suggest analogies of similarity and point to differences which may be significant; so classifications are important not only for definitions but also as aids for structuring ideas, and suggesting new experiments and theories.

KINDS OF VISUAL ILLUSIONS

It is not surprising that schemes of classification have turned out to be important for the physical sciences: chemistry with the periodic table of the elements; evolution of stars with the Main Sequence and other classes; the Linnean taxonomy of plants, with phyla, species, genera, varieties and so on. This was profoundly affected by explanations from Darwinian evolution though with a danger of circularity – when supposed sequences of evolutionary development are used to suggest classes, which are then used to justify the supposed evolutionary sequence.

Appropriateness of classes depends very much on uses. An ancient Chinese encyclopedia, the *Celestial Emporium of Benevolent Knowledge* (according to Ornstein and Ehrlich 1991) classified the animal kingdom thus:

Animals are divided into

Those that belong to the emperor
Embalmed ones
Those that are trained
Suckling pigs
Mermaids
Fabulous ones
Stray dogs
Those that are included in this classification
Those that tremble as if they were mad
Innumerable ones
Those drawn with a very fine camel-hair brush
Others
Those that have broken a flower vase
Those that resemble flies at a distance

Whatever its uses this could hardly have advanced Chinese science; but for all their dangers classifications clearly are very important in the natural and the biological sciences. So we might expect an appropriate taxonomy for perception – with its even odder phenomena of illusions – to be useful for focusing on what puzzles us about the distorting windows to the world by which we see and hear, taste and touch what seems to be reality.

To put phenomena of illusions in their place we might start with their appearances but, just as for physical phenomena, as we come to explain them the phenomena that look similar or even identical can turn out to be essentially different. As for chemicals or plants or stars, we should expect that some phenomena of perception will change their categories as explanations change, and as we come to understand differently or more deeply. How then can we set up categories that are likely to be useful and not misleading, for the un-natural science of illusions? There is no way of *deducing* appropriate categories. They must be *posited*, by a dangerous leap of imagination. Having made such a leap we may agree it was dangerous, but has it landed us upon anything useful? Well, let's leap – and see where we land!

For this classification to reach beneath appearances it will need and may suggest theoretical assumptions. Although its structure should be tolerant to considerable variations of explanation, we do need to start with some acceptable assumptions for its take-off. The basic assumption will be that perceptions are *descriptions* or, more specifically, that perceptions are predictive *hypotheses*. This accepts the Helmholtzian (Helmholtz 1856) view of perceptions as unconscious inferences from sensory data. The extension, that perceptions are predictive hypotheses, accepts that perceptions are descriptions and suggests that illusions are much like errors in science (Gregory 1980a, 1980b, 1981). The alternative 'direct' theories – holding that perceptions are given immediately by sensory inputs (Gibson 1950) – suppose that there is little or even no information processing by the senses or the brain for perception. These accounts play down phenomena of illusions, as they are hard to explain without active intermediary processes (Gregory 1970a), so on this paradigm of perception these intriguing phenomena are ignored or left entirely unexplained.

Accepting that perceptions are actively created brain descriptions suggests that we may find appropriate categories of perceptual illusions in *errors of language*. This is our dangerous leap! This is our take-off for putting illusions in their place.

ERRORS OF LANGUAGE

It may be that structures of language have derived from the ways the world has been classified over millions of years in pre-human perception. This helps to explain how language could have developed so rapidly, on the biological timescale, if it was a 'take-over' of ancient perceptual classifications of objects and situations of pre-human dramatic importance (Gregory 1971). On such a view of the relation of language to perception we may look with some confidence to errors in language for suggesting classes of perceptual illusions. In its mysterious development, the key 'invention' of language accepts certain objects (or shapes or sounds) as *standing for* quite other objects, or concepts or whatever – as shared symbols. For putting illusions in their place, let's use this notion that language and perception are closely linked by noting the principle errors of language. These it seems to me are of four kinds: *Ambiguities, Distortions, Paradoxes, Fictions.* Let's look at examples:

Four kinds of language errors

Ambiguous:	John looks funny.
Distortion:	He is miles taller than his father.
Paradox:	John's sister is a dark-haired blonde.
Fiction:	She is a little green girl from Mars.

One might add Confusion, such as 'John's green taller miles father Mars'. But this is failure to describe or represent, so it corresponds to sensations rather than to perceptions. I shall leave this out, as confusion is not an error of perception but is, rather, lack of perception. Confusion might, though, be included for some purposes.

We should expect to find different kinds of errors – illusions – produced at each different stage of visual processing, from object to experience, or to sensory-guided behaviour. Let's look now at what seem to be very different stages of perception – where we should expect to find very different sources of illusions.

SOURCES OF ILLUSIONS

As we are looking for basically similar and different kinds of illusions, not merely different or similar *appearances*, we may classify illusions in terms of their causes. This takes us to essentially different stages of vision (here we are looking only at visual perception) where there are very different kinds of processes, and so very different causes of illusion. These are: *Physical*, *Physiological* and *Cognitive* stages of visual perception.

Three stages of vision

• The first is what happens in the physical world between the object and the retinas of the eyes. Errors generated here I shall call *Physical* illusions.
• The second is the physiology of the visual pathway and relevant physiological processes of the brain itself. Errors here I shall call *Physiological* illusions.
• The third and last stage is cognitive processes – carried out by the physiology of the brain. Errors stemming from these rule-following and knowledge-based procedures, I shall call *Cognitive* illusions.

We should expect different kinds of causes of illusions from these stages of perception but some arising from different stages and having very different causes may appear similar. How do we recognise deep differences when surface appearances are similar, or even identical? The first – Physical – does not present problems when the physical cause (reflection, refraction, diffraction, etc. of light) is identified, as the physics of optics and of the eye itself is very fully understood. But with the last two – Physiological and Cognitive – we are almost on our own in a tricky philosophical minefield. Yet this is extremely important. The distinction between Physiological and Cognitive is the crucial distinction between the sciences of physiology and psychology, where explanations can be very different.

The notion that perception is physically brain-based, so the mind is not a balloon floating above our heads, is a fairly new idea, though there are strong hints of a physical basis of mind in Aristotle's writings of over two thousand years ago. The notion of the brain as a physical machine was advanced against great opposition by Julian Offray de la Mettrie in 1748. Now this is held as a fundamental assumption by the great majority if not by quite all brain scientists.

Just how to distinguish between processes of physiology and cognition is, however, somewhat controversial. A different kind of example might help. Consider a pocket calculator. It may give a wrong answer for the same three causal reasons.

1. A *Physical* error: a wrong number may be entered. (Occurring before the device is reached).
2. A *Physiological* error: A failure of function. (Perhaps due to a low battery).
3. A *Cognitive* error: (i) An inappropriate operating rule (such as dividing when multiplying is appropriate); or (ii) a false assumption, (such as a corner is 90 degrees, when it isn't).

These we can use for classifying kinds of causes of illusions: Physical – Physiological – Cognitive. (Actually Cognitive is of two kinds – wrong rules, and false assumptions – but we will not bother with this distinction here).

Errors of language will suggest the classes of appearances of visual illusions seen as phenomena: Ambiguities – Distortions – Paradoxes – Fictions.

So now we have the basis for a classification of illusions:

CLASSES OF VISUAL ILLUSIONS

I Physical illusions

Ambiguities

Mist
Shadows

Distortions

Of space: Stick-in-water
Of velocity: Stroboscope

EVEN ODDER PERCEPTIONS

Paradoxes

Mirrors (seeing oneself in the wrong place, and duplicated)

Fictions

Rainbows
Moiré patterns

II Physiological illusions

Ambiguities

Size–distance, for a single stationary eye

Distortions

Adaptations to tilt or curvature
The 'Cafe Wall' (Fig. 27.1)

Paradoxes

(when visual channels disagree)
After-effect of motion
Moving yet not changing position or size

Fictions

After-images
Autokinetic effect
Migraine patterns

III Cognitive illusions

Ambiguities

Necker Cube (Fig. 27.2)
Jastrow's Duck-Rabbit (Fig. 14.1)
Rubin's Vase-Faces (Fig. 27.4)
Staircase illusion (Fig. 27.3)

Distortions

Muller-Lyer 'arrows' (Fig. 27.5)
Ponzo – 'railway lines' (Fig. 27.6)
Poggendorf – displacement (Fig. 27.7)

Paradoxes

Penrose Impossible Triangle (Fig. 27.8)
Escher's pictures

Fictions

Kanizsa Triangle (Fig. 19.1)
Filling-in of the Blind Spot and Scotomas

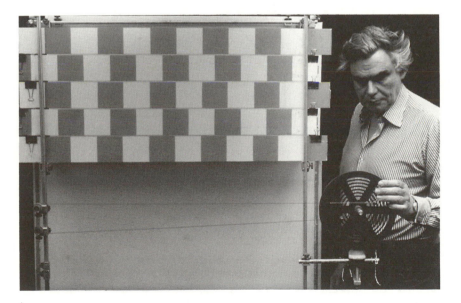

Figure 27.1 The café wall. These long illusory wedges are remarkable, being large-scale distortions produced by a symmetrical smaller-scale pattern. This is impossible! There must be two processes, the first being small-scale wedges which are integrated, giving the large-scale distortion. This is a 'physiological' distortion illusion.

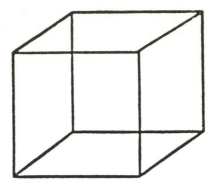

Figure 27.2 Necker Cube

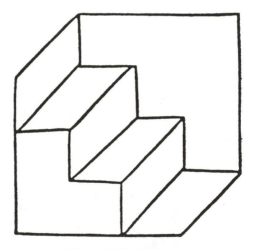

Figure 27.3 Staircase

This taxonomy of visual phenomena has a low resolution. It is not hard to add sub-classes – Species, Varieties and so on – under the major categories: Physical, Physiological and Cognitive.

Assigning causes can be highly controversial, so we should not expect complete agreement on which phenomena belong in which category. I have given my preferences. Others may want to shift some of the phenomena to different categories. This an empirical matter

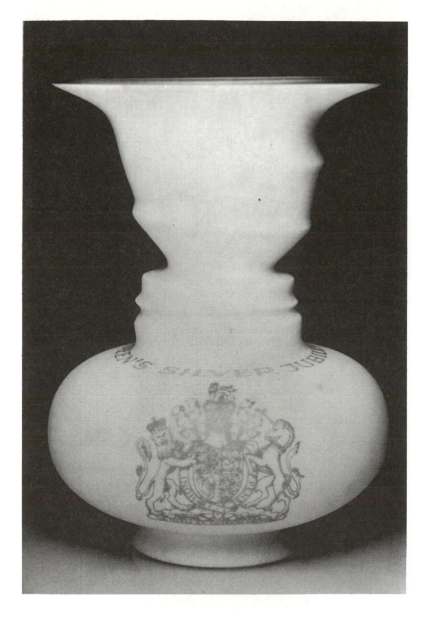

Figure 27.4 Rubin's Vase-Faces. This is a sophisticated version – working with the actual object. If rotated, the lips move as though the Queen is talking to the Duke of Edinburgh.

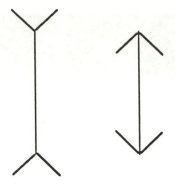

Figure 27.5 The Muller-Lyer arrows. These (and the Ponzo and Poggendorff illusions) are regarded here as 'cognitive' distortion illusions.

Figure 27.6 The Ponzo railway lines

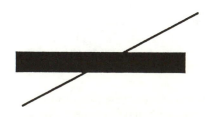

Figure 27.7 The Poggendorf displacement figure

Figure 27.8 The Penroses' Impossible Triangle. Originally designed by Lionel and Roger Penrose, this is the most famous impossible figure. Try hiding a corner – and it will seem entirely possible. The brain, or mind, assumes the three sides are touching – though they need not be touching in depth.

requiring experiments. What is needed are litmus tests for identifying kinds of illusions. This takes us to technical questions, and leads to new experiments. Many of the well-known illusions are, however, clearly Physical, Physiological or Cognitive.

An illusion may occur from several causes (Halpern 1981) and so may enter more than one explanation-category, though usually there is a main cause. For example, the autokinetic effect of a dim light in a field of darkness apparently moving (surely the origin of many flying saucers) is believed to be due to fluctuating physiological imbalances of the eyes' positioning system which normally keeps the world stable when we move our eyes; but there is a cognitive component which rejects the (unlikely) illusory movement of large objects (Gregory and Zangwill 1963).

It might be objected of the Physical illusions that they are not themselves ambiguous (or distorted, paradoxical or fictional), but this is not the suggestion. These categories all refer to supposed causes

257

or origins. Thus mist can originate perceptual ambiguity even though mist is not itself ambiguous. Similarly, mirrors produce visual paradoxes though they are not themselves, as objects, paradoxical. Whether illusions occur depends on characteristics of perception. Some diving birds can even avoid errors from the (Physical) bent-stick effect of refraction by water, though we are fooled. In principle, we might literally see through refractive distortions and mirror paradoxes, but this is beyond our perceptual abilities. So we can only see through them conceptually.

Several Physical illusions have practical importance. The stroboscope allows moving machinery to be examined as though it were stationary, and was a key to the origins of the cinema. (See 'Michael Faraday's Perception', p. 231.)

The most dramatic and useful Physical fiction is holograms. Several Physical illusions are described by Tolansky (1964) and a very full account is given by Mineart (1954) of naturally occurring, especially meteorological phenomena. I once saw two suns of about equal brightness, in the early evening, from Kew Gardens in London. This odd phenomenon of atmospheric refraction lasted at least ten minutes.

Physiological illusions include all manner of neural losses and interactions which produce degenerated or distorted neural signals, including those induced by drugs. Illusions of Physiological adaptation are experimentally useful for teasing out characteristics of neural channels (Blakemore and Sutton 1969). Presumably, the apparitions of schizophrenia lie in the Physiological category, though some may be due to bugs of cognition, perhaps like errors or bugs in computer programs. The distinction between Physiological and Cognitive is very important for diagnosis and treatment.

Cognitive illusions are the most difficult to investigate, but their study can be highly rewarding for their theoretical implications and for their use by artists (Gombrich 1960; 1982) of dramatic cognitive Ambiguities, Paradoxes, and Fictions. Ambiguities are clearly cognitive when they depend on balanced probabilities of alternative 'hypotheses', such as the Necker Cube (Fig. 27.2), the Jastrow duck-rabbit (Fig. 14.1), and probably Rubin's Vase-Faces (Fig. 27.4).

A very different, clearly cognitive example is the Size–Weight illusion which involves vision and touch: smaller objects of the same scale weight feel heavier than larger objects of the same scale weight. Evidently, the larger object sets up an expectation of being heavier. In this case, this is a false expectation. (This may suggest that signals of weight from the limbs are compared with an 'internal' expected weight, like a Wheatstone Bridge used in electrical measurements (Ross and Gregory 1964.)

A purely visual example which is also related to probabilities, is the Hollow Mask. Though actually hollow it looks like a normal nose-sticking-out face – as a hollow face is so unlikely this hypothesis is rejected, though it happens to be true.

Distortion illusions evoke the most controversy. How does one show that a perceptual phenomenon is Cognitive, rather than Physiological? By the principle of Ockham's Razor – that the simplest explanation is to be preferred – one should start with Physical or Physiological possibilities. To make a Cognitive claim, one has to show that it is due to misleading assumptions, or to misleading rule-following leading perception astray.

Here we reach tendentious issues of how much of perception is given 'bottom-up' from sensory signals, how much 'top-down' from stored knowledge. And we may add 'side-ways' rules or algorithms which may be misleading. The notion here is that they are introduced 'side-ways' like programs on floppy disks in a personal (the most personal!) computer. (See also 'Mind in a Black Box', pp. 140–1.)

Rules, including legal laws, allow knowledge from the past to be applied to dealing with the present and to predicting the future. But when the present is unusual, the guiding Rules from the past can lead to error. This is bound to happen from time to time, for rules must be broader than individual events and so they cannot define them and we cannot always make fair judgments. Rules work best when there are simple, common features applying to many objects and situations. For vision this is so for the perspective geometry of retinal images, which provide generally safe rules for seeing three-dimensional object shapes from two-dimensional perspective retinal images, pictures or photographs. These rules of perspective work fine for normal objects; but queer-shaped objects, such as the Ames Demonstrations (Ittleson 1952), have shapes that violate the assumptions of parallel sides and right-angular corners of normal familiar objects. (see 'Adelbert Ames', p. 238.) The well-known 'geometrical' illusions of perspective drawings probably produce distortions due to mis-scaling of size, shape and distance (Gregory 1963, 1966) when the perspective is inappropriate to the true depth.

If there were 'floppy disks' of modified rules for perspective for flat pictures (or for the odd shapes of Ames's objects) then these illusions should not occur. The snag is they are seen with the rules which apply to normal three-dimensional objects. If one handled pictures and Ames's objects so that the illusions *mattered*, then our visual systems might write special floppies for pictures and odd objects.

A litmus test for Cognitive rather than Physiological distortion is whether the illusion is destroyed when the figures are seen in the depth appropriate to their perspective. This is so for the Muller-Lyer, the Ponzo and the Pogendorf figures (Gregory and Harris 1975). It is not so for the quite similar-appearing Café Wall distortion (Gregory and Heard 1979), which evidently is a physiological illusion, with its origin in the retinas.

Cognitive Fictions such as Kanizsa's Triangle (Fig. 19.1) are especially intriguing. This is like three cakes with missing triangular slices facing each other: a ghostly triangular surface is seen suspended over the missing parts of the 'cakes'. These illusory surfaces seem to be visual postulates of nearer eclipsing surfaces, accounting for unlikely gaps (Gregory 1972). Cognitive Fictions are most likely present continuously and have useful functions. They fill in gaps in sensory signals and they help us to see objects, though they are partly hidden.

The blind spot of the eyes, where the optic nerve leaves the retina, is not seen. Why don't we see a great black blodge near the edge of vision? For this local loss of sight is just the same as the image of a large black object. And we know that retinal after images are 'projected' to appear as external objects. If blind spots were seen as objects, this would be disturbing, even threatening. Do we simply ignore such scotomas? Or is it that they are actively filled in? A recent experiment (Ramachandran and Gregory 1991) suggests that they are filled in, by rather low-level cognitive pattern-completion. In this experiment one can actually see what one's own brain has created to fill the gaps in vision – nothing less than one's private virtual reality. (See 'Virtually Real', p. 81).

By revealing unconscious knowledge, assumptions and operating rules of vision, illusions reveal hidden depths of our minds. The classes of illusions put forward here were suggested from errors of language. This is based on the concept that both perceptions and language are descriptions – and so may have some deep similarities. Could there be still deeper links between language and perception?

Ludwig Wittgenstein, in the *Tractatus* (1922, 4.01) held his Picture Theory of meaning: that the logical structure beneath the grammar of sentences is like the structure of pictures:

The proposition is a picture of reality. The proposition is a model of the reality as we think it is.

Then he says (4.011):

Language disguises the thought; so that from the external form of the clothes one cannot infer the form of the thought they clothe, because the external form of the clothes is constructed with quite another object than to let the form of the body be recognized.

The silent adjustments to understand colloquial language are enormously complicated.

And Wittgenstein refers to errors (4.023):

The proposition constructs a world with the help of a logical scaffolding, and therefore one can actually see in the proposition all the logical features possessed of reality if it is true. One can *draw conclusions* from a false proposition.

We have tried to draw conclusions from illusions.

REFERENCES

Blakemore, C. and Sutton, P.(1969) 'Size Adaptation: a New After-effect', *Science*, 166, 245–7.

Gibson, J.J. (1950) *The Visual World*. (Boston, Mass.: Houghton Mifflin).

Gombrich, E.H. (1960) *Art and Illusion: A Study on the Psychology of Pictorial Representation*. (London: Phaidon).

Gombrich, E.H. (1982) *The Image and the Eye: Further Studies in the Psychology of Pictorial Representation*. (London: Phaidon).

Gregory, R.L. (1963) 'Distortion of Visual Space as Inappropriate Constancy Scaling.' *Nature*, 199, 678–91.

Gregory, R.L. (1966) (4th ed. 1990) *Eye and Brain*. (London: Weidenfeld).

Gregory, R.L. (1970a) 'Choosing a Paradigm for Perception', in: E.C. Carterette and M.P. Friedman (eds) *Handbook of Perception* Vol. 1, Ch. 3.

Gregory, R.L. (1970b) *The Intelligent Eye*. (London: Weidenfeld).

Greory, R.L. (1971) 'The Grammar of Vision', *The Listener*, 19 Feb. 242–4. Reprinted in: Gregory, R.L. (1974) *Concepts and Mechanisms of Perception* pp. 622–9.

Gregory, R.L. (1972) 'Cognitive Contours', *Nature*, 238, 5358, 51–2.

Gregory, R.L. (1980a) 'Perceptions as Hypotheses' *Philosophical Transactions of the Royal Society of London, B*, 290, 181–97.

Gregory, R.L. (1980b) 'The Confounded Eye', in: R.L. Gregory and E.H. Gombrich (eds). *Illusion in Nature and Art* (London: Duckworth).

Gregory, R.L. (1981) *Mind in Science*. (London: Weidenfeld).

Gregory, R.L. and Harris, J.P. (1975) 'Illusion Destruction by Appropriate Scaling', *Perception*, 4, 203–20.

Gregory, R.L. and Heard, P. (1979) 'Border Locking and the Café Wall Illusion', *Perception* 8, 4, 365–80.

Gregory, R.L. and Zangwill, O.L. (1963) 'The Origin of the Autokinetic Effect', *Quarterly Journal of Experimental Psychology*, 15, 252–6.

Halpern, D.F. (1981) 'The Determinants of Illusory-contour Perception', *Perception*, 10, 2, 199–213.

Ittleson, W.H. (1952) *The Ames Demonstrations in Perception*. (Princeton, N.J.: Princeton University Press).

Kanizsa, G. (1979) *Organization of Vision: Essays on Gestalt Perception*. (New York: Praeger).

Mettrie, Julian Offray de la (1748) *L'Homme Machine*.

Minnaert, M. (1954) *The Nature of Light and Colour in the Open Air* (London: Dover).

Ornstein, R. and Ehrlich, P. (1991) *New World New Mind: Changing the Way We Think to Save the Future*. (London: Paladin), p. 90.

Ramachandran, V.S. and Gregory, R.L. (1991) 'Perceptual Filling-in of Artificially Induced Scotomas in Human Vision', *Nature* 350, 6320, 699–702.

Robinson, J.O. (1972) *The Psychology of Visual Illusion*. (London: Hutchinson).

Ronchi, V. (1970) *The Nature of Light: An Historical Survey* (V. Barocas, trans.). (London: Heinemann).

Ross, H.E. and Gregory, R.L. (1964) 'Is the Weber Fraction a Function of Physical or Perceived Input?', *Quarterly Journal of Experimental Psychology*, 16, 2, 116–22.

Sabra, A.I. (1989) (trans.) *The Optics of Ibn Al-Haytham*, 2 vols. (London: The Warburg Institute).

Tolansky, S. (1964) *Curiosities of Light Rays and Light Waves* (London: Vaneda).

Wittgenstein, Ludwig (1922) *Tractatus Logico-Philosophicus*. (C.K. Ogden, trans.). (London: Kegan Paul. International Library of Psychology Philosophy and Scientific Method).

INDEX